AF496763

LITTLE
LIBRARY

Univ. of
CALIFORNIA

DANTE BY GIOTTO.
From the fresco (before restoration)
in the Bargello at Florence

THE VISION

OF

DANTE ALIGHIERI

Translated by

HENRY FRANCIS CARY, M.A.

PART II.—PURGATORY

REVISED, WITH AN INTRODUCTION
By PAGET TOYNBEE, M.A.

WITH A FRONTISPIECE
From the Portrait of Dante by
GIOTTO

LONDON
METHUEN & CO.
36 ESSEX STREET W.C.
MDCCCCI

UNIV. OF
CALIFORNIA

CONTENTS

578886

251190

PREFATORY NOTE

IN the present edition of Cary's *Purgatory* (as in the case of the *Hell*) the notes have been subjected to revision. A paragraph here and there has been omitted, as being no longer strictly relevant, sundry errors have been corrected, and an occasional note has been added in square brackets. Also, the index has been recast.

In the Introduction is included a short sketch of the genesis and history of Cary's translation, which constitute an interesting, and by no means unimportant, chapter in literary history. This would naturally have found a place in the Introduction to the first part, had not the allotted space—" tutte le carte ordite "—in that volume been necessarily taken up by the account of Dante's life, and other general introductory matter. This sketch, however, is not inappropriately prefixed to the *Purgatory*, inasmuch as it was with this portion of the *Divina Commedia* that Cary made his first essay in the translation of Dante.

The representation of Dante which forms the

frontispiece of this volume is reproduced (by kind
permission of Messrs. Alinari of Florence) from a
photograph of the drawing made in 1840, by Mr.
Seymour Kirkup, of the then newly discovered
portrait by Giotto in the Bargello at Florence—a
drawing which has a special value, as having been
executed before the character of the likeness had
been hopelessly altered, in the process of the
"restoration" of the fresco, by the Florentine
painter Marini.

PAGET TOYNBEE.

October 19, 1900.

INTRODUCTION

I

CARY'S TRANSLATION

IT appears from an entry in Cary's *Journal*,[1] as well as from a passage in the preface to the first edition of his *Vision of Dante*, that he began his translation with the *Purgatorio*, in January 1797, eight years before the publication of his version of the *Inferno*. His reason for starting with the second *cantica*, instead of with the *Inferno*, was doubtless the fact that two English versions of the latter were already in existence, and had been published a few years before, namely, one by Charles Rogers, which appeared in 1782, and another by Henry Boyd, which appeared in 1785.

Even while an undergraduate at Oxford, Cary was studying the *Purgatorio*. In a letter to Miss Anna Seward, dated from Christ Church, 7th May 1792, in which he recommends her to read Dante, he says :—

"I subjoin two passages from the *Purgatorio*,

---

[1] *Memoir of the Rev. Henry Francis Cary, M.A.*, by his son, London, 1847, vol. i. p. 103.

because the poem is less known than the *Inferno*. The third canto begins with this comparison, so exquisitely drawn from nature :—

'As the sheep come out of the fold, some alone, others in pairs, others three together, the rest stand fearful, putting their eyes and noses to the ground, and whatever the first does, all the others do the same, crowding at her back, if she makes a stand, simple and tranquil, and yet do not know the reason why they stop, so this crowd of spirits stopt at our approach,' etc.[1]

"Speaking of the swift motion of a spirit that flew from them, he says :—

'I never saw the lighted vapours at the beginning of the night cut the serene air so swiftly, nor when the sun is setting, the clouds of autumn.'[2]

"Such are the sketches of Dante's pencil. . . . Everything becomes interesting at this period of reviving literature, and I am infinitely delighted with Dante, as an historian of his own time; so that I am collecting anecdotes, so plentifully interspersed among his works, for my amusement."[3]

[1] It is interesting to compare this rendering with the version of later years :—

> "As sheep, that step from forth their fold, by one,
> Or pairs, or three at once; meanwhile the rest
> Stand fearfully, bending the eye and nose
> To ground, and what the foremost does, that do
> The others, gathering round her if she stops,
> Simple and quiet, nor the cause discern;
> So saw I moving," etc.
> *Purg.* iii. 79-85.

[2] In the later version :—

> "Ne'er saw I fiery vapours with such speed
> Cut through the serene air at fall of night,
> Nor August's clouds athwart the setting sun," etc.
> *Purg.* v. 37-39.

[3] *Memoir of Cary*, vol. i. pp. 43-44.

Miss Seward's response was not encouraging, and had Cary's enthusiasm for Dante been less ardent, her matter-of-fact criticism might have quenched it altogether. She replies :—

"I confess I cannot perceive the high value of the simile you were so good to translate for me from Dante. It is undoubtedly a natural description of the manners and habits of a flock of sheep; but what truth, what sublimity, what beauty you can see in comparing a crowd of spirits, or ghosts, to them, I cannot conceive. If sheep are such silly imitators of their leader, why are we to suppose a troop of ghosts would all put their eyes and noses to the ground because the first might do so, in the same sort of ambition with which the clown tumbles after Harlequin? and so I can discern no apposition in this vaunted simile, without which a simile is but on a level with his, who said, 'even as a wheelbarrow goes rumble rumble, even so that man lends another sixpence.'"[1]

Although Cary began his translation with the *Purgatorio,* the first portion published was the *Inferno,* which appeared in two volumes in 1805 and 1806, accompanied by the Italian text. In his original preface (which was omitted in later editions) Cary gives an account of his motives in making the translation, and he incidentally furnishes an interesting criticism on the version of Henry Boyd, which had been published in 1802.

"The following work," he writes, "is offered to the publick with the earnest hope that it may be serviceable to the cause of Literature and the interests

1 *Letters of Anna Seward,* vol. iii. pp. 142-143.

of Virtue, as it will tend to facilitate the study of one of the most sublime and moral, but certainly one of the most obscure,[1] writers in any language.

" An edition of Dante, with a literal prose translation, was considered as a *desideratum* by the late Earl of Orford, who probably would have met with as little difficulty in the original as most of his learned cotemporaries; and the sentiments of that Nobleman, in however little value they may deservedly be held on subjects of far higher importance, yet in matters of taste at least were of no mean authority.[2]

" In the ensuing pages I have aimed at not only adding to the original text a translation so faithful as, with the assistance of the notes, to enable one moderately skilled in the Italian tongue to understand my author; but at producing a work which shall not

[1] Considerable amusement was caused to Cary's friends by a misprint in the notice of his book which appeared in the *Gentleman's Magazine* in June 1805. Cary is made to describe Dante not as "one of the most *obscure*," but as "certainly one of the most *obscene* writers in any language." Miss Seward writes to him from Lichfield on 8th August of that year :—" We are all much amused by the ridiculous misquotation in the *Gentleman's Magazine* in its review of your Dante. . . . while the literati will instantly perceive the mistake, it is likely to procure the circulation of your work amongst a certain and numerous class of beings, those gross voluptuaries, to whom chaste poesy is a dead letter."—*Letters*, vol. vi. p. 229.

[2] Horace Walpole's opinion is recorded in Pinkerton's *Walpoliana* (vol. ii. p. 26, second ed.) :—" Dante is a difficult author. I wish we had a complete translation in prose, with the original on the opposite page, like the French one of the *Inferno*, printed at Paris in 1776." The French translation here referred to was one of no value by Montonnet de Clairfons, who, whenever he met with a difficulty, omitted the passage in which it occurred. In 1782, the year in which Charles Rogers' version of the *Inferno* appeared, Horace Walpole had spoken of Dante, in a letter to William Mason, as "extravagant, absurd, disgusting, in short a Methodist Parson in Bedlam"!

be totally devoid of interest to the mere English reader. The difficulty of such an attempt will be most faithfully appreciated by those who are most competent to judge of the genius and character, both of the two languages and of the poet, which I design to illustrate. They will be disposed, I trust, to regard with a lenient eye many passages that may wear the appearance of coarseness or negligence, but which have perhaps cost me as much pains as any other parts of the poem. If the judgment of an Italian of eminence in the literary history of his country is to be relied on, my author is responsible for many such blemishes. In a letter to Lorenzo de Medici, Pico de Mirandola says 'Dante is at times harsh, rough, and meagre, generally deficient in elegance and address.' Nearly the same has by some of our critics been said of Milton, and with still less reason. But I do not wish to shelter myself under an imputation so unfavourable and so unjust; and am furnished with a better apology in the avowal of Dante himself, who, in the dedication of the *Paradiso* to his Veronese patron, declares that he had principally used a diction low and familiar.

"To the labours of Mr. Boyd we are indebted for the only view that has yet appeared in English of the *Divina Commedia ;* but whatever praise that gentleman's translation may deserve in other respects, it must be owned that it takes so great a latitude in its interpretation as not to answer one

principal purpose, to which the present is adapted,
that of affording an easy introduction to such as are
desirous of forming an acquaintance with the Italian
poet himself." [1]

[1] Boyd's translation of the *Inferno* was published in 1785; the
translation of the whole *Commedia* appeared in three volumes in
1802. Cary's strictures on the "latitude of his interpretation"
were certainly not undeserved. Here is Boyd's version of the
simile of the sheep, of which Cary's rendering both in prose and
verse has been given above (see p. x.):—

> " As Tenants of the fold in groupes advance,
>   And some strange form peruse with timid glance,
>   Each with uplifted head, and startled eye ;
>   Thro' each the sympathy of wild amaze
>   Contagious runs, till all, attentive, gaze
>   On the new prodigy, they know not why.
>
>   As they, obsequious to their trembling guide,
>   Move, rally, stop, and shift from side and side ;
>   So in slow countermarch," etc,

The reviewer of Boyd's *Inferno* in the *Gentleman's Magazine* for
May, 1785, points out several flagrant instances of the translator's
amplifications, one of which is the expansion of Dante's three
lines

> " Quegli è Omero poeta sovrano,
>   L' altro è Orazio satiro, che viene,
>   Ovidio è 'l terzo, e l' ultimo Lucano,"
>
> (*Inf.* iv. 88-90)

into the following *nine* :—

> " 'Tis mighty Homer, first of bards ! who sung
>   How on the flying rear Achilles hung,
>   And all the terrors of Scamander's field !
>
>   Near him, the master of the Latian lyre,
>   Who civiliz'd the rude Satyric Choir,
>   And bade them mingle with the polished throng ;
>   And mighty Lucan stain'd with civil blood,
>   With him who to the swans on Ister's flood
>   In exile sung his sweetly plaintive song !"

Another sample, from the well-known opening lines of the poem,
will show how greatly superior was Cary's version in fidelity and
diction to that of his immediate predecessor :—

> " When life had labour'd up her midmost stage,
>   And, weary with her mortal pilgrimage,
>   Stood in suspense upon the point of Prime ;
>   Far in a pathless grove I chanc'd to stray,
>   Where scarce imagination dares display,
>   The gloomy scen'ry of the savage clime."

Cary's venture did not meet with the encouragement it deserved. One of his most severe critics was his friend, Miss Anna Seward—a high literary authority in those days. She not only expressed her distaste for the subject-matter of the poem, but further charged the translation with " obscurity and vulgarism." Writing in August 1806, in acknowledgment of the second volume, she says :—

" This second part of the *Inferno* increases my wonder at the longevity of Dante's fame. Few are the passages of genuine poetry, of power to mitigate the ridiculous infelicity of the plot ; an epic poem consisting wholly of dialogue and everlasting egotism ! . . . the terrible graces of the *Inferno* lose all their dignity in butcherly, gridiron, and intestinal exhibitions, which become fatal to our esteem for the contriver. . . . In several passages you have not been able to remove the veil of inflated and dense obscurity which envelops the meaning of this fire and smoke poet. . . . I think if you had fully comprehended the enigmas you have Anglicised, you would, by more perspicuous language, have enabled your readers to understand them also, though perhaps at the expense of some portion of that literality unfortunately the first object of so many translators."[1]

After referring to one passage of the poem as containing " the filthiest horridness I ever met without the limits of this volume, for within it there is yet transcending filthiness," Miss Seward goes on to take Cary to task for making use of expressions (" such as *folk* for *souls* in hell, *tell on't*

---

[1] *Letters,* vol. vi. pp. 302 ff.

b

for *tell of it, liker, maul,* and other similar vulgarisms ") which debase his blank-verse. In a
second letter she returns to the charge, quoting a
number of passages in which she declares Cary to
have failed in his translation, either through want
of perspicuity or through want of dignity. Cary
made a very spirited defence, and had little difficulty
in justifying the expressions complained of as
" vulgarisms " by references to parallel usages in
Shakespeare and Milton, whom Miss Seward had
held up to him as his proper models.

Miss Seward, however, did Cary one great
service in connection with his translation — she
introduced it to the notice of Scott, who had
come to Lichfield to pay her a visit on his way
back from London in May 1807, " having
diverged from the great road to Scotland for the
purpose." In a letter to Cary, written from
Lichfield a day or two after Scott's visit, she
says :—

" I shewed Mr. Scott the passage in your Dante which
mentions his work, and the Magician it celebrates.[1]
He had heard of your translation, but not read it. On
looking at a few of the passages, and comparing them
with the original, he said there was power and skill in
having breathed so much spirit into a translation so
nearly literal; but he confessed his inability to find
pleasure in that author, even in his own language,
which Mr. Scott perfectly understands. The plan, he

---

[1] In his note on *Inferno,* xx. 116, where Dante mentions the
wizard Michael Scot, Cary had quoted the account given by Scott
in his notes to the *Lay of the Last Minstrel.*

said, appeared to him unhappy, as it was singular, and the personal malignity and strange mode of revenge, presumptuous and uninteresting. However, he promised to examine your English version more largely when he could find leisure." [1]

Cary's version of the *Purgatorio*, which he finished towards the end of 1807,[2] did not see the light until seven years later, when it was issued as one of the three small volumes in which the complete translation of the whole of the *Commedia* first made its appearance. The translation itself had been completed in May 8, 1812, as is recorded in Cary's *Journal* under that date ("Finished my translation of Dante's *Commedia* — began the 16th of Jan.[3] 1797"). The two years which elapsed before its publication were chiefly taken up with the compilation of the notes. The little notice attracted by his version of the *Inferno*, published nearly eight years before, made it impossible for Cary to find a publisher for the whole work. He was consequently obliged to publish it at his own expense, and in a cheap form, which was not calculated to further its fortunes with the public. Writing to a friend on December 28, 1813, he says :—

"The book is a cheap one, if the quantity alone be considered. The price is only twelve shillings for the

---

[1] *Letters*, vol. vi. pp. 339-340. See also Lockhart's *Life of Sir Walter Scott*, vol. ii. pp. 121-122.

[2] *Memoir of Cary*, vol. i. p. 253.

[3] Printed *June*; but there is no doubt about the correct date, for in his *Journal* for January 16, 1797, is the entry :— "Translated Dante, *Purgatorio*, part of the first Canto."

three volumes in boards; and though they are diminutive in size, yet they contain letter-press in abundance. They will come out on the first of next month." [1]

The subsequent fate of the work forms a curious chapter in literary history. It was very highly praised in the *Gentleman's Magazine*, and disposed of with "two or three lines of very contemptuous mention" in the *Critical Review*; after which, for the next four years, it appears to have remained entirely unnoticed. Its sudden leap into fame was due to an accidental meeting of Cary with the poet Coleridge in the year 1817, which is thus described by Cary's son, who was with his father at the time :—

"At the retired village of Littlehampton occurred one of the most important incidents (I might almost call it an event), of my father's life, that is, his becoming acquainted with Coleridge. The manner of their introduction is perhaps not devoid of interest.

"Several hours of each day were spent by Mr. Cary in reading the Classics with the writer of this memoir, who was then only thirteen years of age. After a morning of toil over Greek and Latin composition, it was our custom to walk on the sands and read Homer aloud, a practice adopted partly for the sake of the sea-breezes, and not a little, I believe, in order that the pupil might learn to read *ore rotundo*, having to raise his voice above the noise of the sea that was breaking at our feet. For several consecutive days Coleridge crossed us in our walks. The sound of the Greek, and especially the expressive countenance of the tutor, attracted his notice;

---

[1] *Memoir of Cary*, vol. i. p. 283.

so one day, as we met, he placed himself directly in my father's way and thus accosted him: ' Sir, yours is a face I *should* know: I am Samuel Taylor Coleridge.' His person was not unknown to my father, who had already pointed him out to me as the great genius of our age and country. . . .

"The close of our walk found Coleridge at our family dinner-table. Amongst other topics of conversation Dante's ' divine ' poem was mentioned: Coleridge had never heard of my father's translation, but took a copy home with him that night. On the following day, when the two friends met for the purpose of taking their daily stroll, Coleridge was able to recite whole pages of the version of Dante, and, though he had not the original with him, repeated passages of that also, and commented on the translation. Before leaving Littlehampton he expressed his determination to bring the version of Dante into public notice; and this, more than any other single person, he had the means of doing in his course of lectures delivered in London during the winter months. . . .

"In the month of February 1818, Coleridge, in a lecture on Dante, being the tenth in his course, made mention of my father's translation. Of the terms in which he introduced it no record has been preserved. In his *Literary Remains* (vol. i. p. 161,) edited by Mr. Henry Nelson Coleridge, the following memorandum is made in his Notes for this lecture :—' Here to speak of Mr. Cary's translation.'

"The effect of his commendation, however, was no other than might have been expected. The work, which had been published four years, but had remained in utter obscurity, was at once eagerly sought after. About a thousand copies of the first edition that remained on hand were immediately disposed of; in less than three months a new edition was called for. The *Edinburgh* and *Quarterly Reviews* re-echoed the praises that had been sounded by Coleridge, and henceforth the claims of the translator of Dante to literary distinction were universally admitted."[1]

It appears from a letter written to a friend by Cary in June 1818, that he received £125 for the second edition of his Dante, which was published in the following year, as well as £109 for the remainder of the first edition.[2]

The vogue of the translation at this time was such that, as Cary records with gratification, a year after the issue of the new edition the Master of the Charterhouse gave a large order for the work, "for the use of his boys to turn into Latin verse," which order could not be supplied.[3]

As was to be expected, the demand for the book after a time fell off considerably, and a third edition was not called for until 1831, twelve years after the publication of the second, of which it was a reprint.[4] The sale, however, continued steadily if slowly, and Cary had the satisfaction of seeing a fourth edition, with numerous corrections and additions, issued from the press a few months

---

[1] *Memoir of Cary*, vol. ii. pp. 17.foll.

[2] *Memoir of Cary*, vol. ii. p. 32,

[3] *Memoir of Cary*, vol. ii. p. 54. Apparently this order was for the original cheap edition.

[4] It is a testimony to the popularity of Cary's translation even at that early date, that it was thought worth while to publish a pirated edition, a reprint of the second English edition, in America (at Philadelphia in 1822). As a consequence it was decided to issue the fourth edition at such a low price (rbs. 6d.) as to prevent a recurrence of this proceeding. Cary, oddly enough, was inclined to condone the piracy, which he preferred to regard as "no more than a fair competition between the two countries."—See *Memoir of Cary*, vol. ii. p. 327.

before his death in 1844, when he was in his seventy-second year.[1]   Since his death the translation has been repeatedly reprinted both in England and America.   In England, in spite of numerous rivals, it still holds its own as the standard translation.   In America it has now to a large extent been superseded by Longfellow's version, which was first published in 1867, the *Inferno* having been privately printed in 1865, on the occasion of the celebration at Florence of the sixth centenary of Dante's birth, and the *Purgatorio* in the following year.

II

THE "PURGATORIO"

Purgatory, the place of purgation and of preparation for the life of eternal blessedness,[2] according to Dante's conception, consists of an island-mountain, formed by the earth which retreated before Lucifer as he fell from Heaven into the abyss of Hell.[3] This mountain, which has the form of an immense truncated cone, rises out of the ocean in the centre of the southern hemisphere, where, according to the Ptolemaic system of cosmography followed by

---

[1] A cheaper edition, a reprint of the fourth, in double columns, was issued in this same year by the same publisher (William Smith) at 6s.

[2]

> " That second region . . .
> In which the human spirit from sinful blot
> Is purged, and for ascent to Heaven prepares."
> *Purg.* i. 4–6.

[3] *Inferno*, xxxiv. 122–126.

Dante, there was nothing (except, of course, in Dante's view, the mountain of Purgatory) save a vast expanse of water. The mountain is the exact antipodes of Jerusalem,[1] the central point of the northern hemisphere, where Christ suffered for the sin of Adam committed in the Garden of Eden (*i.e.* the Terrestrial Paradise at the summit of the mountain).

The lower part of the mountain is not a department of Purgatory proper, but forms an Ante-purgatory, where are located the spirits of those who died without having availed themselves of the means of penitence offered by the Church. These are divided into four classes. The first consists of those who died in contumacy of the Church, and only repented at the last moment ; these have to remain in Ante-purgatory for a period thirty-fold that during which they had been contumacious, unless the period is shortened by the prayers of others on their behalf.[2] The second class consists of those who in indolence and indifference put off their repentance until just before their death ; these are detained outside Purgatory for a period equal to that of their lives upon earth, unless it be shortened by prayers on their behalf.[3] The third class consists of those who died a violent death, without absolution, but repented at the last moment ; these are detained under the same conditions as the last class ; during their detention they circle round

---

[1] *Purgatorio*, ii. 3, iv. 68, xxvii. 2.
[2] *Purgatorio*, iii. 136–141.   [3] *Purgatorio*, iv. 130–135.

and round, chanting the *Miserere*.[1] The fourth class consists of kings and princes who deferred their repentance owing to the pressure of temporal interests; these, who are detained for the same period as the last two classes, are placed in a valley full of flowers, and are guarded at night by two angels against the attacks of a serpent.[2]

Purgatory proper, which is entered by a gate guarded by an angel, consists of seven concentric terraces, each about seventeen feet wide,[3] which rise in succession with diminished circuit[4] as they approach the summit, where is situated the Terrestrial Paradise. The ascent to the gate of Purgatory is by three steps of diverse colours, the first of which is of polished white marble; the second is of rock, almost black, rough and burnt as with fire, and cracked across its length and breadth, in the shape of a cross; the third and topmost is of porphyry of a bright blood-red colour. The threshold of the gate, whereon is seated the guardian angel, is of adamantine rock.[5]

The terraces within the gate are connected by steep and narrow stairways, the steps of which become successively less steep as each terrace is

[1] *Purgatorio*, v. 22–24, 52–57.
[2] *Purgatorio*, vii. 64–84, viii. 22–39.
[3] *Purgatorio*, x. 22–24, xiii. 4–5.
[4] *Purgatorio*, xiii. 4–6.
[5] *Purgatorio*, ix. 76–77, 94–105. These three steps are symbolical of the state of mind with which penance is to be approached, and denote respectively, as Maria Rossetti interprets, "candid confession, mirroring the whole man; mournful contrition, breaking the hard heart of the gazer on the Cross; love, all aflame, offering up in satisfaction the life-blood of body, soul, and spirit." (*Shadow of Dante*, p. 112.)

surmounted. Each of the seven terraces or circles corresponds to one of the seven deadly sins, from the traces of which the soul is there purged. The seven terraces, together with Ante-purgatory and the Terrestrial Paradise, form nine divisions, thus corresponding to the nine circles of Hell, and the nine spheres of Paradise. At the foot of the mountain is stationed Cato of Utica as guardian; at the entrance to Purgatory proper, and at the approach to each of the terraces, stands an angel, who chants one of the Beatitudes to comfort those who are purging them of their sins.

In the first circle, where the sin of *pride* is purged, the angel sings *Beati pauperes spiritu,* " Blessed are the poor in spirit." In the second circle, where the sin of *envy* is purged, the angel sings *Beati misericordes,* " Blessed are the merciful." In the third circle, where the sin of *wrath* is purged, the angel sings *Beati pacifici,* " Blessed are the peacemakers." In the fourth circle, where the sin of *sloth* is purged, the angel sings *Beati qui lugent,* " Blessed are they that mourn." In the fifth circle, where the sin of *avarice* is purged, the angel sings *Beati qui sitiunt justitiam,* " Blessed are they who thirst after justice." In the sixth circle, where the sin of *gluttony* is purged, the angel sings *Beati qui esuriunt justitiam,* " Blessed are they who hunger after justice." In the seventh circle, where the sin of *lust* is purged, the angel sings *Beati mundo corde,* " Blessed are the pure in heart."

The system of purgation is explained to Dante by his guide Virgil as follows : [1]—love exists in every creature, and as, if rightly directed, it is the spring of every good action, so, if ill directed, it is the spring of every evil action; love may err through a bad object (thus giving birth to *pride, envy, anger*), through defect of vigour in pursuit of good (thus giving birth to *sloth*), through excess of vigour in the same (thus giving birth to *avarice, gluttony*, and *lust*).

The manner of purgation is threefold, consisting in, firstly, a material punishment intended to mortify the evil passions and incite to virtue; secondly, a subject for meditation, bearing on the sin purged, and its opposite virtue, with examples of persons conspicuous for the one or the other drawn from sacred and profane history; thirdly, a prayer, whereby the soul is purified and strengthened in the grace of God.

In the Terrestrial Paradise are two streams, Lethe and Eunoe, the former of which washes away the remembrance of sin, while the latter strengthens the remembrance of good deeds.

The time occupied by Dante in passing through Purgatory was four days—one day (Easter day) in Ante-purgatory; [2] two days (Easter Monday [3] and Easter Tuesday [4]) in Purgatory proper; and one

---

[1] *Purgatorio*, xvii.–xviii.
[2] *Purgatorio*, i. 19–ix. 9.
[3] *Purgatorio*, ix. 13–xviii. 76.
[4] *Purgatorio*, xix. 1.–xxvii. 89.

day (Easter Wednesday) in the Terrestrial Paradise.[1]

> "O'er better waves to speed her rapid course
> The light bark of my genius lifts the sail,
> Well pleased to leave so cruel sea behind."[2]

The feeling of relief experienced by Dante on emerging from the gloom of Hell once more under the canopy of heaven, "once more to see the stars," [3] is a feeling which is in great measure likewise experienced by his readers. To pass from the *Inferno* to the *Purgatorio* is to pass from the atmosphere of the prison-house to the free air of the mountain-side, whence, like Dante, we may "descry from afar the quivering of the sea before the flying breath of dawn." [4] Here we exchange the spectacle of the doomed and the desperate in everlasting torment, for the companionship of beings, who suffer indeed, but to whom hope is not denied, for whom prayers may yet avail.

The secret of the attraction of the *Purgatorio*, as compared with the *Inferno* on the one hand, and the *Paradiso* on the other, is revealed in a word by Dean Church—"the *Purgatorio* is more human."

"In spite (says the same writer) of famous episodes, the eternal memorials of the world's sin and woe, we shrink from the relentless and hopeless terrors of the *Inferno*, from its audacities, from its grotesque

---

[1] *Purgatorio*, xxvii. 94–xxxiii. 103.
[2] *Purgatorio*, i. 1–3.
[3] *Inferno*, xxxiv. 139.
[4] *Purgatorio*, i. 115–117.

brutalities. . . . And, with all the serene splendour of the *Paradiso*, most readers, at least most beginners, find it more difficult to enter into than even the *Inferno*. It is possible to follow in imagination the miseries of those who suffer; but who can divine or conceive what is thought or felt by spirits on the other side of death, beyond temptation and weakness and pain, glorified and made perfect? But the *Purgatorio* is a great parable of the discipline on earth of moral agents, of the variety of their failures and needs, of the variety of their remedies. We understand the behaviour of those who are undergoing their figurative processes of purification. . . . We understand their resignation, their thankful submission to the chastisement which is to be the annealing to strength and peace. . . . We understand the aim and purpose which sustain them, the high-hearted courage which endures, the steady hope which knows that all is well. . . .

"In another way also the *Purgatorio* is more human in its interest than the *Inferno* and the *Paradiso*. It abounds with local touches, reminiscences of actual places and scenes, which had impressed themselves on the mind of a man who had travelled much and observed keenly the features of a landscape, the circumstances of a perilous adventure, the enjoyment of an interesting or happy day. Such touches are indeed wanting in none of the books, but they are more frequent in the *Purgatorio*. Each of the cantos which describe the climbing of the sacred mountain, or the wanderings along its ledges, shows some special mark of the experience of a man who was familiar with the rough and dangerous paths by which travellers had to cross Alps or Apennines; who had noted their characteristic appearances and difficulties: the soft falling of the accumulating snow, the apparently hopeless steepness of some sheer precipice barring the way; who had been surprised far from shelter by the night; who had woke up by sea-shore or mountain to the gradual glories of the dawn; who had been excited and cheered by the sudden meeting with fellow-travellers on his desolate road. He delights to recall, by name or place, some scene which dwells in his memory. . . . He likes to recall some perhaps momentary thrill, such as that which pierces the voyager who has just parted from his friends, when he hears at sea the evening bell over the waters ' seeming to mourn the day which is dying.'[1]

"In the *Purgatorio* the poet finds companions who are neither below him, nor hopelessly enstranged from him, as in the *Inferno*, nor far above him, as in the *Paradiso*: they are still almost creatures of flesh and blood, certainly human characters, capable of effort, pain, and self-command, going through their training as he is going through his, though on a higher level, having in view the aims and hopes which lead him on, praying the prayers which he prays, singing the psalms which he sings, receiving the absolution which is vouchsafed to him.'

A further attraction in the *Purgatorio* is supplied by the scenery and surroundings. Instead of being confounded by the horrors and pitchy blackness of Hell, or bewildered by the almost dazzling radiance of the heavenly spheres, we find ourselves here in the presence of the beauties of nature and of art, in a world where music and poetry, painting and sculpture, still charm the ear aud eye, and where the heart is gladdened, amid flowers and trees

---

[1] *Purgatorio*, viii. 5–6: "Squilla di lontano, Che paia il giorno pianger che muore"—the original of Gray's "curfew tolls the knell of parting day."

[2] Introduction by the Dean of St. Paul's (R. W. Church) to *Readings on the Purgatorio of Dante*, by the Honble. William Warren Vernon, 1897, vol. i. pp. xiii. foll.

and streams, by the light of the sun and of the stars.

The *Purgatorio* is especially rich in beautiful and touching episodes, such as that (in the second Canto) of the meeting of Dante with

> "His Casella, whom he woo'd to sing;
> Met in the milder shades of Purgatory";—

his interview (in the third Canto) with the comely and accomplished Manfred, the hapless King of Sicily;—the account given (in the fifth Canto) by Buonconte da Montefeltro of his death at Campaldino, and of the fate of his body after the battle;—the sudden kindling into life of the Mantuan Sordello (in the sixth Canto), at the name of his native place pronounced by Virgil, at whom he had previously been gazing "haughty and disdainful, like a lion in repose";—the meeting of Statius and Virgil, and the former's account (in the twenty-second Canto) of how by Virgil's means he had been converted to Christianity, wherein Virgil did "as one who goes by night bearing a lantern, and helps not himself, but shows the way to those who come behind";—the appearance of Matilda (in the twenty-eighth Canto) gathering flowers along the banks of the stream in the Terrestrial Paradise, singing as she goes;—and lastly (in the thirtieth Canto), Dante's distress at finding Virgil gone, "Virgil his beloved father," at the very moment when at last Beatrice reveals her

presence, the moment for which he had thirsted
during ten long years.[1]

These are some of the " beauties of Dante " con-
tained in the *Purgatorio ;* but it should be borne in
mind, as Dean Church is careful to remind us, that
" Dante certainly did not intend to be read only
in fine passages "—to be properly understood, and
properly appreciated, he must be read as a whole,
and studied as a whole.

To Dante's readers, as to Dante himself, the
passage through the *Purgatorio* is a preparation for
higher things.   Few who read this second *Cantica*
with due attention and with due reverence will fail
to feel something of what Dante felt after tasting
the waters of Eunoe—

> " Back turned I from that wave most blest,
>   Fresh, as fresh plant with fresh leaves dressed,
>   Prepared, all clean from cares,
>   To mount unto the stars." [2]

---

[1] *Purgatorio,* xxxii. 2.
[2] *Purgatorio,* xxxiii. 142-145 (Shadwell's translation):—

> " Io ritornai dalla santissim' onda
>   Rifatto sì, come piante novelle
>   Rinnovellate di novella fronda,
> Puro e disposto a salire alle stelle."

THE VISION OF DANTE

PURGATORY

CANTO I

ARGUMENT

The Poet describes the delight he experienced at issuing a little before dawn from the infernal regions, into the pure air that surrounds the isle of Purgatory; and then relates how, turning to the right, he beheld four stars never seen before but by our first parents, and met on his left the shade of Cato of Utica, who, having warned him and Virgil what is needful to be done before they proceed on their way through Purgatory, disappears; and the two poets go towards the shore, where Virgil cleanses Dante's face with the dew, and girds him with a reed, as Cato had commanded.

O'ER better waves [1] to speed her rapid course
The light bark of my genius lifts the sail,
Well pleased to leave so cruel sea behind;
And of that second region will I sing,
In which the human spirit from sinful blot
Is purged, and for ascent to Heaven prepares.
    Here, O ye hallow'd Nine! for in your train
I follow, here the deaden'd strain revive;
Nor let Calliope refuse to sound

[1] *O'er better waves.*] So Berni, Orl. Inn. lib. ii. c. i.

    Per correr maggior acqua alza le vele,
    O debil navicella del mio ingegno.

1

A somewhat higher song, of that loud tone
Which when the wretched birds of chattering note [1]
Had heard, they of forgiveness lost all hope.

Sweet hue of eastern sapphire, that was spread
O'er the serene aspect of the pure air,
High up as the first circle, [2] to mine eyes
Unwonted joy renew'd, soon as I 'scaped
Forth from the atmosphere of deadly gloom,
That had mine eyes and bosom fill'd with grief.
The radiant planet, [3] that to love invites,
Made all the orient laugh, [4] and veil'd beneath
The Pisces' light, [5] that in his escort came.

To the right hand I turned, and fix'd my mind
On the other pole attentive, where I saw
Four stars [6] ne'er seen before save by the ken

[1] *Birds of chattering note.*] For the fable of the daughters of
Pierus who challenged the muses to sing, and were by them
changed into magpies, see Ovid, *Met.* lib. v. fab. 5.

[2] *The first circle.*] Either, as some suppose, the moon ; or, as
Lombardi (who likes to be as far off the rest of the commentators as
possible) will have it, the highest circle of the stars.

[3] *Planet.*] Venus.

[4] *Made all the orient laugh.*] Hence Chaucer, Knight's Tale :

And all the orisont laugheth of the sight.

It is sometimes read "orient."

[5] *The Pisces' light.*] The constellation of the Fish veiled by the
more luminous body of Venus, then a morning star.

[6] *Four stars.*] Venturi observes that "Dante here speaks as a
poet, and almost in the spirit of prophecy ; or, what is more likely,
describes the heaven about that pole according to his own invention. In our days," he adds, "the cross, composed of four stars,
three of the second and one of the third magnitude, serves as a
guide to those who sail from Europe to the south ; but in the age
of Dante these discoveries had not been made :" yet it appears
probable, that either from long tradition, or from the relation of
later voyagers, the real truth might not have been unknown to our
Poet. Seneca's prediction of the discovery of America may be
accounted for in a similar manner. But whatever may be thought
of this, it is certain that the four stars are here symbolical of the
four cardinal virtues, Prudence, Justice, Fortitude, and Temperance.
See Canto xxxi. v. 105. M. Artaud mentions a globe constructed
by an Arabian in Egypt, with the date of the year 622 of the
Hegira, corresponding to 1225 of our era, in which the southern
cross is positively marked. See his Histoire de Dante, ch. xxxi.
and xl. 8°. Par. 1841.

Of our first parents.[1]   Heaven of their rays
Seem'd joyous.   Oh thou northern site ! bereft
Indeed, and widow'd, since of these deprived.

As from this view I had desisted, straight
Turning a little towards the other pole,
There from whence now the wain [2] had disappear'd,
I saw an old man [3] standing by my side
Alone, so worthy of reverence in his look,
That ne'er from son to father more was owed.
Low down his beard, and mix'd with hoary white,
Descended, like his locks, which, parting, fell
Upon his breast in double fold.   The beams
Of those four luminaries on his face
So brightly shone, and with such radiance clear
Deck'd it, that I beheld him as the sun.

"Say who are ye, that stemming the blind stream,
Forth from the eternal prison-house have fled ?"
He spoke and moved those venerable plumes.[4]

[1] *Our first parents.*]   In the terrestrial paradise, placed, as we
shall see, by our Poet, on the summit of Purgatory.
[2] *The wain.*]   Charles's Wain, or Boötes.
[3] *An old man.*]   Cato.

Secretosque pios ; his dantem jura Catonem.
Virg. Æn. viii. 670.

The commentators, and Lombardi amongst the rest, might have
saved themselves and their readers much needless trouble if they
would have consulted the prose writings of Dante with more
diligence.   In the Convito (iv. 28) he has himself declared his
opinion of the illustrious Roman.   "Quale uomo, etc."   "What
earthly man was more worthy to follow God than Cato ?
Certainly none."   And again : "Nel nome di cui, etc."   "In
whose name, whatever needs be said concerning the signs of
nobility may be concluded ; for, in him, that nobility displays them
all throughout all ages."

[4] *Venerable plumes.*]   Insperata tuæ quum veniet pluma
superbiæ.
Hor. Carm. lib. iv. ode 10.
The same metaphor has occurred in Hell, Canto xx. 41.

—— the plumes,
That mark'd the better sex.

It is used by Ford in the Lady's Trial, act iv. sc. 2.

—— Now the down
Of softness is exchanged for plumes of age.

" Who hath conducted, or with lantern sure
Lights you emerging from the depth of night,
That makes the infernal valley ever black ?
Are the firm statutes of the dread abyss
Broken, or in high heaven new laws ordain'd,
That thus, condemn'd, ye to my caves approach ? "
 My guide, then laying hold on me, by words
And intimations given with hand and head,
Made my bent knees and eye submissive pay
Due reverence ; then thus to him replied :
 " Not of myself I come ; a Dame from heaven [1]
Descending, him besought me in my charge
To bring. But since thy will implies, that more
Our true condition I unfold at large,
Mine is not to deny thee thy request.
This mortal ne'er hath seen the furthest gloom ; [2]
But erring by his folly had approach'd
So near, that little space was left to turn.
Then, as before I told, I was despatch'd
To work his rescue ; and no way remain'd
Save this which I have ta'en. I have display'd
Before him all the regions of the bad ;
And purpose now those spirits to display,
That under thy command are purged from sin.
How I have brought him would be long to say.
From high descends the virtue, by whose aid
I to thy sight and hearing him have led.

---

[1] *A Dame from heaven.*] Beatrice. See Hell, ii. 54.
[2] *The furthest gloom.*] L'ultima sera.
So Ariosto, O. F. Canto xxxiv. st. 59.

 Che non han visto ancor l'ultima sera.

And Filicaja, Canto ix. Al Sonno.

 L'ultima sera.

And Mr. Mathias, Canzone a Guglielmo Roscoe premessa alla
Storia della Poesia Italiana, p. 13.

 Di morte non vedrà l'ultima sera.

Now may our coming please thee.   In the search
Of liberty he journeys : that how dear,
They know who for her sake have life refused.
Thou knowest, to whom death for her was sweet
In Utica, where thou didst leave those weeds,
That in the last great day will shine so bright.
For us the eternal edicts are unmoved :
He breathes, and I of Minos am not bound,[1]
Abiding in that circle, where the eyes
Of thy chaste Marcia[2] beam, who still in look
Prays thee, O hallow'd spirit ! to own her thine.
Then by her love we implore thee, let us pass
Through thy seven regions ;[3] for which, best thanks
I for thy favour will to her return,
If mention there below thou not disdain."

    "Marcia so pleasing in my sight was found,"
He then to him rejoin'd, "while I was there,
That all she ask'd me I was fain to grant.
Now that beyond the accursed stream she dwells,
She may no longer move me, by that law,[4]

[1] *Of Minos am not bound.*]   See Hell, v. 4.
[2] *Marcia.*]   —— Da fœdera prisci
         Illibata tori : da tantum nomen inane
         Connubii : liceat tumulo scripsisse, Catonis
         Martia.   *Lucan, Phars.* lib. ii. 344.

Our author's habit of putting an allegorical interpretation on
everything, a habit which appears to have descended to that age
from certain fathers of the church, is nowhere more apparent than
in his explanation of this passage. See Convito (iv. 28.) "Marzia
fu vergine, etc." "Marcia was a virgin, and in that state she
signifies childhood ; then she came to Cato, and in that state she
represents youth ; she then bare children, by whom are represented
the virtues that we have said belong to that age." Dante would
surely have done well to remember his own rule laid down in the
De Monarch. lib. iii. "Advertendum, etc." "Concerning the
mystical sense it must be observed that we may err in two ways,
either by seeing it where it is not, or by taking it otherwise than it
ought to be taken."

[3] *Through thy seven regions.*]   The seven rounds of Purgatory,
in which the seven capital sins are punished.

[4] *By that law.*]   When he was delivered by Christ from limbo, a
change of affections accompanied his change of place.

Which was ordain'd me, when I issued thence.
Not so, if Dame from heaven, as thou sayst,
Moves and directs thee; then no flattery needs.
Enough for me that in her name thou ask.
Go therefore now: and with a slender reed [1]
See that thou duly gird him, and his face
Lave, till all sordid stain thou wipe from thence.
For not with eye, by any cloud obscured,
Would it be seemly before him to come,
Who stands the foremost minister in heaven.
This islet all around, there far beneath,
Where the wave beats it, on the oozy bed
Produces store of reeds.   No other plant,
Cover'd with leaves, or harden'd in its stalk,
There lives, not bending to the water's sway.
After, this way return not; but the sun
Will show you, that now rises, where to take [2]
The mountain in its easiest ascent."

He disappear'd; and I myself upraised
Speechless, and to my guide retiring close,
Toward him turn'd mine eyes.   He thus began:
"My son! observant thou my steps pursue.
We must retreat to rereward; for that way
The champain to its low extreme declines."

The dawn had chased the matin hour of prime,
Which fled before it, so that from afar
I spied the trembling of the ocean stream. [3]

---

[1] *A slender reed.*] The reed is here supposed, with sufficient probability, to be meant for a type of simplicity and patience.

[2] *Where to take.*] "Prendere il monte," a reading which Lombardi claims for his favourite Nidobeatina edition, is also found in Landino's of 1484.

[3] *I spied the trembling of the ocean stream.*]

        Conobbi il tremolar della marina.

So Trissino in the Sofonisba.

        E resta in tremolar l'onda marina.

And Fortiguerra, Ricciardetto, Canto ix. st. 17.

        —— visto il tremolar della marina.

We traversed the deserted plain, as one
Who, wander'd from his track, thinks every step
Trodden in vain till he regain the path.
  When we had come, where yet the tender dew
Strove with the sun, and in a place where fresh
The wind breathed o'er it, while it slowly dried;
Both hands extended on the watery grass
My master placed, in graceful act and kind.
Whence I of his intent before apprized,
Stretch'd out to him my cheeks suffused with tears.
There to my visage he anew restored
That hue which the dun shades of hell conceal'd.
  Then on the solitary shore arrived,
That never sailing on its waters saw
Man that could after measure back his course,
He girt me in such manner as had pleased
Him who instructed; and O strange to tell!
As he selected every humble plant,
Wherever one was pluck'd another [1] there
Resembling, straightway in its place arose.

CANTO II

ARGUMENT

They behold a vessel under conduct of an angel, coming over the
waves with spirits to Purgatory, among whom, when the passengers
have landed, Dante recognises his friend Casella; but, while they
are entertained by him with a song, they hear Cato exclaiming
against their negligent loitering, and at that rebuke hasten forward
to the mountain.

Now had the sun [2] to that horizon reach'd,
That covers, with the most exalted point

---

[1] *Another.*] From Virg. Æn. lib. vi. 143. Primo avulso non
deficit alter.
[2] *Now had the sun.*] Dante was now antipodal to Jerusalem; so

Of its meridian circle, Salem's walls;
And night, that opposite to him her orb
Rounds, from the stream of Ganges issued forth,
Holding the scales,[1] that from her hands are dropt
When she reigns highest:[2] so that where I was,
Aurora's white and vermeil-tinctured cheek
To orange turn'd [3] as she in age increased.
    Meanwhile we linger'd by the water's brink,
Like men,[4] who, musing on their road, in thought
Journey, while motionless the body rests.
When lo! as, near upon the hour of dawn,
Through the thick vapours [5] Mars with fiery beam
Glares down in west, over the ocean floor;
So seem'd, what once again I hope to view,
A light, so swiftly coming through the sea,
No winged course might equal its career.
From which when for a space I had withdrawn
Mine eyes, to make inquiry of my guide,
Again I look'd, and saw it grown in size
And brightness: then on either side appear'd
Something, but what I knew not, of bright hue,

that while the sun was setting with respect to that place, which he
supposes to be the middle of the inhabited earth, to him it was
rising.   See Routh's Reliquæ Sacræ, tom. iii. p. 256.   So Fazio
degli Uberti, Dittamondo, lib. vi. cap. vi.

> —— questo monte è quello
> Ch' in mezzo il mondo apunto si divisa.

[1] *The scales.*]   The constellation Libra.
[2] *When she reigns highest.*]   "Quando soverchia" is (according
to Venturi, whom I have followed) "when the autumnal equinox is
passed."   Lombardi supposes it to mean "when the nights begin to
increase, that is, after the summer solstice."
[3] *To orange turn'd.*]   "L'aurora già di vermiglia cominciava
appressandosi il sole a divenir rancia."   Boccaccio, Decam. G. iii.
at the beginning.   See notes to Hell, xxiii. 101.
[4] *Like men.*]   Che va col cuore e col corpo dimora.
So Frezzi.   E mentre il corpo posa, col cor varca.
                              Il Quadrir. lib. iv. cap. 8.
[5] *Through the thick vapours.*]   So in the Convito (ii. 14).   "Esso
pare, etc."   "He (Mars) appears more or less inflamed with heat,
according to the thickness or rarity of the vapours that follow him.

And by degrees from underneath it came
Another.   My preceptor silent yet
Stood, while the brightness, that we first discern'd,
Open'd the form of wings : then when he knew
The pilot, cried aloud, " Down, down ; bend low
Thy knees ; behold God's angel : fold thy hands :
Now shalt thou see true ministers indeed.
Lo ! how all human means he sets at nought ;
So that nor oar he needs, nor other sail
Except his wings,[1] between such distant shores.
Lo ! how straight up to heaven he holds them
      rear'd,
Winnowing the air [2] with those eternal plumes,
That not like mortal hairs fall off or change."
    As more and more toward us came, more bright
Appear'd the bird of God, nor could the eye
Endure his splendour near : I mine bent down.
He drove ashore in a small bark so swift
And light, that in its course no wave it drank.
The heavenly steersman at the prow was seen,
Visibly written Blessed in his looks.
Within, a hundred spirits and more there sat.
    " In Exitu [3] Israel de Egypto,"
All with one voice together sang, with what
In the remainder of that hymn is writ.
Then soon as with the sign of holy cross
He bless'd them, they at once leap'd out on
      land :
He, swiftly as he came, return'd.   The crew,

---

[1] *Except his wings.*]   Hence Milton :
        Who after came from earth, sailing arrived
        Wafted by angels.   *P. L.* b. iii. ver. 521.

[2] *Winnowing the air.*]
            Trattando l'aere con l'eterne penne.

So Filicaja, canz. viii. st. 11.   Ma trattar l'aere coll' eterne piume.
    [3] *In Exitu.*]   " When Israel came out of Egypt."   Ps. cxiv.

There left, appear'd astounded with the place,
Gazing around, as one who sees new sights.
  From every side the sun darted his beams,
And with his arrowy radiance [1] from mid heaven
Had chased the Capricorn, when that strange
    tribe,
Lifting their eyes toward us : " If ye know,
Declare what path will lead us to the mount."
  Them Virgil answer'd : " Ye suppose, perchance,
Us well acquainted with this place : but here,
We, as yourselves, are strangers.   Not long erst
We came, before you but a little space,
By other road so rough and hard, that now
The ascent will seem to us as play."   The spirits,
Who from my breathing had perceived I lived,
Grew pale with wonder.   As the multitude
Flock round a herald sent with olive branch,
To hear what news he brings, and in their haste
Tread one another down ; e'en so at sight
Of me those happy spirits were fix'd, each one
Forgetful of its errand to depart
Where, cleansed from sin, it might be made all fair.
  Then one I saw darting before the rest
With such fond ardour to embrace me, I
To do the like was moved.   O shadows vain !

---

[1] *With his arrowy radiance.*] So Milton :

> —— and now went forth the morn :
> —— from before her vanish'd night,
> Shot through with orient beams.   *P. L.* b. vi. ver. 15.

This has been regarded by some critics as a conceit, into which
Milton was betrayed by the Italian poets ; but it is in truth
authorised by one of the correctest of the Grecians.

> Ὂν αἰόλα νὺξ ἐναριζομένα
> τίκτει, κατευνάζει τε, φλογιζόμενον
> Ἅλιον.   *Sophocles, Trachin.* 96.

  Ecco dinanzi a te fugge repente
Saettata la notte. *Marini, Son. al Sig. Cinthio Aldobrandino.*

Except in outward semblance : thrice my hands [1]
I clasp'd behind it, they as oft return'd
Empty into my breast again.   Surprise
I need must think was painted in my looks,
For that the shadow smiled and backward drew.
To follow it I hasten'd, but with voice
Of sweetness it enjoin'd me to desist.
Then who it was I knew, and pray'd of it,
To talk with me it would a little pause.
It answer'd : " Thee as in my mortal frame
I loved, so loosed from it I love thee still,
And therefore pause : but why walkest thou here ? "

    " Not without purpose once more to return,
Thou find'st me, my Casella,[2] where I am,[3]
Journeying this way ;" I said : " but how of thee
Hath so much time been lost ? "[4]   He answer'd
        straight :

[1] *Thrice my hands.*]

        Ter conatus ibi collo dare brachia circum,
        Ter frustra comprensa manus effugit imago ;
        Par levibus ventis volucrique simillima somno.
                        Virg. Æn. ii. 794.

Compare Homer, Od. xi. 205.
    The incident in the text is pleasantly alluded to in that delightful
book, the Capricci del Botaio of Gelli (Opere. Milan. 1805, v. ii.
p. 26), of which there is an English translation entitled " The Fear-
full Fancies of the Florentine Cooper. Written in Toscane, by
John Baptist Gelli, one of the free studie of Florence. And for re-
creation translated into English by W. Barker." 8°. *Lond.* 1599.
    [2] *My Casella.*] A Florentine, celebrated for his skill in music,
" in whose company," says Landino, " Dante often recreated his
spirits, wearied by severer studies." See Dr. Burney's History of
Music, vol. ii. cap. iv. p. 322. Milton has a fine allusion to this
meeting in his sonnet to Henry Lawes.

        Dante shall give fame leave to set thee higher
        Than his Casella, whom he wooed to sing,
        Met in the milder shades of Purgatory.

    [3] *Where I am.*] " Là dove io son." Lombardi understands this
differently : " Not without purpose to return again to the earth,
where I am ; that is, where I usually dwell."
    [4] *Hath so much time been lost.*] There is some uncertainty in
this passage.   If we read

        Ma a te com' era tanta terra tolta ?

"No outrage hath been done to me, if he,[1]
Who when and whom he chooses takes, hath oft
Denied me passage here ; since of just will
His will he makes.   These three months past[2] in-
    deed,
He, whoso chose to enter, with free leave
Hath taken ; whence I wandering by the shore[3]
Where Tiber's wave grows salt, of him gain'd kind
Admittance, at that river's mouth, toward which
His wings are pointed ; for there always throng
All such as not to Acheron descend."
  Then I : "If new law taketh not from thee
Memory or custom of love-tuned song,
That whilom all my cares had power to 'swage ;
Please thee therewith a little to console
My spirit, that encumber'd with its frame,
Travelling so far, of pain is overcome."
  "Love, that discourses in my thoughts,"[4] he then
Began in such soft accents, that within
The sweetness thrills me yet.   My gentle guide,

with the Nidobeatina and Aldine editions, and many MSS., it sig-
nifies "why art thou deprived of so desirable a region as that of
Purgatory? why dost thou not hasten to be cleansed of thy sins?"
If with the Academicians della Crusca, we read,

Diss 'io, ma a te come tant' ora è tolta?

which is not destitute of authority to support it, and which has the
advantage over the other, as it marks Dante's speech from Casella's,
then it must mean as I have translated it, "why hast thou lost so
much time in arriving here?"   Lombardi, who is for the former
reading, supposes Casella to be just dead ; those, who prefer the
latter, suppose him to have been dead some years, but now only
just arrived.

  [1] *He.*]   The conducting angel.

  [2] *These three months past.*]   Since the time of the Jubilee, during
which all spirits not condemned to eternal punishment were supposed
to pass over to Purgatory as soon as they pleased.

  [3] *The shore.*]   Ostia.

  [4] *"Love, that discourses in my thoughts."*]

"Amor che nella mente mi ragiona."

  The first verse of a canzone in the Convito (iii. 1) of Dante, which
he again cites in his treatise de Vulg. Eloq. lib. ii. cap. 6.

And all who came with him, so well were pleased,
That seem'd nought else might in their thoughts have
      room.
    Fast fix'd in mute attention to his notes
We stood, when lo! that old man venerable
Exclaiming, "How is this, ye tardy spirits?
What negligence detains you loitering here?
Run to the mountain to cast off those scales,
That from your eyes the sight of God conceal."
    As a wild flock of pigeons, to their food
Collected, blade or tares, without their pride
Accustom'd, and in still and quiet sort,
If aught alarm them, suddenly desert
Their meal, assail'd by more important care;
So I that new-come troop beheld, the song
Deserting, hasten to the mountain's side,
As one [1] who goes, yet, where he tends, knows not.
    Nor with less hurried step did we depart.

CANTO III

ARGUMENT

Our Poet, perceiving no shadow except that cast by his own body,
is fearful that Virgil has deserted him; but he is freed from that
error, and both arrive together at the foot of the mountain: on
finding it too steep to climb, they inquire the way from a troop of
spirits that are coming towards them, and are by them shown which
is the easiest ascent. Manfredi, king of Naples, who is one of these
spirits, bids Dante inform his daughter Costanza, queen of Arragon,
of the manner in which he had died.

THEM sudden flight had scatter'd o'er the plain,
Turn'd towards the mountain, whither reason's voice

---

[1] *As one.*] Com' uom, che va, nè sa dove riesca.
So Frezzi: Come chi va, nè sa dove camina.
                              Il Quadrir. lib. i. cap. 3.

Drives us: I, to my faithful company
Adhering, left it not.   For how, of him
Deprived, might I have sped? or who, beside,
Would o'er the mountainous tract have led my steps?
He, with the bitter pang of self-remorse,
Seem'd smitten.   O clear conscience, and upright!
How doth a little failing wound thee sore.[1]
  Soon as his feet desisted (slackening pace)
From haste, that mars all decency of act,[2]
My mind, that in itself before was wrapt,
Its thought expanded, as with joy restored;
And full against the steep ascent I set
My face, where highest[3] to heaven its top o'erflows.
  The sun, that flared behind, with ruddy beam
Before my form was broken; for in me
His rays resistance met.   I turn'd aside
With fear of being left, when I beheld
Only before myself the ground obscured.
When thus my solace, turning him around,
Bespake me kindly: "Why distrustest thou?
Believest not I am with thee, thy sure guide?
It now is evening there, where buried lies

---

[1] *How doth a little failing wound thee sore.*]
  Ch' era al cor picciol fallo amaro morso.
                    Tasso, G. L. Canto x. st. 59.
[2] *Haste, that mars all decency of act.*]   Aristotle in his Physiog.
c. iii. reckons it among the ἀναιδοῦς σημεῖα, "the signs of an im-
pudent man," that he is ἐν ταῖς κινήσεσιν ὀξὺς, "quick in his
motions."   Compare Sophocles, Electra, 878.
            Τὸ κόσμιον μεθεῖσα.
  Joy, my dear sister, wings my quick return,
  And with more speed than decency allows.   *Potter.*

[3] *Where highest.*]   Lombardi proposes, with some hesitation, a
different meaning from that which has hitherto been affixed to the
words,

          Che 'nverso 'l ciel più alto si dislaga;

and would construe them, "that raises itself higher than every other
mountain above the sea;" "sopra l'allagamento delle acque del
mare."   The conjecture is at least ingenious, and has obtained new
force by the arguments of Monti in his Proposta.

The body in which I cast a shade, removed
To Naples[1] from Brundusium's wall.   Nor thou
Marvel, if before me no shadow fall,
More than that in the skyey element
One ray obstructs not other.   To endure
Torments of heat and cold extreme, like frames
That virtue hath disposed, which, how it works,
Wills not to us should be reveal'd.   Insane,
Who hopes our reason may that space explore,
Which holds three persons in one substance knit.
Seek not the wherefore, race of human kind;
Could ye have seen the whole, no need had been
For Mary to bring forth.   Moreover, ye
Have seen such men desiring fruitlessly;[2]
To whose desires, repose would have been given,
That now but serve them for eternal grief.
I speak of Plato, and the Stagirite,
And others many more."   And then he bent
Downwards his forehead, and in troubled mood[3]
Broke off his speech.   Meanwhile we had arrived
Far as the mountain's foot, and there the rock
Found of so steep ascent, that nimblest steps
To climb it had been vain.   The most remote,
Most wild, untrodden path, in all the tract
'Twixt Lerice and Turbia,[4] were to this
A ladder easy and open of access.

[1] *To Naples.*]   Virgil died at Brundusium, from whence his body
is said to have been removed to Naples.

[2] *Desiring fruitlessly.*]   See Hell, Canto iv. 39.

[3] *In troubled mood.*]   Because he himself (Virgil) was amongst the
number of spirits, who thus desired without hope.

[4] *'Twixt Lerice and Turbia.*]   At that time the two extremities of
the Genoese republic ; the former on the east, the latter on the west.
A very ingenious writer has had occasion, for a different purpose, to
mention one of these places as remarkably secluded by its mountainous situation.   "On an eminence among the mountains, between
the two little cities, Nice and Monaco, is the village of Torbia, a
name formed from the Greek τρόπαια."   *Mitford on the Harmony
of Language*, sect. xv. p. 351, 2nd edit.

"Who knows on which hand now the steep
    declines,
My master said, and paused; "so that he may
Ascend, who journeys without aid of wing?"
And while, with looks directed to the ground,
The meaning of the pathway [1] he explored,
And I gazed upward round the stony height;
On the left hand appear'd to us a troop ·
Of spirits, that toward us moved their steps;
Yet moving seem'd not, they so slow approach'd.
    I thus my guide address'd: "Upraise thine eyes:
Lo! that way some, of whom thou mayst obtain
Counsel, if of thyself thou find'st it not."
    Straightway he look'd, and with free speech
    replied:
"Let us tend thither: they but softly come.
And thou be firm in hope, my son beloved."
    Now was that crowd from us distant as far,
(When we some thousand steps, [2] I say, had past,)
As at a throw the nervous arm could fling;
When all drew backward on the massy crags
Of the steep bank, and firmly stood unmoved,
As one, who walks in doubt, might stand to look.
    "O spirits perfect! O already chosen!"
Virgil to them began: "by that blest peace,
Which, as I deem, is for you all prepared,
Instruct us where the mountain low declines,
So that attempt to mount it be not vain.
For who knows most, him loss of time most grieves."

---

[1] *The meaning of the pathway.*] Lombardi reads,

—— tenea 'l viso basso,
Esaminando del cammin la mente,

and explains it, "he bent down his face, his mind being occupied
with considering their way to ascend the mountain." I doubt much
whether the words can bear that construction.

[2] *When we some thousand steps.*] Mr. Carlyle puts a query to
my former translation of this passage. It was certainly erroneous.

As sheep,[1] that step from forth their fold, by
    one,
Or pairs, or three at once; meanwhile the rest
Stand fearfully, bending the eye and nose
To ground, and what the foremost does, that do
The others, gathering round her if she stops,
Simple and quiet, nor the cause discern;
So saw I moving to advance the first,
Who of that fortunate crew were at the head,
Of modest mien, and graceful in their gait.
When they before me had beheld the light
From my right side fall broken on the ground,
So that the shadow reach'd the cave; they
    stopp'd,
And somewhat back retired: the same did all
Who follow'd, though unweeting of the cause.
    "Unask'd of you, yet freely I confess,
This is a human body which ye see.
That the sun's light is broken on the ground,
Marvel not: but believe, that not without
Virtue derived from Heaven, we to climb
Over this wall aspire."   So them bespake
My master; and that virtuous tribe rejoin'd:
"Turn, and before you there the entrance lies;"
Making a signal to us with bent hands.
    Then of them one began.   "Whoe'er thou
    art,
Who journey'st thus this way, thy visage turn;
Think if me elsewhere thou hast ever seen."
    I towards him turn'd, and with fix'd eye beheld.

---

[1] *As sheep.*] The imitative nature of these animals supplies our
Poet with another comparison, in his Convito (i. 11). "Questi sono
da chiamare pecore, etc." "These may be called flocks of sheep
and not men; for if one sheep should throw himself down a
precipice of a thousand feet, all the rest would follow; and if one
for any cause in passing a road should leap, all the rest would do
the same, though they saw nothing to leap over."

2

Comely and fair, and gentle of aspect
He seem'd, but on one brow a gash was mark'd.
   When humbly I disclaim'd to have beheld
Him ever : " Now behold ! " he said, and show'd
High on his breast a wound : then smiling spake.
   " I am Manfredi,[1] grandson to the Queen
Costanza : [2] whence I pray thee, when return'd,
To my fair daughter [3] go, the parent glad

  [1] *Manfredi.*] King of Naples and Sicily, and the natural son of
Frederick II. He was lively and agreeable in his manners, and
delighted in poetry, music, and dancing. But he was luxurious and
ambitious, void of religion, and in his philosophy an Epicurean.
See G. Villani, lib. vi. cap. xlvii. and Mr. Mathias's Tiraboschi,
vol. i. p. 99. He fell in the battle with Charles of Anjou in 1265,
alluded to in Canto xxviii. of Hell, ver. 13, or rather in that which
ensued in the course of a few days at Benevento. But the successes
of Charles were so rapidly followed up, that our author, exact as he
generally is, might not have thought it necessary to distinguish
them in point of time; for this seems the best method of re-
conciling some little apparent inconsistency between him and the
annalist. "Dying excommunicated, King Charles did not allow of
his being buried in sacred ground, but he was interred near the
bridge of Benevento ; and on his grave there was cast a stone by
everyone of the army, whence there was formed a great mound of
stones. But some have said, that afterwards, by command of the
Pope, the Bishop of Cosenza took up his body and sent it out of the
kingdom, because it was the land of the church ; and that it was
buried by the river Verde, on the borders of the kingdom and of
Campagna. This, however, we do not affirm." G. Villani, Hist.
lib. vii. cap. ix. Manfredi and his father are spoken of by our
Poet in his De Vulg. Eloq. lib. i. cap. 12, with singular commendation. "Siquidem illustres, etc." "Those illustrious worthies,
Frederick the Emperor, and his well-born son Manfredi, manifested
their nobility and uprightness of form, as long as fortune remained,
by following pursuits worthy of men, and disdained those which are
suited only to brutes. Such, therefore, as were of a lofty spirit, and
graced with natural endowments, endeavoured to walk in the track
which the majesty of such great princes had marked out for them :
so that whatever was in their time attempted by eminent Italians,
first made its appearance in the court of crowned sovereigns ; and
because Sicily was a royal throne, it came to pass that whatever
was produced in the vernacular tongue by our predecessors was
called Sicilian ; which neither we nor our posterity shall be able to
change."

  [2] *Costanza.*] See Paradise, Canto iii. 121.

  [3] *My fair daughter.*] Costanza, the daughter of Manfredi, and
wife of Peter III., King of Arragon, by whom she was mother to
Frederick, King of Sicily, and James, King of Arragon. With the
latter of these she was at Rome 1296. See G. Villani, lib. viii. cap.
xviii. and notes to Canto vii.

Of Aragonia and Sicilia's pride;
And of the truth inform her, if of me
Aught else be told.   When by two mortal blows
My frame was shatter'd, I betook myself
Weeping to him, who of free will forgives.
My sins were horrible : but so wide arms
Hath goodness infinite, that it receives
All who turn to it.   Had this text divine
Been of Cosenza's shepherd better scann'd,
Who then by Clement [1] on my hunt was set,
Yet at the bridge's head my bones had lain,
Near Benevento, by the heavy mole
Protected; but the rain now drenches them,
And the wind drives, out of the kingdom's
     bounds,
Far as the stream of Verde,[2] where, with lights
Extinguish'd, he removed them from their bed.
Yet by their curse we are not so destroy'd,
But that the eternal love may turn, while hope [3]
Retains her verdant blossom.   True it is,
That such one as in contumacy dies
Against the holy church, though he repent,
Must wander thirty-fold for all the time
In his presumption past; if such decree
Be not by prayers of good men shorter made.
Look therefore if thou canst advance my bliss;

---

[1] *Clement.*]   Pope Clement IV.
[2] *The stream of Verde.*]   [The ancient Liris, now called the
Gargliano; it formed one of the boundaries between the Papal
States and the kingdom of Naples. Cf. Par. viii. 63.]   The
"extinguished lights" formed part of the ceremony at the interment
of one excommunicated.

> Passa la mora di Manfrè, cui lava
>   Il Verde. ——
> *Uberti, Dittamondo*, lib. iii. cap. i., as corrected by Perticari.

[3] *Hope.*]   Mentre che la speranza ha fior del verde.
So Tasso, G. L. Canto xix. st. 53.
> —— infin che verde è fior di speme.

Revealing to my good Costanza, how
Thou hast beheld me, and beside, the terms
Laid on me of that interdict; for here
By means of those below much profit comes."

CANTO IV

ARGUMENT

Dante and Virgil ascend the mountain of Purgatory, by a steep
and narrow path pent in on each side by rock, till they reach a part
of it that opens into a ledge or cornice.   There seating themselves,
and turning to the east, Dante wonders at seeing the sun on their
left, the cause of which is explained to him by Virgil; and while
they continue their discourse, a voice addresses them, at which
they turn, and find several spirits behind the rock, and amongst the
rest one named Belacqua, who had been known to our Poet on
earth, and who tells that he is doomed to linger there on account
of his having delayed his repentance to the last.

When [1] by sensations of delight or pain,
That any of our faculties hath seized,

---

[1] *When.*]   It must be owned the beginning of this Canto is
somewhat obscure.   Vellutello refers, for an elucidation of it, to the
reasoning of Statius in the twenty-fifth Canto.   Perhaps some
illustration may be derived from the following passage in the
Summa Theologiæ of Thomas Aquinas. "Some say that in
addition to the vegetable soul, which was present from the first,
there supervenes another soul, which is the sensitive, and again, in
addition to that, another,[which is the intellective.   And so there
are in man three souls, one of which exists potentially with regard
to another : but this has been already disproved.   And accordingly
others say that that same soul, which at first was merely vegetative,
is, through action of the seminal virtue, carried forward till it
reaches to that point, in which, being still the same, it nevertheless
becomes sensitive ; and at length the same by an ulterior pro-
gression is led on till it becomes intellective ; not, indeed, through
the seminal virtue acting in it, but by virtue of a superior agent,
that is, God, enlightening it from without." (This opinion he next
proceeds so confute.) "Dicunt ergo quidam quòd supra animam
vegetabilem, quæ primo inerat, supervenit alia anima, quæ est
sensitiva, supra illam iterum alia quæ est intellectiva.   Et sic sunt
in homine tres animæ, quarum una est in potentia ad aliam, quòd
supra improbatum est.   Et ideo alii dicunt quod illa eadem anima,
quæ primo fuit vegetativa tantum, postmodum per actionem

Entire the soul collects herself, it seems
She is intent upon that power alone ;
And thus the error is disproved, which holds
The soul not singly lighted in the breast.
And therefore whenas aught is heard or seen,
That firmly keeps the soul toward it turn'd,
Time passes, and a man perceives it not.
For that, whereby we hearken, is one power ;
Another that, which the whole spirit hath :
This is as it were bound, while that is free.

   This found I true by proof, hearing that spirit,
And wondering ; for full fifty steps [1] aloft
The sun had measured, unobserved of me,
When we arrived where all with one accord
The spirits shouted, "Here is what ye ask."

   A larger aperture oft-times is stopt,
With forked stake of thorn by villager,
When the ripe grape imbrowns, than was the path
By which my guide, and I behind him close,
Ascended solitary, when that troop
Departing left us.   On Sanleo's [2] road
Who journeys, or to Noli [3] low descends,
Or mounts Bismantua's [4] height, must use his feet ;
But here a man had need to fly, I mean

virtutis, quæ est in semine, perducitur ad hoc, ut ipsa eadem fiat
sensitiva ; et tandem ipsa eadem perducitur ad hoc, ut ipsa eadem
fiat intellectiva, non quidem per virtutem activam seminis, sed per
virtutem superioris agentis, scilicet Dei deforis illustrantis."
Thom. Aquin. Opera, Edit. Venet. 1595, tom. x. *Summa Theolog.*
1ma Pars. Quæstio cxviii. *Art.* ii.   See also Lettere di Fra
Guittone, 4°. *Roma*, 1745, p. 15 ; and Routh's note on the Gorgias
of Plato, p. 451.

  [1] *Full fifty steps.*]   Three hours and twenty minutes, fifteen
degrees being reckoned to an hour.

  [2] *Sanleo.*]   A fortress on the summit of Montefeltro.   The
situation is described by Troya, Veltro Allegorico, p. 11.   It is a
conspicuous object to travellers along the cornice on the riviera
di Genoa.

  [3] *Noli.*]   In the Genoese territory, between Finale and Savona.

  [4] *Bismantua.*]   A steep mountain in the territory of Reggio.

With the swift wing [1] and plumes of high desire,
Conducted by his aid, who gave me hope,
And with light furnish'd to direct my way.
  We through the broken rock ascended, close
Pent on each side, while underneath the ground
Ask'd help of hands and feet.   When we arrived
Near on the highest ridge of the steep bank,
Where the plain level open'd, I exclaim'd,
"O Master! say, which way can we proceed?"
  He answer'd, "Let no step of thine recede.
Behind me gain the mountain, till to us
Some practised guide appear."   That eminence
Was lofty, that no eye might reach its point;
And the side proudly rising, more than line [2]
From the mid quadrant to the centre drawn.
I, wearied, thus began: "Parent beloved!
Turn and behold how I remain alone,
If thou stay not."—"My son!" he straight replied,
"Thus far put forth thy strength;" and to a track
Pointed, that, on this side projecting, round
Circles the hill.   His words so spurr'd me on,
That I, behind him, clambering, forced myself,
Till my feet press'd the circuit plain beneath.
There both together seated, turn'd we round
To eastward, whence was our ascent: and oft
Many beside have with delight look'd back.
  First on the nether shores I turn'd mine eyes,
Then raised them to the sun, and wondering mark'd
That from the left [3] it smote us.   Soon perceived
That poet sage, how at the car of light

---

[1] *With the swift wing.*]   Compare Paradise, Canto xxxiii. 17.
[2] *More than line.*]   It was much nearer to being perpendicular
than horizontal.
[3] *From the left.*]   Vellutello observes an imitation of Lucan in
this passage :
  Ignotum vobis, Arabes, venistis in orbem,
  Umbras mirati nemorum non ire sinistras.   *Phars.* lib. iii. 248.

Amazed [1] I stood, where 'twixt us and the north
Its course it enter'd.   Whence he thus to me :
" Were Leda's offspring [2] now in company
Of that broad mirror, that high up and low
Imparts his light beneath, thou mightst behold
The ruddy Zodiac nearer to the Bears
Wheel, if its ancient course it not forsook.
How that may be, if thou wouldst think ; within
Pondering, imagine Sion with this mount
Placed on the earth, so that to both be one
Horizon, and two hemispheres apart,
Where lies the path [3] that Phaëton ill knew
To guide his erring chariot : thou wilt see [4]
How of necessity by this, on one,
He passes, while by that on the other side ;
If with that clear view thine intellect attend."

   "Of truth, kind teacher ! " I exclaim'd, " so
     clear
Aught saw I never, as I now discern,
Where seem'd my ken to fail, that the mid orb [5]

---

[1] *Amazed.*]   He wonders that being turned to the east he should see the sun on his left, since in all the regions on this side of the tropic of Cancer it is seen on the right of one who turns his face towards the east ; not recollecting that he was now antipodal to Europe, from whence he had seen the sun taking an opposite course.

[2] *Were Leda's offspring.*]   "As the constellation of the Gemini is nearer the Bears than Aries is, it is certain that if the sun, instead of being in Aries, had been in Gemini, both the sun and that portion of the Zodiac made ' ruddy ' by the sun, would have been seen to ' wheel nearer to the Bears.'   By the ' ruddy Zodiac ' must necessarily be understood that portion of the Zodiac affected or made red by the sun ; for the whole of the Zodiac never changes, nor appears to change, with respect to the remainder of the heavens."—*Lombardi.*

[3] *The Path.*]   The ecliptic.

[4] *Thou wilt see.*]   "If you consider that this mountain of Purgatory, and that of Sion, are antipodal to each other, you will perceive that the sun must rise on opposite sides of the respective eminences."

[5] *That the mid orb.*]   "That the equator (which is always situated between that part where, when the sun is, he causes

Of the supernal motion (which in terms
Of art is call'd the Equator, and remains
Still 'twixt the sun and winter) for the cause
Thou hast assign'd, from hence toward the north
Departs, when those, who in the Hebrew land
Were dwellers, saw it towards the warmer part.
But if it please thee, I would gladly know,
How far we have to journey: for the hill
Mounts higher, than this sight of mine can mount."
    He thus to me: " Such is this steep ascent,
That it is ever difficult at first,
But more a man proceeds, less evil grows.[1]
When pleasant it shall seem to thee, so much
That upward going shall be easy to thee
As in a vessel to go down the tide,
Then of this path thou wilt have reach'd the end.
There hope to rest thee from thy toil.   No more
I answer, and thus far for certain know."
As he his words had spoken, near to us
A voice there sounded: " Yet ye first perchance
May to repose you by constraint be led."
At sound thereof each turn'd; and on the left
A huge stone we beheld, of which nor I
Nor he before was ware.   Thither we drew;
And there were some, who in the shady place
Behind the rock were standing, as a man
Through idleness might stand.   Among them one,
Who seem'd to be much wearied, sat him down,
And with his arms did fold his knees about,
Holding his face between them downward bent.

summer, and the other where his absence produces winter) recedes
from this mountain towards the north, at the time when the Jews
inhabiting Mount Sion saw it · depart towards the south."—
Lombardi.
  [1] *But more a man proceeds, less evil grows.*] Because in ascending he gets rid of the weight of his sins.

"Sweet Sir!" I cried, "behold that man who
    shows
Himself more idle than if laziness
Were sister to him."   Straight he turn'd to us,
And, o'er the thigh lifting his face, observed,
Then in these accents spake: "Up then, proceed,
Thou valiant one."   Straight who it was I knew;
Nor could the pain I felt (for want of breath
Still somewhat urged me) hinder my approach.
And when I came to him, he scarce his head
Uplifted, saying, "Well hast thou discern'd,
How from the left the sun his chariot leads."

His lazy acts and broken words my lips
To laughter somewhat moved; when I began:
"Belacqua,[1] now for thee I grieve no more.
But tell, why thou art seated upright there.
Waitest thou escort to conduct thee hence?
Or blame I only thine accustom'd ways?"
Then he: "My brother! of what use to mount,
When, to my suffering, would not let me pass
The bird of God,[2] who at the portal sits?
Behoves so long that heaven first bear me round
Without its limits, as in life it bore;
Because I, to the end, repentant sighs
Delay'd; if prayer do not aid me first,
That riseth up from heart which lives in grace.
What other kind avails, not heard in heaven?"

Before me now the poet, up the mount

----

[1] *Belacqua.*] Concerning this man, the commentators afford no
information, except that in the margin of the Monte Casino MS.
there is found this brief notice of him: "Iste Belacqua fuit optimus
magister cithararum, et leutorum, et pigrissimus homo in operibus
mundi sicut in operibus animæ." "This Belacqua was an excellent
master of the harp and lute, but very negligent in his affairs both
spiritual and temporal." *Lettera di Eustazio Dicearcheo ad
Angelio Sidicino*, 4to, Roma, 1801.

[2] *The bird of God.*] Here are two other readings, "Uscier" and
"Angel," "Usher" and "Angel" of God.

Ascending, cried : " Haste thee : for see the sun
Has touch'd the point meridian ; and the night
Now covers with her foot Marocco's shore."[1]

CANTO V

ARGUMENT

They meet with others, who had deferred their repentance till
they were overtaken by a violent death, when sufficient space being
allowed them, they were then saved ; and amongst these, Giacopo
del Cassero, Buonconte da Montefeltro, and Pia, a lady of Sienna.

Now had I left those spirits, and pursued
The steps of my conductor ; when behind,
Pointing the finger at me, one exclaim'd :
" See, how it seems as if the light not shone
From the left hand[2] of him beneath,[3] and he,
As living, seems to be led on."   Mine eyes
I at that sound reverting, saw them gaze,
Through wonder, first at me ; and then at me
And the light broken underneath, by turns.
" Why are thy thoughts thus riveted," my guide
Exclaim'd, "that thou hast slack'd thy pace? or how
Imports it thee, what thing is whisper'd here ?

[1] *Marocco's shore.*] Cuopre la notte già col piè Marocco. Hence,
perhaps, Milton :

> Damasco, or Marocco, or Trebisond. *P. L.* b. i. 584.

instead of Morocco, as he elsewhere calls it :

> Morocco, and Algiers, and Tremisen. *P. L.* b. xi. 404.

If the vowels were to change places, the verse would in both
instances be spoiled.

[2] *——It seems as if the light not shone*
From the left hand.] The sun was, therefore, on the right of
our travellers. For, as before, when seated and looking to the east
from whence they had ascended, the sun was on their left ; so now
that they have risen and are again going forward, it must be on the
opposite side of them.

[3] *Of him beneath.*] Of Dante, who was following Virgil up the
mountain, and therefore was the lower of the two.

Come after me, and to their babblings leave
The crowd.   Be as a tower,[1] that, firmly set,
Shakes not its top for any blast that blows.
He, in whose bosom thought on thought shoots out,
Still of his aim is wide, in that the one
Sicklies and wastes to nought the other's strength."

    What other could I answer, save "I come?"
I said it, somewhat with that colour tinged,
Which oft-times pardon meriteth for man.

    Meanwhile traverse along the hill there came,
A little way before us, some who sang
The "Miserere" in responsive strains.
When they perceived that through my body I
Gave way not for the rays to pass, their song
Straight to a long and hoarse exclaim they changed;
And two of them, in guise of messengers,
Ran on to meet us, and inquiring ask'd:
"Of your condition we would gladly learn."

    To them my guide.   "Ye may return, and bear
Tidings to them who sent you, that his frame
Is real flesh.   If, as I deem, to view
His shade they paused, enough is answer'd them:
Him let them honour: they may prize him well."

    Ne'er saw I fiery vapours[2] with such speed

---

[1] *Be as a tower.*]   Sta come torre ferma.
So Berni, Orl. Inn. lib. i. canto xvi. st. 48.

> In quei due piedi sta fermo il gigante
> Com' una torre in mezzo d'un castello.

And Milton, *P. L.* b. i. 591.   Stood like a tower.

[2] *Ne'er saw I fiery vapours.*]   Imitated by Tasso, G. L. canto
xix. st. 62.

> Tal suol fendendo liquido sereno
> Stella cader della gran madre in seno.

And by Milton, *P. L.* b. iv. 558.

> —— Swift as a shooting star
> In autumn thwarts the night, when vapours fired
> Impress the air.

Compare Statius, Theb. i. 92.

> Ilicet igne Jovis, lapsisque citatior astris.

Cut through the serene air at fall of night,
Nor August's clouds athwart the setting sun,
That upward these did not in shorter space
Return ; and, there arriving, with the rest
Wheel back on us, as with loose rein a troop.
  "Many," exclaim'd the bard, "are these, who throng
Around us : to petition thee, they come.
Go therefore on, and listen as thou go'st."
  "O spirit ! who go'st on to blessedness,
With the same limbs that clad thee at thy birth,"
Shouting they came : "a little rest thy step.
Look if thou any one amongst our tribe
Hast e'er beheld, that tidings of him there [1]
Thou mayst report.   Ah, wherefore go'st thou on ?
Ah, wherefore tarriest thou not ?   We all
By violence died, and to our latest hour
Were sinners, but then warn'd by light from heaven ;
So that, repenting and forgiving, we
Did issue out of life at peace with God,
Who, with desire to see him, fills our heart."
  Then I : "The visages of all I scan,
Yet none of ye remember.   But if aught
That I can do may please you, gentle spirits !
Speak, and I will perform it ; by that peace,
Which, on the steps of guide so excellent
Following, from world to world, intent I seek."
  In answer he began : "None here distrusts
Thy kindness, though not promised with an oath ;
So as the will fail not for want of power.
Whence I, who sole before the others speak,
Entreat thee, if thou ever see that land [2]

---

[1] *There.*] Upon the earth.
[2] *That land.*] The Marca d'Ancona, between Romagna and
Apulia, the kingdom of Charles of Anjou.

Which lies between Romagna and the realm
Of Charles, that of thy courtesy thou pray
Those who inhabit Fano, that for me
Their adorations duly be put up,
By which I may purge off my grievous sins.
From thence I came.[1]   But the deep passages,
Whence issued out the blood [2] wherein I dwelt,
Upon my bosom in Antenor's land [3]
Were made, where to be more secure I thought.
The author of the deed was Este's prince,
Who, more than right could warrant, with his wrath
Pursued me.   Had I towards Mira fled,
When overta'en at Oriaco, still
Might I have breathed.   But to the marsh I sped ;
And in the mire and rushes tangled there
Fell, and beheld my life-blood float the plain."

     Then said another : " Ah ! so may the wish,
That takes thee o'er the mountain, be fulfill'd,
As thou shalt graciously give aid to mine.
Of Montefeltro I ;[4] Buonconte I :
Giovanna [5] nor none else have care for me ;
Sorrowing with these I therefore go."   I thus :
" From Campaldino's field what force or chance

---

    [1] *From thence I came.*]   Giacopo del Cassero, a citizen of Fano, who having spoken ill of Azzo da Este, Marquis of Ferrara, was by his orders put to death.   Giacopo was overtaken by the assassins at Oriaco, a place near the Brenta, from whence if he had fled towards Mira, higher up on that river, instead of making for the marsh on the sea-shore, he might have escaped.

    [2] *The blood.*]   Supposed to be the seat of life.

    [3] *Antenor's land.*]   The city of Padua, said to be founded by Antenor.   This implies a reflection on the Paduans.   See Hell, xxxii. 89.   Thus G. Villani calls the Venetians " the perfidious descendants from the blood of Antenor, the betrayer of his country, Troy."   Lib. xi. cap. lxxxix.

    [4] *Of Montefeltro I.*]   Buonconte (son of Guido da Montefeltro, whom we have had in the twenty-seventh Canto of Hell) fell in the battle of Campaldino (1289), fighting on the side of the Aretini.   In this engagement our Poet is said to have taken part.   See Fazio degli Uberti, Dittamondo, lib. ii. cap. xxix.

    [5] *Giovanna*].   The wife of Buonconte.

Drew thee, that ne'er thy sepulture was known ? "
  "Oh ! " answer'd he, "at Casentino's foot
A stream there courseth, named Archiano, sprung
In Apennine above the hermit's seat.[1]
E'en where its name is cancel'd,[2] there came I,
Pierced in the throat,[3] fleeing away on foot,
And bloodying the plain. Here sight and speech
Fail'd me ; and, finishing with Mary's name,
I fell, and tenantless my flesh remain'd.
I will report the truth ; which thou again
Tell to the living. Me God's angel took,[4]
Whilst he of hell exclaim'd : 'O thou from
    heaven :
'Say wherefore hast thou robb'd me ? Thou of
    him
'The eternal portion bear'st with thee away,
'For one poor tear [5] that he deprives me of.
'But of the other, other rule I make.'
  "Thou know'st how in the atmosphere collects
That vapour dank, returning into water
Soon as it mounts where cold condenses it.
That evil will,[6] which in his intellect
Still follows evil, came ; and raised the wind
And smoky mist, by virtue of the power

---

[1] *The hermit's seat.*] The hermitage of Camaldoli.

[2] *Where its name is cancel'd.*] That is, between Poppi and Bibbiena, where the Archiano falls into the Arno.

[3] *Throat.*] In the former editions it was printed " heart." Mr. Carlyle has observed the error.

[4] *Me God's angel took.*] Cum autem finem vitæ explesset servus Dei aspiciens vidit diabolum simul et Angelum ad animam stantem ac unum quemque illam sibi tollere festinantem. *Alberici Visio,* § 18.

[5] *For one poor tear.*] Visum est quod angelus Domini lachrimas quas dives ille —— fuerat in ampulla teneret. *Alberici Visio,* § 18.

[6] *That evil will.*] The devil. Lombardi refers us to Albertus Magnus de Potentiâ Dæmonum. This notion of the Evil Spirit having power over the elements, appears to have arisen from his being termed the " prince of the air," in the New Testament.

Given by his nature.   Thence the valley, soon
As day was spent, he cover'd o'er with cloud,
From Pratomagno to the mountain range;[1]
And stretch'd the sky above; so that the air
Impregnate changed to water.   Fell the rain;
And to the fosses came all that the land
Contain'd not; and, as mightiest streams are wont,
To the great river, with such headlong sweep,
Rush'd, that nought stay'd its course.   My stiffen'd
    frame
Laid at his mouth, the fell Archiano found,
And dash'd it into Arno; from my breast
Loosening the cross, that of myself I made
When overcome with pain.   He hurl'd me on,
Along the banks and bottom of his course;
Then in his muddy spoils encircling wrapt."

  "Ah! when thou to the world shalt be return'd,
And rested after thy long road," so spake
Next the third spirit; "then remember me.
I once was Pia.[2]   Sienna gave me life;
Maremma took it from me.   That he knows,
Who me with jewel'd ring had first espoused."

1 *From Pratomagno to the mountain range.*] From Pratomagno
(which divides the lower Valdarno from Casentino,) as far as to the
Apennine.
  2 *Pia.*] She is said to have been a Siennese lady, of the family
of Tolommei, secretly made away with by her husband, Nello
della Pietra of the same city, in Maremma, where he had some
possessions.

CANTO VI

ARGUMENT

Many besides, who are in like case with those spoken of in the last
Canto, beseech our Poet to obtain for them the prayers of their
friends, when he shall be returned to this world. This moves him
to express a doubt to his guide, how the dead can be profited by
the prayers of the living; for the solution of which doubt he is
referred to Beatrice. Afterwards he meets with Sordello the
Mantuan, whose affection, shown to Virgil his countryman, leads
Dante to break forth into an invective against the unnatural
divisions with which Italy, and more especially Florence, was
distracted.

WHEN from their game of dice men separate,
He who hath lost remains in sadness fix'd,
Revolving in his mind [1] what luckless throws
He cast: but, meanwhile, all the company
Go with the other; one before him runs,
And one behind his mantle twitches, one
Fast by his side bids him remember him.
He stops not; and each one, to whom his hand
Is stretch'd, well knows he bids him stand aside;
And thus [2] he from the press defends himself.
E'en such was I in that close-crowding throng;

---

[1] *Revolving in his mind.*]   —— Riman dolente
                Ripetendo le volte, e triste impara.

Lombardi explains this: "that the loser remains by himself, and
taking up the dice casts them over again, as if to learn how he may
throw the numbers he could wish to come up." There is something
very natural in this; but whether the sense can be fairly deduced
from the words, is another question.

[2] *And thus.*]   The late Archdeacon Fisher pointed out to me a
passage in the Novella de la Gitanilla of Cervantes, Ed. Valentia,
1797, p. 12, from which it appears that it was usual for money to be
given to bystanders at play by winners; and as he well remarked:
"Dante is therefore describing, with his usual power of observation,
what he had often seen, the shuffling, boon-denying exit of the
successful gamester."

And turning so my face around to all,
And promising, I 'scaped from it with pains.
  Here of Arezzo him[1] I saw, who fell
By Ghino's cruel arm; and him beside,[2]
Who in his chase was swallow'd by the stream.
Here Frederic Novello,[3] with his hand
Stretch'd forth, entreated; and of Pisa he,[4]
Who put the good Marzucco to such proof
Of constancy.   Count Orso[5] I beheld;
And from its frame a soul dismiss'd for spite
And envy, as it said, but for no crime;
I speak of Peter de la Brosse:[6] and here,

[1] *Of Arezzo him.*] Benincasa, a judge of Arezzo, eminent for his skill in jurisprudence, who having condemned to death Turrino da Turrita, brother of Ghino di Tacco, for his robberies in Maremma, was murdered by Ghino while he was sitting as assessor in the papal audit-office at Rome.   Ghino was not only suffered to escape in safety, but (as the commentators inform us) obtained so high a reputation by the liberality with which he was accustomed to dispense the fruits of his plunder, and treated those who fell into his hands with so much courtesy, that he was afterwards invited to Rome, and knighted by Boniface VIII.   A story is told of him by Boccaccio, G. x. N. 2.

[2] *Him beside.*] Cione, or Ciacco, or Guccio, de' Tarlatti of Arezzo. He is said to have been carried by his horse into the Arno, and there drowned, while he was in pursuit of certain of his enemies.

[3] *Frederic Novello.*] Son of the Conte Guido da Battifolle, and slain by one of the family of Bostoli.

[4] *Of Pisa he.*] Farinata degli Scornigiani of Pisa.   His father Marzucco, who had entered the order of the Frati Minori, so entirely overcame the feelings of resentment, that he even kissed the hands of the slayer of his son, and, as he was following the funeral, exhorted his kinsmen to reconciliation.   The eighteenth and thirtieth in the collection of Guittone d'Arezzo's Letters are addressed to Marzucco. The latter is in verse.

[5] *Count Orso.*] Son of Napoleone da Cerbaia, slain by Alberto da Mangona, his cousin.

[6] *Peter de la Brosse.*] Secretary of Philip III. of France.   The courtiers, envying the high place which he held in the king's favour, prevailed on Mary of Brabant to charge him falsely with an attempt upon her person; for which supposed crime he suffered death.   So say the Italian commentators.   Henault represents the matter very differently: "Pierre de la Brosse, formerly barber to St. Louis, afterwards the favourite of Philip, fearing the too great attachment of the king for his wife Mary, accuses this princess of having poisoned Louis, eldest son of Philip, by his first marriage.   This calumny is discovered by a nun of Nivelle in Flanders.   La Brosse is hung." *Abrégé Chron.* 1275, etc.   The Deputati, or those

3

While she yet lives, that lady of Brabant,
Let her beware ; lest for so false a deed
She herd with worse than these.   When I was freed
From all those spirits, who pray'd for others' prayers
To hasten on their state of blessedness ;
Straight I began : " O thou, my luminary !
It seems expressly in thy text [1] denied,
That heaven's supreme decree can ever bend
To supplication ; yet with this design
Do these entreat.   Can then their hope be vain ?
Or is thy saying not to me reveal'd ? "
    He thus to me : " Both what I write is plain,
And these deceived not in their hope ; if well
Thy mind consider, that the sacred height
Of judgment [2] doth not stoop, because love's flame
In a short moment all fulfils, which he,
Who sojourns here, in right should satisfy.
Besides, when I this point concluded thus,
By praying no defect could be supplied ;
Because the prayer had none access to God.
Yet in this deep suspicion rest thou not
Contented, unless she assure thee so,
Who betwixt truth and mind infuses light :
I know not if thou take me right ; I mean
Beatrice.   Her thou shalt behold above, [3]
Upon this mountain's crown, fair seat of joy."

deputed to write annotations on the Decameron, suppose that Boccaccio, in the Giornata, ii. Novella 9, took the story from this passage in Dante, only concealing the real names and changing the incidents in some parts, in order not to wound the feelings of those whom, as it was believed, these incidents had so lately befallen. Ediz. Giunti. 1573, p. 40.

[1] *In thy text.*]   He refers to Virgil, Æn. lib. vi. 376.

    Desine fata deûm flecti sperare precando.

[2]   —— *The sacred height*
    Of judgment.]   So Shakspeare, Measure for Measure, act ii. sc. 2.
        If he, which is the top of judgment.

[3] *Above.*]   See Purgat. xxx. 32.

Then I : "Sir! let us mend our speed ; for
   now
I tire not as before : and lo ! the hill [1]
Stretches its shadow far." He answer'd thus :
"Our progress with this day shall be as much
As we may now dispatch ; but otherwise
Than thou supposest is the truth. For there
That canst not be, ere thou once more behold
Him back returning, who behind the steep
Is now so hidden, that, as erst, his beam
Thou dost not break. But lo ! a spirit there
Stands solitary, and toward us looks :
It will instruct us in the speediest way."
   We soon approach'd it. O thou Lombard
   spirit !
How didst thou stand, in high abstracted mood,
Scarce moving with slow dignity thine eyes.
It spoke not aught, but let us onward pass,
Eyeing us as a lion on his watch. [2]
But Virgil, with entreaty mild, advanced,
Requesting it to show the best ascent.
It answer to his question none return'd ;
But of our country and our kind of life
Demanded. When my courteous guide began,
"Mantua," the shadow, in itself absorb'd, [3]
Rose towards us from the place in which it stood,
And cried, "Mantuan ! I am thy countryman,

---

[1] *The hill.*] It was now past the noon.

[2] *Eyeing us as a lion on his watch.*] A guisa di leon quando si posa. A line taken by Tasso, G. L. can. x. st. 56.

[3] *The shadow, in itself absorb'd.*] I had before translated "The solitary shadow" ; and have made the alteration in consequence of Monti's just remark on the original, that "tutta in se romita" does not mean "solitary," but "collected, concentrated in itself." See his Proposta under "Romito." Vellutello had shown him the way to this interpretation, when he explained the words by "tutta in se raccolta e sola." Petrarch applies the expression to the spirit of Laura, when departing from the body. See his Triumph of Death, cap. i. v. 152.

Sordello."[1]   Each the other then embraced.
   Ah, slavish Italy! thou inn of grief! [2]
Vessel without a pilot in loud storm!
Lady no longer of fair provinces,
But brothel-house impure! this gentle spirit,
Even from the pleasant sound of his dear land
Was prompt to greet a fellow citizen
With such glad cheer: while now thy living ones [3]
In thee abide not without war; and one
Malicious gnaws another; ay, of those
Whom the same wall and the same moat contains.
Seek, wretched one! around thy sea-coasts wide;

[1] *Sordello.*]   The history of Sordello's life is wrapt in the obscurity of romance.   That he distinguished himself by his skill in Provençal poetry is certain; and many feats of military prowess have been attributed to him.   He was born [at Goito, near Mantua,] towards the end of the twelfth, and died about the middle of the succeeding century.   Tiraboschi, who terms him the most illustrious of all the Provençal poets of his age, has taken much pains to sift all the notices he could collect relating to him, and has particularly exposed the fabulous narrative which Platina has introduced on this subject in his history of Mantua.   Honourable mention of his name is made by our Poet in the treatise de Vulg. Eloq. lib. i. cap. 15, where it is said that, remarkable as he was for eloquence, he deserted the vernacular language of his own country, not only in his poems, but in every other kind of writing.   Tiraboschi had at first concluded him to be the same writer whom Dante elsewhere (De Vulg. Eloq. lib. ii. c. 13) calls Gottus Mantuanus, but afterwards gave up that opinion to the authority of the Conte d'Arco and the Abate Bettinelli.   By Bastero, in his Crusca Provenzale, Ediz. Roma, 1724, p. 94, amongst Sordello's MS. poems in the Vatican are mentioned "Canzoni, Tenzoni, Cobbole," and various "Serventesi," particularly one in the form of a funeral song on the death of Blancas, in which the poet reprehends all the reigning princes in Christendom.   This last was well suited to attract the notice of our author.   Mention of Sordello will recur in the notes to the Paradise, ix. 32.   Since this note was written, many of Sordello's poems have been brought to light by the industry of M. Raynouard in his *Choix des Poésies des Troubadours* and his *Lexique Roman.*   [An account of Sordello will be found in the *Vita e Poesie di Sordello di Goito* by C. de Lollis (1896).]

[2] *Thou inn of grief.*]   S' io son d'ogni dolore ostello e chiave.
Son. II. 6, in the Vita Nuova.

—— Thou most beauteous inn,
Why should hard-favour'd grief be lodged in thee?
Shakspeare, Richard II. act v. sc. 1.

[3] *Thy living ones.*]   Compare Milton, *P. L.* b. ii. 496, etc.

Then homeward to thy bosom turn; and mark,
If any part of thee sweet peace enjoy.
What boots it, that thy reins Justinian's hand [1]
Refitted, if thy saddle be unprest?
Nought doth he now but aggravate thy shame.
Ah, people! thou obedient still shouldst live,
And in the saddle let thy Cæsar sit,
If well thou marked'st that which God commands. [2]
   Look how that beast to fellness hath relapsed,
From having lost correction of the spur,
Since to the bridle thou hast set thine hand,
O German Albert! [3] who abandon'st her
That is grown savage and unmanageable,
When thou shouldst clasp her flanks with forked
      heels.
Just judgment from the stars fall on thy blood;
And be it strange and manifest to all;
Such as may strike thy successor [4] with dread;
For that thy sire [5] and thou have suffer'd thus,
Through greediness of yonder realms detain'd,
The garden of the empire to run waste.
Come, see the Capulets and Montagues, [6]

---

[1] *Justinian's hand.*] "What avails it that Justinian delivered thee from the Goths and reformed thy laws, if thou art no longer under the control of his successors in the empire?"

[2] *That which God commands.*] He alludes to the precept—"Render unto Cæsar the things which are Cæsar's."

[3] *O German Albert!*] The Emperor Albert I. succeeded Adolphus in 1298, and was murdered in 1308. See Par. Canto xix. 114.

[4] *Thy successor.*] The successor of Albert was Henry of Luxemburgh, by whose interposition in the affairs of Italy our Poet hoped to have been reinstated in his native city.

[5] *Thy sire.*] The Emperor Rodolph, too intent on increasing his power in Germany to give much of his thoughts to Italy, "the garden of the empire."

[6] *Capulets and Montagues.*] Our ears are so familiarised to the names of these rival houses in the language of Shakspeare, that I have used them instead of the "Montecchi" and "Cappelletti." They are said to have been two powerful Ghibelline families of Verona. In some parts of that play, of which they form the leading characters, our great dramatic poet seems to have been not a little indebted to

The Filippeschi and Monaldi,[1] man
Who carest for nought! those sunk in grief, and these
With dire suspicion rack'd.   Come, cruel one!
Come, and behold the oppression of the nobles,
And mark their injuries; and thou mayst see
What safety Santafiore can supply.[2]
Come, and behold thy Rome,[3] who calls on thee,
Desolate widow, day and night with moans,
" My Cæsar, why dost thou desert my side?"
Come, and behold what love among thy people :
And if no pity touches thee for us,
Come, and blush for thine own report.   For me,
If it be lawful, O Almighty Power!
Who wast in earth for our sakes crucified,
Are thy just eyes turn'd elsewhere? or is this
A preparation, in the wondrous depth
Of thy sage counsel made, for some good end,
Entirely from our reach of thought cut off?
So are the Italian cities all o'erthrong'd
With tyrants, and a great Marcellus[4] made
Of every petty factious villager.

the Hadriana of Luigi Groto, commonly called Il cieco d'Adria.
See Walker's Historical Memoir on Italian Tragedy, 4to. 1799,
§ i. p. 49.

[1] *Filippeschi and Monaldi.*]   Two other rival families in Orvieto.

[2] *What safety Santafiore can supply.*]   A place between Pisa and
Sienna.   What he alludes to is so doubtful, that it is not certain
whether we should not read " come si cura "—" How Santafiore is
governed."   Perhaps the event related in the note to v. 58, Canto
xi. may be pointed at.

[3] *Come and behold thy Rome.*]   Thus in the Latin Epistle to the
Cardinals, which has been lately discovered in the Laurentian
library, and has every appearance of being Dante's: "Romam urbem,
nunc utroque lumine destitutam, nunc Hannibali nedum aliis miser-
andam, solam sedentem et viduam, prout superius proclamatur,
qualis est, pro modulo nostræ imaginis, ante mortales oculos affigatis
omnes."   Opere minori di Dante, tom. iii. Pte ii. p. 270, 12°. *Fir.*
1840.

[4] *Marcellus.*]   ——.Un Marcel diventa
            Ogni villan che parteggiando viene.
Repeated by Alamanni in his Coltivazione, lib. i.   He probably
means the Marcellus who opposed Julius Cæsar.

My Florence! thou mayst well remain unmoved
At this digression, which affects not thee:
Thanks to thy people, who so wisely speed.
Many have justice in their heart, that long
Waiteth for counsel to direct the bow,
Or ere it dart unto its aim: but thine
Have it on their lips' edge.   Many refuse [1]
To bear the common burdens: readier thine
Answer uncall'd, and cry, "Behold I stoop!"
  Make thyself glad, for thou hast reason now,
Thou wealthy! thou at peace! thou wisdom-fraught!
Facts best will witness if I speak the truth.
Athens and Lacedæmon, who of old
Enacted laws, for civil arts renown'd,
Made little progress in improving life
Towards thee, who usest such nice subtlety,
That to the middle of November scarce
Reaches the thread thou in October weavest.
How many times within thy memory,
Customs, and laws, and coins, and offices
Have been by thee renew'd, and people changed.
  If thou remember'st well and canst see clear,
Thou wilt perceive thyself like a sick wretch, [2]
Who finds no rest upon her down, but oft
Shifting her side, short respite seeks from pain.

---

[1] *Many refuse.*]   He appears to have been of Plato's mind, that in a commonwealth of worthy men, place and power would be as much declined as they are now sought after and coveted. κινδυνεύει πόλις ἀνδρῶν ἀγαθῶν εἰ γένοιτο, περιμαχητὸν ἂν εἶναι τὸ μὴ ἄρχειν, ὥσπερ νῦν τὸ ἄρχειν. Πολιτ. Lib. A.

[2] *A sick wretch.*]   Imitated by the Cardinal de Polignac in his Anti-Lucretius, lib. i. 1052.

> Ceu lectum peragrat membris languentibus æger,
> In latus alterne lævum dextrumque recumbens:
> Nec juvat: inde oculos tollit resupinus in altum:
> Nusquam inventa quies; semper quæsita: quod illi
> Primum in deliciis fuerat, mox torquet et angit:
> Nec morbum sanat, nec fallit tædia morbi.

CANTO VII 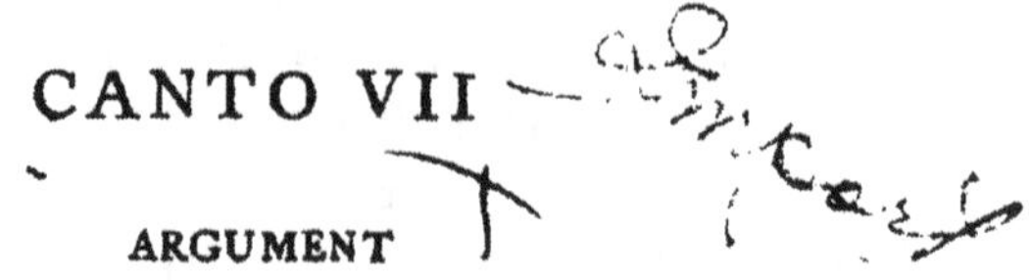

ARGUMENT

The approach of night hindering further ascent, Sordello conducts our Poet apart to an eminence, from whence they behold a pleasant recess, in form of a flowery valley, scooped out of the mountain ; where are many famous spirits, and among them the Emperor Rodolph, Ottocar king of Bohemia, Philip III. of France, Henry of Navarre, Peter III. of Arragon, Charles I. of Naples, Henry III. of England, and William, Marquis of Montferrat.

AFTER their courteous greetings joyfully
Seven times exchanged, Sordello backward drew
Exclaiming, "Who are ye?" — "Before this
    mount
By spirits worthy of ascent to God
Was sought, my bones had by Octavius' care
Been buried.   I am Virgil ; for no sin
Deprived of heaven, except for lack of faith."
So answer'd him in few my gentle guide.

   As one, who aught before him suddenly
Beholding, whence his wonder riseth, cries,
" It is, yet is not," wavering in belief ;
Such he appeared ; then downward bent his eyes,
And, drawing near with reverential step,
Caught him, where one of mean estate might clasp
His lord.[1]   " Glory of Latium ! " he exclaim'd,
" In whom our tongue its utmost power display'd ;
Boast of my honour'd birth-place ! what desert[2]

[1] —— *Where one of mean estate might clasp
His lord.*] So Ariosto, Orl. F. c. xxiv. st. 19.

    E l'abbracciaro, ove il maggior s'abbraccia,
    Col capo nudo e col ginocchio chino.

[2] *What desert.*] So Frezzi :

    Qual grazia, o qual destin m' ha fatto degno
    Che io ti veggia.   *Il Quadrir.* lib. iv. cap. 9.

Of mine, what favour, rather, undeserved,
Shows thee to me ?   If I to hear that voice
Am worthy, say if from below thou comest,
And from what cloister's pale." — " Through
  every orb
Of that sad region," he replied, "thus far
Am I arrived, by heavenly influence led :
And with such aid I come.   Not for my doing,[1]
But for not doing, have I lost the sight
Of that high Sun, whom thou desirest, and who
By me too late was known.   There is a place[2]
There underneath, not made by torments sad,
But by dun shades alone ; where mourning's voice
Sounds not of anguish sharp, but breathes in sighs.
There I with little innocents abide,
Who by death's fangs were bitten, ere exempt
From human taint.   There I with thòse abide,
Who the three holy virtues[3] put not on,
But understood the rest,[4] and without blame
Follow'd them all.   But, if thou know'st, and can'st,
Direct us how we soonest may arrive,
Where Purgatory its true beginning takes."
He answer'd thus : " We have no certain place
Assign'd us : upwards I may go, or round.
Far as I can, I join thee for thy guide.
But thou beholdest now how day declines ;
And upwards to proceed by night, our power
Excels : therefore it may be well to choose
A place of pleasant sojourn.   To the right
Some spirits sit apart retired.   If thou

[1] *Not for my doing.*] I am indebted to the kindness of Mr.
Lyell for pointing out to me that three lines of the original were
here omitted in the former editions of this translation.
[2] *There is a place.*] Limbo. See Hell, Canto iv. 24.
[3] *The three holy virtues.*] Faith, Hope, and Charity.
[4] *The rest.*] Prudence, Justice, Fortitude, and Temperance.

Consentest, I to these will lead thy steps:
And thou wilt know them, not without delight."
  "How chances this?" was answer'd: "whoso
      wish'd
To ascend by night, would he be thence debarr'd
By other, or through his own weakness fail?"
  The good Sordello then, along the ground
Trailing his finger, spoke: "Only this line[1]
Thou shalt not overpass, soon as the sun
Hath disappear'd; not that aught else impedes
Thy going upwards, save the shades of night.
These, with the want of power, perplex the will.
With them thou haply mightst return beneath,
Or to and fro around the mountain's side
Wander, while day is in the horizon shut."
  My master straight, as wondering at his speech,
Exclaim'd: "Then lead us quickly, where thou
      sayst
That, while we stay, we may enjoy delight."
  A little space we were removed from thence,
When I perceived the mountain hollow'd out,
Even as large valleys[2] hollow'd out on earth.
  "That way," the escorting spirit cried, "we
      go,
Where in a bosom the high bank recedes:
And thou await renewal of the day."
  Betwixt the steep and plain, a crooked path
Led us traverse into the ridge's side,
Where more than half the sloping edge expires.
Refulgent gold, and silver thrice refined,

---

[1] *Only this line.*] "Walk while ye have the light, lest darkness
come upon you; for he that walketh in darkness, knoweth not
whither he goeth." John xii. 35.

[2] *As large valleys.*] Viatores enim per viam rectam dum
ambulant, campum juxta viam cernentes spatiosum et pulchrum,
oblitique itineris, dicunt intra se, Iter per campum istum faciamus,
etc. Alberici Visio, § 28.

And scarlet grain and ceruse, Indian wood [1]
Of lucid dye serene, fresh emeralds [2]
But newly broken, by the herbs and flowers
Placed in that fair recess, in colour all
Had been surpass'd, as great surpasses less.
Nor nature only there lavish'd her hues,
But of the sweetness [3] of a thousand smells
A rare and undistinguish'd fragrance made.

"Salve Regina," [4] on the grass and flowers,
Here chanting, I beheld those spirits sit,
Who not beyond the valley could be seen.

"Before the westering sun sink to his bed,"
Began the Mantuan, who our steps had turn'd,
"'Mid those, desire not that I lead ye on.
For from this eminence ye shall discern
Better the acts and visages of all,
Than, in the nether vale, among them mix'd.
He, who sits high above the rest, and seems
To have neglected that he should have done,

[1] *Indian wood.*] Indico legno lucido e sereno.
It is a little uncertain what is meant by this. Indigo, although it is extracted from a herb, seems the most likely. Monti in his Proposta maintains it to be ebony.

[2] *Fresh emeralds.*]
> Under foot the violet,
> Crocus, and hyacinth with rich inlay
> Broider'd the ground, more colour'd than with stone
> Of costliest emblem.   *Milton, P. L.* b. iv. 703.

> Zaffir, rubini, oro, topazj, e perle,
> E diamanti, e crisoliti e giacinti
> Potriano i fiori assimigliar, che per le
> Liete piagge v'avea l'aura dipinti;
> Sì verdi l'erbe, che potendo averle
> Qua giù ne foran gli smeraldi vinti.
>   *Ariosto, Orl. Fur.* Canto xxxiv. st. 49.

[3] *The sweetness.*]
> E quella ai fiori, ai pomi, e alla verzura
> Gli odor diversi depredando giva,
> E di tutti faceva una mistura,
> Che di soavità l'alma notriva.   *Ibid.* st. 51.

[4] *Salve Regina.*] The beginning of a prayer to the Virgin. It is sufficient here to observe, that in similar instances I shall either preserve the original Latin words or translate them, as it may seem best to suit the purpose of the verse.

And to the others' song moves not his lip,
The Emperor Rodolph [1] call, who might have
   heal'd
The wounds wherof fair Italy hath died,
So that by others she revives but slowly.
He, who with kindly visage comforts him,
Sway'd in that country,[2] where the water springs,
That Moldaw's river to the Elbe, and Elbe
Rolls to the ocean: Ottocar [3] his name:
Who in his swaddling clothes was of more worth
Than Winceslaus his son, a bearded man,
Pamper'd with rank luxuriousness and ease.
And that one with the nose deprest,[4] who close
In counsel seems with him of gentle look,[5]
Flying expired, withering the lily's flower.
Look there, how he doth knock against his breast.
The other ye behold, who for his cheek
Makes of one hand a couch, with frequent sighs.
They are the father and the father-in-law
Of Gallia's bane:[6] his vicious life they know
And foul; thence comes the grief that rends them
   thus.

[1] *The Emperor Rodolph.*] See the last Canto, v. 104. He died in 1292.

[2] *That country.*] Bohemia.

[3] *Ottocar.*] King of Bohemia, who was killed in battle with Rodolph, near Vienna, August 26, 1278. Winceslaus II. his son, who succeeded him in the kingdom of Bohemia, died in 1305. The latter is again taxed with luxury in the Paradise, xix. 123.

[4] *That one with the nose deprest.*] Philip III. of France, father of Philip IV. He died in 1285, at Perpignan, in his retreat from Arragon.

[5] *Him of gentle look.*] Henry of Navarre, father of Joan married to Philip IV. of France, whom Dante calls "mal di Francia"—"Gallia's bane."

[6] *Gallia's bane.*] G. Villani, lib. vii. cap. cxlvi., speaks with equal resentment of Philip IV. "In 1291, on the night of the calends of May, Philip le Bel, King of France, by advice of Biccio and Musciatto Franzesi, ordered all the Italians, who were in his country and realm, to be seized, under pretence of seizing the money-lenders, but thus he caused the good merchants also to be

" He, so robust of limb,[1] who measure keeps
In song with him of feature prominent,[2]
With every virtue bore his girdle braced.
And if that stripling,[3] who behind him sits,
King after him had lived, his virtue then
From vessel to like vessel had been pour'd ;
Which may not of the other heirs be said.
By James and Frederick[4] his realms are held ;
Neither the better heritage obtains.
Rarely[5] into the branches of the tree ·

seized and ransomed ; for which he was much blamed and held in great abhorrence. And from thenceforth the realm of France fell evermore into degradation and decline. And it is observable, that between the taking of Acre and this seizure in France, the merchants of Florence received great damage and ruin of their property."

[1] *He, so robust of limb.*] Peter III., called the Great, King of Arragon, who died in 1285, leaving three sons, Alonzo, James, and Frederick. The two former succeeded him in the kingdom of Arragon, and Frederick in that of Sicily. See G. Villani, lib. vii. cap. cii., and Mariana, lib. xiv. cap. 9. He is enumerated among the Provençal poets by Millot, Hist. Litt. des Troubadours, tom. iii. p. 150.

[2] *Him of feature prominent.*] " Dal maschio naso "—" with the masculine nose." Charles I., King of Naples, Count of Anjou, and brother of St. Louis. He died in 1285. The annalist of Florence remarks, that " there had been no sovereign of the house of France, since the time of Charlemagne, by whom Charles was surpassed either in military renown and prowess, or in the loftiness of his understanding." G. Villani, lib. vii. cap. xciv. We shall, however, find many of his actions severely reprobated in the twentieth Canto.

[3] *That stripling.*] Alonzo III., King of Arragon, the eldest son of Peter III., who died in 1291, at the age of 27. He was a young prince of virtue sufficient to have justified the eulogium and the hopes of Dante. See Mariana, lib. xiv. cap. 14.

[4] *By James and Frederick.*] See note to Canto iii. 112.

[5] *Rarely.*]   Full well can the wise poet of Florence,
              That hight Dantes, speake in this sentence ;
              Lo ! in such manner rime is Dantes tale.
              Full selde upriseth by his branches smale
              Prowesse of man, for God of his goodnesse
              Woll that we claim of him our gentlenesse :
              For of our elders may we nothing claime
              But temporal thing, that men may hurt and maime.
                      Chaucer, Wife of Bathe's Tale.

Compare Homer, Od. b. ii. v. 276. Pindar. Nem. xi. 48, and Euripides, Electra, 369.

Doth human worth mount up : and so ordains
He who bestows it, that as his free gift
It may be call'd.   To Charles [1] my words apply
No less than to his brother in the song ;
Which Pouille and Provence now with grief
        confess.
So much that plant degenerates from its seed,
As, more than Beatrix and Margaret,
Costanza [2] still boasts of her valorous spouse.
    " Behold the king of simple life and plain,
Harry of England, [3] sitting there alone :
He through his branches better issue [4] spreads.
    " That one, who, on the ground, beneath the
        rest,
Sits lowest, yet his gaze directs aloft,
Is William, that brave Marquis, [5] for whose cause,

[1] *To Charles.*] " Al Nasuto "—" Charles II., King of Naples, is
no less inferior to his father Charles I. than James and Frederick
to theirs, Peter III."   See Canto xx. 78, and Paradise, Canto xix.
125.

[2] *Costanza.*]   Widow of Peter III.   She has been already
mentioned in the third Canto, v. 112.   By Beatrix and Margaret
are probably meant two of the daughters of Raymond Berenger,
Count of Provence ; the latter married to St. Louis of France, the
former to his brother Charles of Anjou, King of Naples.   See
Paradise, Canto vi. 135.   Dante therefore considers Peter as the
most illustrious of the three monarchs.

[3] *Harry of England.*]   Henry III.   The contemporary annalist
speaks of this king in similar terms.   G. Villani, lib. v. cap. iv.
" From Richard was born Henry, who reigned after him, who was
a plain man and of good faith, but of little courage."   With the
exception of the last part of the sentence, which must be changed
for its opposite, we might well imagine ourselves to be reading the
character of our present venerable monarch. (A.D. 1819.)   Fazio
degli Uberti, Dittamondo, I. iv. cap. xxv., where he gives the
characters of our Norman kings, speaks less respectfully of Henry.
Capitoli xxiii.-xxv. lib. iv. of this neglected poem appear to deserve
the notice of our antiquarians.

[4] *Better issue.*]   Edward I.   " From the said Henry was born
the good king Edward, who reigns in our times, who has done
great things, whereof we shall make mention in due place."   G.
Villani, ibid.

[5] *William, that brave Marquis.*]   William, Marquis of
Montferrat, was treacherously seized by his own subjects, at
Alessandria in Lombardi, A.D. 1290, and ended his life in prison.

The deed of Alexandria and his war
Makes Montferrat and Canavese weep."

CANTO VIII

ARGUMENT

Two angels, with flaming swords broken at the points, descend to keep watch over the valley, into which Virgil and Dante entering by desire of Sordello, our Poet meets with joy the spirit of Nino, the judge of Gallura, one who was well known to him. Meantime three exceedingly bright stars appear near the pole, and a serpent creeps subtly into the valley, but flees at hearing the approach of those angelic guards. Lastly, Konrad Malaspina predicts to our Poet his future banishment.

Now was the hour that wakens fond desire
In men at sea, and melts their thoughtful heart
Who in the morn have bid sweet friends fare-
    well,
And pilgrim newly on his road with love
Thrills, if he hear the vesper bell from far,[1]
That seems to mourn for the expiring day:[2]
When I, no longer taking heed to hear,
Began, with wonder, from those spirits to mark
One risen from its seat, which with its hand
Audience implored.   Both palms it join'd and
    raised,
Fixing its stedfast gaze toward the east,
As telling God, "I care for nought beside."

See G. Villani, lib. vii. cap. cxxxv. A war ensued between the people of Alessandria and those of Montferrat and the Canavese, now a part of Piedmont.

[1] *Hear the vesper bell from far.*]
    I hear the far-off curfew sound.   *Milton's Penseroso.*

[2] *That seems to mourn for the expiring day.*]
    The curfew tolls the knell of parting day.   *Gray's Elegy.*

" Te Lucis Ante," [1] so devoutly then
Came from its lip, and in so soft a strain,
That all my sense [2] in ravishment was lost.
And the rest after, softly and devout,
Follow'd through all the hymn, with upward gaze
Directed to the bright supernal wheels.

Here, reader! [3] for the truth make thine eyes keen:
For of so subtle texture is this veil,
That thou with ease mayst pass it through unmark'd.

I saw that gentle band silently next
Look up, as if in expectation held,
Pale and in lowly guise ; and, from on high,
I saw, forth issuing descend beneath,

[1] *Te Lucis Ante.*] " Te lucis ante terminum," says Lombardi,
is the first verse of the hymn sung by the church in the last part of
the sacred office termed compieta, a service which our Chaucer
calls " complin."

[2] *All my sense.*] Fece me a me uscir di mente.
Me surpuerat mihi.

Horat. Carm. lib. iv. od. 13.

[3] *Here, reader!*] Lombardi's explanation of this passage, by
which the commentators have been much perplexed, though it may
be thought rather too subtle and fine-spun, like the veil itself
spoken of in the text, cannot be denied the praise of extraordinary
ingenuity. " This admonition of the poet to his reader," he
observes, " seems to relate to what has been before said, that these
spirits sung the whole of the hymn 'Te lucis ante terminum'
throughout, even that second strophe of it—

Procul recedant somnia,
Et noctium phantasmata,
Hostemque nostrum comprime,
Ne polluantur corpora ;

and he must imply, that these souls, being incorporeal, did not offer
up this petition on their own account, but on ours, who are yet in
this world ; as he afterwards makes those other spirits, who repeat
the Pater Noster, expressly declare, when after that prayer they add,

This last petition, dearest Lord ! is made
Not for ourselves, etc.   Canto xi.

As, therefore, if we look through a very fine veil, the sight easily
passes on, without perceiving it, to objects that lie on the other
side ; so here the poet fears that our mind's eye may insensibly pass
on to contemplate these spirits, as if they were praying for the
relief of their own wants; without discovering the veil of our wants,
with which they invest themselves in the act of offering up this
prayer."

Two angels, with two flame-illumined swords,
Broken and mutilated of their points.
Green as the tender leaves but newly born,
Their vesture was, the which, by wings as green
Beaten, they drew behind them, fann'd in air.
A little over us one took his stand;
The other lighted on the opposing hill;
So that the troop were in the midst contain'd.

Well I descried the whiteness on their heads;
But in their visages the dazzled eye
Was lost, as faculty [1] that by too much
Is overpower'd. " From Mary's bosom both
Are come," exclaim'd Sordello, "as a guard
Over the vale, 'gainst him, who hither tends,
The serpent." Whence, not knowing by which path
He came, I turn'd me round; and closely press'd,
All frozen, to my leader's trusted side.

Sordello paused not: "To the valley now
(For it is time) let us descend; and hold
Converse with those great shadows: haply much
Their sight may please ye." Only three steps down
Methinks I measured, ere I was beneath,
And noted one who look'd as with desire
To know me. Time was now that air grew dim;
Yet not so dim, that, 'twixt his eyes and mine,
It clear'd not up what was conceal'd before.
Mutually towards each other we advanced.
Nino, thou courteous judge! [2] what joy I felt,
When I perceived thou wert not with the bad.

---

[1] *As faculty*.] My earthly by his heavenly overpower'd

    As with an object, that excels the sense,
    Dazzled and spent.
Milton, P. L. b. viii. 457.

[2] *Nino, thou courteous judge*.] Nino di Gallura de' Visconti, nephew to Count Ugolino de' Gherardeschi, and betrayed by him. See notes to Hell, Canto xxxiii.

4

No salutation kind on either part
Was left unsaid.   He then inquired : " How long,
Since thou arrived'st at the mountain's foot,
Over the distant waves ? "—" Oh ! " answer'd I,
" Through the sad seats of woe this morn I came ;
And still in my first life, thus journeying on,
The other strive to gain."   Soon as they heard
My words, he and Sordello backward drew,
As suddenly amazed.   To Virgil one,
The other to a spirit turn'd, who near
Was seated, crying : " Conrad ! [1] up with speed :
Come, see what of his grace high God hath will'd."
Then turning round to me : " By that rare mark
Of honour, which thou owest to him, who hides
So deeply his first cause it hath no ford ;
When thou shalt be beyond the vast of waves,
Tell my Giovanna,[2] that for me she call
There, where reply to innocence is made.
Her mother,[3] I believe, loves me no more ;
Since she has changed the white and wimpled folds,[4]
Which she is doom'd once more with grief to wish.

[1] *Conrad.*]   Currado, father to Moroello Malaspina.
[2] *My Giovanna.*]   The daughter of Nino, and wife of Riccardo da
Camino of Trevigi, concerning whom see Paradise, c. ix. 48.
[3] *Her mother.*]   Beatrice, Marchioness of Este, wife of Nino,
and after his death married to Galeazzo de' Visconti of Milan.   It
is remarked by Lombardi, that the time which Dante assigns to this
journey, and consequently to this colloquy with Nino Visconti, the
beginning, that is, of April, is prior to the time which Bernardino
Corio, in his history of Milan, part the second, fixes for the nuptials
of Beatrice with Galeazzo ; for he records her having been betrothed
to that prince after the May of this year (1300), and her having been
solemnly espoused at Modena on the 29th of June.   Besides, however, the greater credit due to Dante, on account of his having lived
at the time when these events happened, another circumstance in
his favour is the discrepancy remarked by Giovambatista Giraldi
(Commentar. delle cose di Ferrara) in those writers by whom the
history of Beatrice's life has been recorded.   Nothing can set the
general accuracy of our Poet, as to historical facts, in a stronger
point of view, than the difficulty there is in convicting him of even
so slight a deviation from it as is here suspected.
[4] *The white and wimpled folds.*]   The weeds of widowhood.

By her it easily may be perceived,
How long in woman lasts the flame of love,
If sight and touch do not relume it oft.
For her so fair a burial will not make
The viper,[1] which calls Milan to the field,
As had been made by shrill Gallura's bird."[2]

He spoke, and in his visage took the stamp
Of that right zeal, which with due temperature
Glows in the bosom.   My insatiate eyes
Meanwhile to heaven had travel'd, even there
Where the bright stars are slowest, as a wheel
Nearest the axle; when my guide inquired:
"What there aloft, my son, has caught thy gaze?"

I answered: "The three torches,[3] with which here
The pole is all on fire."   He then to me:
"The four resplendent stars, thou saw'st this morn,
Are there beneath; and these, risen in their stead."

While yet he spoke, Sordello to himself
Drew him, and cried: "Lo there our enemy!"
And with his hand pointed that way to look.

Along the side, where barrier none arose
Around the little vale, a serpent lay,
Such haply as gave Eve the bitter food.[4]

---

[1] *The viper.*] The arms of Galeazzo and the ensign of the Milanese.

[2] *Shrill Gallura's bird.*] The cock was the ensign of Gallura, Nino's province in Sardinia. Hell, xxii. 80, and notes. It is not known whether Beatrice had any further cause to regret her nuptials with Galeazzo, than a certain shame which appears, however unreasonably, to have attached to a second marriage.

[3] *The three torches.*] The three evangelical virtues, Faith, Hope, and Charity. These are supposed to rise in the evening, in order to denote their belonging to the contemplative; as the four others, which are made to rise in the morning, were probably intended to signify that the cardinal virtues belong to the active life: or perhaps it may mark the succession, in order of time, of the Gospel to the heathen system of morality.

[4] *Such haply as gave Eve the bitter food.*] Compare Milton's description of that serpent in the ninth book of the Paradise Lost.

Between the grass and flowers, the evil snake
Came on, reverting oft his lifted head;
And, as a beast that smooths its polish'd coat,
Licking his back.   I saw not, nor can tell,
How those celestial falcons from their seat
Moved, but in motion each one well descried.
Hearing the air cut by their verdant plumes,
The serpent fled; and, to their stations, back
The angels up return'd with equal flight.

The spirit, (who to Nino, when he call'd,
Had come), from viewing me with fixed ken,
Through all that conflict, loosen'd not his sight.

"So may the lamp,[1] which leads thee up on high,
Find, in thy free resolve, of wax so much,
As may suffice thee to the enamel'd height,"
It thus began: "If any certain news
Of Valdimagra,[2] and the neighbour part
Thou know'st, tell me, who once was mighty there.
They call'd me Conrad Malaspina; not
That old one;[3] but from him I sprang.   The love
I bore my people is now here refined."

"In your domains," I answer'd, "ne'er was I.
But, through all Europe, where do those men dwell,
To whom their glory is not manifest?
The fame, that honours your illustrious house,
Proclaims the nobles, and proclaims the land;
So that he knows it, who was never there.
I swear to you, so may my upward route
Prosper, your honour'd nation not impairs
The value of her coffer and her sword.

---

[1] *May the lamp.*]   "May the divine grace find so hearty a co-
operation on the part of thy own will, as shall enable thee to ascend
to the terrestrial paradise, which is on the top of this mountain."
[2] *Valdimagra.*]   See Hell, Canto xxiv. 144, and notes.
[3] *That old one.*]   The grandfather of Conrad Malaspina, who was
also of that name.

Nature and use give her such privilege,
That while the world is twisted from his course
By a bad head, she only walks aright,
And has the evil way in scorn."   He then:
"Now pass thee on: seven times the tired sun [1]
Revisits not the couch, which with four feet
The forked Aries covers, ere that kind
Opinion shall be nail'd into thy brain
With stronger nails than other's speech can drive;
If the sure course of judgment be not stay'd."

CANTO IX

ARGUMENT

Dante is carried up the mountain, asleep and dreaming, by Lucia;
and, on wakening, finds himself, two hours after sunrise, with
Virgil, near the gate of Purgatory, through which they are admitted
by the angel deputed by Saint Peter to keep it.

Now the fair consort of Tithonus old, [2]
Arisen from her mate's beloved arms,
Look'd palely o'er the eastern cliff; her brow,
Lucent with jewels, glitter'd, set in sign

[1] *Seven times the tired sun.*] "The sun shall not enter into the
constellation of Aries seven times more, before thou shalt have still
better cause for the good opinion thou expressest of Valdimagra, in
the kind reception thou shalt there meet with." Dante was hospit-
ably received by one of the Malaspina during his banishment,
A.D. 1306.

[2] *Now the fair consort of Tithonus old.*]

La concubina di Titone antico.

So Tassoni, Secchia Rapita, c. viii. st. 15.

La puttanella del canuto amante. Venturi, after some of the old
commentators, interprets this to mean an Aurora, or dawn of the
moon; but this seems highly improbable. From what follows, it
may be conjectured that our Poet intends us to understand
that it was now near the break of day.

Of that chill animal,[1] who with his train
Smites fearful nations : and where then we were,
Two steps of her ascent the night had past ;
And now the third was closing up its wing,[2]
When I, who had so much of Adam with me,
Sank down upon the grass, o'ercome with sleep,
There where all five [3] were seated.   In that hour,
When near the dawn the swallow her sad lay,
Remembering haply ancient grief,[4] renews ;
And when our minds, more wanderers from the flesh,
And less by thought restrain'd, are, as 't were, full
Of holy divination in their dreams ;
Then, in a vision, did I seem to view
A golden-feather'd eagle [5] in the sky,
With open wings, and hovering for descent ;
And I was in that place, methought, from whence
Young Ganymede, from his associates 'reft,

[1] *Of that chill animal.*]   The scorpion.
[2] *The third was closing up its wing.*]   The night being divided
into four watches, I think he may mean that the third was past,
and the fourth and last was begun, so that there might be some
faint glimmering of morning twilight ; and not merely, as Lombardi
supposes, that the third watch was drawing towards its close, which
would still leave an insurmountable difficulty in the first verse.   At
the beginning of Canto xv. our Poet makes the evening commence
three hours before sunset, and he may now consider the dawn as
beginning at the same distance from sunrise.   Those who would
have the dawn, spoken of in the first verse of the present Canto,
to signify the rising of the moon, construe the "two steps of her
ascent which the night had past," into as many hours, and not
watches ; so as to make it now about the third hour of the night.
The old Latin annotator on the Monte Casino MS. alone, as far as
I know, supposing the division made by St. Isidore (Orig. lib. 5)
of the night into seven parts to be adopted by our Poet, concludes
that it was the third of these ; and he too, therefore, is for the
lunar dawn.   Rosa Morando ingenuously confesses, that to him the
whole passage is "non esplicabile o almeno difficillimo," inexplicable,
or, at best, extremely difficult.
[3] *All five.*]   Virgil, Dante, Sordello, Nino, and Currado Malaspina.
[4] *Remembering haply ancient grief.*]   Progne having been
changed into a swallow after the outrage done her by Tereus.   See
Ovid, Metam. lib. vi.
[5] *A golden-feather'd eagle.*]   So Chaucer, in the House of Fame,
at the conclusion of the first book and beginning of the second,

Was snatch'd aloft to the high consistory.
"Perhaps," thought I within me, "here alone
He strikes his quarry, and elsewhere disdains
To pounce upon the prey."   Therewith, it seem'd,
A little wheeling in his aëry tour,
Terrible as the lightning, rush'd he down,
And snatch'd me upward even to the fire.
There both, I thought, the eagle and myself
Did burn; and so intense the imagined flames,
That needs my sleep was broken off.   As erst
Achilles shook himself, and round him roll'd
His waken'd eyeballs, wondering where he was,
Whenas his mother had from Chiron fled
To Scyros, with him sleeping in her arms;
(There [1] whence the Greeks did after sunder him;)
E'en thus I shook me, soon as from my face
The slumber parted, turning deadly pale,

represents himself carried up by the "grim pawes" of a golden
eagle.   Much of his description is closely imitated from Dante :—

> Methought I saw an eagle sore.
> . . . .
> It was of golde and shone so bright,
> That never sawe men soche a sight.
> *The House of Fame*, b. i.
> This eagle, of which I have you tolde,
> That with fethirs shone al of golde,
> Whiche that so hie gan to sore,
> I gan beholdin more and more
> To seen her beautee and the wonder,
> But never was that dente of thonder,
> Ne that thinge that men callin foudre,
> That smite sometime a toure to poudre,
> And in his swifte comminge brend,
> That so swithe gan downwarde discende
> As this foule whan that it behelde,
> That I a roume was in the felde,
> And with his grim pawes stronge,
> Within his sharpe nailis longe,
> Me fleyng at a swappe he hent, etc.   *Ibid.* b. ii.

Avis candida columbæ similis adveniens, ... per comam
capitis sua me ore apprehendens ferre sublimem cepit." Alberici
Visio, § i.

[1] *There.*]   Mr. Darley has noted the omission of this line in
the preceding editions.

Like one ice-struck with dread.   Sole at my side
My comfort stood : and the bright sun was now
More than two hours aloft : and to the sea
My looks were turn'd.   "Fear not," my master
     cried,
" Assured we are at happy point.   Thy strength
Shrink not, but rise dilated.   Thou art come
To Purgatory now.   Lo! there the cliff
That circling bounds it.   Lo! the entrance there,
Where it doth seem disparted.   Ere the dawn
Usher'd the day-light, when thy wearied soul
Slept in thee, o'er the flowery vale beneath
A lady came, and thus bespake me : 'I
'Am Lucia. [1]   Suffer me to take this man,
'Who slumbers.   Easier so his way shall speed.'
Sordello and the other gentle shapes
Tarrying, she bare thee up : and, as day shone,
This summit reach'd : and I pursued her steps.
Here did she place thee.   First, her lovely eyes
That open entrance show'd me ; then at once
She vanish'd with thy sleep."   Like one, whose
     doubts
Are chased by certainty, and terror turn'd
To comfort on discovery of the truth,
Such was the change in me : and as my guide
Beheld me fearless, up along the cliff
He moved, and I behind him, towards the height.
   Reader! thou markest how my theme doth rise ;
Nor wonder therefore, if more artfully
I prop the structure.   Nearer now we drew,
Arrived whence, in that part, where first a breach
As of a wall appear'd, I could descry
A portal, and three steps beneath, that led
For inlet there, of different colour each ;

[1] *Lucia.*] See Hell, c. ii. 97, and Paradise, c. xxxii. 123.

And one who watch'd, but spake not yet a word.
As more and more mine eye did stretch its view,
I mark'd him seated on the highest step,
In visage such, as past my power to bear.
Grasp'd in his hand, a naked sword glanced back
The rays so towards me, that I oft in vain
My sight directed. "Speak, from whence ye stand;"
He cried: "What would ye? Where is your
    escort?
Take heed your coming upward harm ye not."
  "A heavenly dame, not skilless of these things,"
Replied the instructor, "told us, even now,
'Pass that way: here the gate is.'"—"And may
    she,
Befriending, prosper your ascent," resumed
The courteous keeper of the gate: "Come then
Before our steps." We straightway thither came.
  The lowest stair [1] was marble white, so smooth
And polish'd, that therein my mirror'd form
Distinct I saw. The next of hue more dark
Than sablest grain, a rough and singed block,
Crack'd lengthwise and across. The third, that
    lay
Massy above, seem'd prophyry, that flamed
Red as the life-blood spouting from a vein.
On this God's angel either foot sustain'd,
Upon the threshold seated, which appear'd
A rock of diamond. Up the trinal steps
My leader cheerly drew me. "Ask," said he,
"With humble heart, that he unbar the bolt."

[1] *The lowest stair.*] By the white step is meant the distinctness
with which the conscience of the penitent reflects his offences; by
the burnt and cracked one, his contrition on their account; and by
that of porphyry, the fervour with which he resolves on the future
pursuit of piety and virtue. Hence, no doubt, Milton describing
"the gate of heaven," *P. L.* b. iii. 516.
    Each stair mysteriously was meant.

Piously at his holy feet devolved
I cast me, praying him for pity's sake
That he would open to me ; but first fell
Thrice on my bosom prostrate.   Seven times [1]
The letter, that denotes the inward stain,
He, on my forehead, with the blunted point
Of his drawn sword, inscribed.   And " Look,"
      he cried,
" When enter'd, that thou wash these scars away."
    Ashes, or earth ta'en dry out of the ground,
Were of one colour with the robe he wore.
From underneath that vestment forth he drew
Two keys,[2] of metal twain : the one was gold,
Its fellow silver.   With the pallid first,
And next the burnish'd, he so ply'd the gate,
As to content me well.   " Whenever one
Faileth of these, that in the key-hole straight
It turn not, to this alley then expect
Access in vain."   Such were the words he spake.
" One is more precious : [3] but the other needs,
Skill and sagacity, large share of each,
Ere its good task to disengage the knot
Be worthily perform'd.   From Peter these
I hold, of him instructed that I err
Rather in opening, than in keeping fast ;
So but the suppliant at my feet implore."
    Then of that hallow'd gate he thrust the door,

[1] *Seven times.*]   Seven P's, to denote the seven sins (Peccata) of
which he was to be cleansed in his passage through Purgatory.
[2] *Two keys.*]   Lombardi remarks, that painters have usually
drawn Saint Peter with two keys, the one of gold and the other of
silver ; but that Niccolo Alemanni, in his Dissertation de Parietinis
Lateranensibus, produces instances of his being represented with one
key, and with three.   We have here, however, not Saint Peter, but
an angel deputed by him.
[3] *One is more precious.*]   The golden key denotes the divine
authority by which the priest absolves the sinners : the silver
expresses the learning and judgment requisite for the due discharge
of that office.

Exclaiming, " Enter, but this warning hear :
He forth again departs who looks behind."
　As in the hinges of that sacred ward
The swivels turn'd, sonorous metal strong,
Harsh was the grating : [1] nor so surlily
Roar'd the Tarpeian, [2] when by force bereft
Of good Metellus, thenceforth from his loss
To leanness doom'd.　Attentively I turn'd,
Listening the thunder that first issued forth ;
And "We praise thee, O God," methought I heard,
In accents blended with sweet melody.
The strains came o'er mine ear, e'en as the sound
Of choral voices, that in solemn chant
With organ [3] mingle, and, now high and clear
Come swelling, now float indistinct away.

[1] *Harsh was the grating.*]

  —— On a sudden open fly
With impetuous recoil and jarring sound
The infernal doors, and on their hinges grate
Harsh thunder.   *Milton, P. L.* b. ii. 882.

[2] *The Tarpeian.*]

  Protinus abducto patuerunt templa Metello.
Tunc rupes Tarpeia sonat : magnoque reclusas
Testatur stridore fores : tunc conditus imo
Eruitur templo multis intactus ab annis
Romani census populi, etc. *Lucan, Ph.* lib. iii. 157.

  The tribune with unwilling steps withdrew,
While impious hands the rude assault renew ;
The brazen gates with thundering strokes resound,
And the Tarpeian mountain rings around.
At length the sacred storehouse, open laid,
The hoarded wealth of ages past displayed. *Rowe.*

[3] *Organ.*]　Organs were used in Italy as early as in the sixth century.　See Tiraboschi, Stor. della Lett. Ital. 4to. vol. iii. lib. iii. cap. i. § 11, where the following description of that instrument is quoted from Cassiodorus, in Psalm 150 :—"Organum itaque est quasi turris diversis fistulis fabricata, quibus flatu follium vox copiosissima destinatur, et ut eam modulatio decora componat, linguis quibusdam ligneis ab interiore parte construitur, quas disciplinabiliter Magistrorum digiti reprimentes grandisonam efficiunt et suavisonam cantilenam."　If I remember right there is a passage in the Emperor Julian's writings, which shows that the organ was not unknown in his time.

CANTO X

ARGUMENT

Being admitted at the gate of Purgatory, our Poets ascend a wind-
ing path up the rock, till they reach an open and level space that
extends each way round the mountain. On the side that rises, and
which is of white marble, are seen artfully engraven many stories of
humility, which whilst they are contemplating, there approach the
souls of those who expiate the sin of pride, and who are bent down
beneath the weight of heavy stones.

WHEN we had past the threshold of the gate,
(Which the soul's ill affection doth disuse,
Making the crooked seem the straighter path,)
I heard its closing sound. Had mine eyes turn'd,
For that offence what plea might have avail'd?
     We mounted up the riven rock, that wound [1]
On either side alternate, as the wave
Flies and advances. " Here some little art
Behoves us," said my leader, " that our steps
Observe the varying flexure of the path."
     Thus we so slowly sped, that with cleft orb
The moon once more o'erhangs her watery couch,
Ere we that strait have threaded. But when
          free,
We came, and open, where the mount above

___

[1] *That wound.*] Venturi justly observes, that the Padre d'Aquino
has misrepresented the sense of this passage in his translation.

>   —— dabat ascensum tendentibus ultra
> Scissa tremensque silex, tenuique erratica motu.

The verb " muover" is used in the same signification in the Inferno,
Canto xviii. 21.

>   Cosi da imo della roccia scogli
>   Moven.
>   —— from the rock's low base
>   Thus flinty paths advanced.

In neither place is actual motion intended to be expressed.

One solid mass retires; I spent with toil,[1]
And both uncertain of the way, we stood,
Upon a plain more lonesome than the roads
That traverse desert wilds.   From whence the brink
Borders upon vacuity, to foot
Of the steep bank that rises still, the space
Had measured thrice the stature of a man:
And, distant as mine eye could wing its flight,
To leftward now and now to right dispatch'd,
That cornice equal in extent appear'd.

   Not yet our feet had on that summit moved,
When I discover'd that the bank, around,
Whose proud uprising all ascent denied,
Was marble white; and so exactly wrought
With quaintest sculpture, that not there alone
Had Polycletus, but e'en nature's self
Been shamed.   The angel (who came down to earth
With tidings of the peace so many years
Wept for in vain, that oped the heavenly gates
From their long interdict) before us seem'd,
In a sweet act, so sculptured to the life,
He look'd no silent image.   One had sworn
He had said "Hail!"[2] for she was imaged there.
By whom the key did open to God's love;
And in her act as sensibly imprest
That word, "Behold the handmaid of the Lord,"
As figure seal'd on wax.   "Fix not thy mind

---

[1] *I spent with toil.*] Dante only was wearied, because he only
had the weight of a bodily frame to encumber him.

[2] *Hail.*]   —— On whom the angel *Hail*
    Bestow'd, the holy salutation used
    Long after to blest Mary, second Eve.
                Milton, P. L. v. 387.

"The basso relievo on the border of the second rock, in Purgatory,
furnished the idea of the Annunziata, painted by Marcello Venusti
from his (Michael Angelo's) design in the sacristy of St. Giov.
Lateran." Fuseli, Lecture iii. note.

On one place only," said the guide beloved,
Who had me near him on that part where lies
The heart of man.   My sight forthwith I turn'd,
And mark'd, behind the virgin mother's form,
Upon that side where he that moved me stood,
Another story graven on the rock.
　　I past athwart the bard, and drew me near,
That it might stand more aptly for my view.
There, in the self-same marble, were engraved
The cart and kine, drawing the sacred ark,
That from unbidden office awes mankind. [1]
Before it came much people; and the whole
Parted in seven quires.   One sense cried "Nay,"
Another, "Yes, they sing."   Like doubt arose
Betwixt the eye and smell, from the curl'd fume
Of incense breathing up the well-wrought toil.
Preceding [2] the blest vessel, onward came
With light dance leaping, girt in humble guise,
Israel's sweet harper: in that hap he seem'd
Less, and yet more, than kingly.   Opposite,
At a great palace, from the lattice forth
Look'd Michol, like a lady full of scorn
And sorrow.   To behold the tablet next,
Which, at the back of Michol, whitely shone,
I moved me.   There, was storied on the rock
The exalted glory of the Roman prince,
Whose mighty worth moved Gregory [3] to earn

---

[1] *That from unbidden office awes mankind.*]   "And when they
came to Nachon's threshing-floor, Uzzah put forth his hand to the
ark of God, and took hold of it; for the oxen shook it."   "And the
anger of the Lord was kindled against Uzzah; and God smote him
there for his error; and there he died by the ark of God."   2 Sam.
vi. 7.

[2] *Preceding.*]   "And David danced before the Lord with all his
might; and David was girded with a linen ephod."   2 Sam. vi. 14.

[3] *Gregory.*]   St. Gregory's prayers are said to have delivered
Trajan from hell.   See Paradise, Canto xx. 40.

His mighty conquest, Trajan the Emperor.[1]
A widow at his bridle stood, attired
In tears and mourning.   Round about them troop'd
Full throng of knights; and overhead in gold
The eagles floated,[2] struggling with the wind.
The wretch appear'd amid all these to say:
"Grant vengeance, Sire! for, woe beshrew this
     heart,
My son is murder'd."   He replying seem'd:
"Wait now till I return."   And she, as one
Made hasty by her grief: "O Sire! if thou
Dost not return?"—"Where I am, who then is,
May right thee."—"What to thee is other's good,
If thou neglect thy own?"—"Now comfort thee;"
At length he answers.   "It beseemeth well
My duty be perform'd, ere I move hence:
So justice wills; and pity bids me stay."

He, whose ken nothing new surveys, produced
That visible speaking, new to us and strange,
The like not found on earth.   Fondly I gazed
Upon those patterns of meek humbleness,
Shapes yet more precious for their artist's sake;
When "Lo!" the poet whisper'd, "where this way

[1] *Trajan the Emperor.*] For this story, Landino refers to two writers, whom he calls "Helinando," of France, by whom he means Elinand, a monk and chronicler, in the reign of Philip Augustus, and "Polycrato," of England, by whom is meant John of Salisbury, author of the Polycraticus de Curialium Nugis, in the twelfth century.   The passage in the text I find nearly a translation from that work, lib. v. c. 8.   The original appears to be in Dio Cassius, where it is told of the Emperor Hadrian, lib. lxix. ἄμιλυ γυναικὸς, κ.τ.λ. "when a woman appeared to him with a suit, as he was on a journey, at first he answered her, 'I have no leisure;' but she crying out to him, 'then reign no longer,' he turned about, and heard her cause." Lombardi refers also to Johannes Diaconus.   Vita S. Gregor. lib. ii. cap. 44; the Euchology of the Greeks, cap. 96; and St. Thomas Aquinas Supplem. Quæst. 73, art. 5 ad 5.   Compare Fazio degli Uberti, Dittamondo, lib. ii. cap. 6.

[2] *The eagles floated.*] See Perticari's Letter on this passage. Opere, vol. iii. p. 552. Ed. Bol. 1823.   The eagles were of metal; not worked on a standard, as Dante supposed.

(But slack their pace) a multitude advance.
These to the lofty steps shall guide us on."
    Mine eyes, though bent on view of novel sights,
Their loved allurement, were not slow to turn.
Reader! I would not that amazed thou miss
Of thy good purpose, hearing how just God
Decrees our debts be cancel'd. Ponder [1] not
The form of suffering. Think on what suc-
    ceeds:
Think that, at worst, beyond the mighty doom
It cannot pass. "Instructor!" I began,
"What I see hither tending, bears no trace
Of human semblance, nor of aught beside
That my foil'd sight can guess." He answering
    thus:
    "So courb'd to earth, beneath their heavy terms
Of torment stoop they, that mine eye at first
Struggled as thine. But look intently thither;
And disentangle with thy labouring view,
What, underneath those stones, approacheth: now,
E'en now, mayst thou discern the pangs of each."
    Christians and proud! O poor and wretched
    ones!
That, feeble in the mind's eye, lean your trust
Upon unstaid perverseness: know ye not
That we are worms, yet made at last to form
The winged insect,[2] imp'd with angel plumes,
That to heaven's justice unobstructed soars?
Why buoy ye up aloft your unfledged souls?

---

[1] *Ponder.*] This is, in truth, an unanswerable objection to the doctrine of Purgatory. It is difficult to conceive how the best can meet death without horror, if they believe it must be followed by immediate and intense suffering.
    [2] *The winged insect.*] L'angelica farfalla.
    The butterfly was an ancient and well-known symbol of the human soul. Venturi cites some lines from the Canzoni Anacreontiche of Magalotti, in which this passage is imitated.

Abortive[1] then and shapeless ye remain,
Like the untimely embryon of a worm.

 As, to support[2] incumbent floor or roof,
For corbel, is a figure sometimes seen,
That crumples up its knees unto its breast;
With the feign'd posture, stirring ruth unfeign'd
In the beholder's fancy; so I saw
These fashion'd, when I noted well their guise.

 Each, as his back was laden, came indeed
Or more or less contracted; and it seem'd
As he, who show'd most patience in his look,
Wailing exclaim'd: "I can endure no more."

[1] *Abortive.*] The word in the original is entomata. Some critics, and Salvini amongst the rest, have supposed that Dante, finding in a vocabulary the Greek word ἔντομα with the article τὰ placed after it to denote its gender, mistook them for one word. From this error he is well exculpated by Rosa Morando in a passage quoted by Lombardi from the Osserv. Parad. III., where it is shown that the Italian word is formed, for the sake of the verse, in analogy with some others used by our Poet; and that Redi himself, an excellent Greek scholar and a very accurate writer, has even in prose, where such licences are less allowable, thus lengthened it. It may be considered as some proof of our author's acquaintance with the Greek language, that in the Convito (i. 10) he finds fault with the version of Aristotle's Ethics made by Taddeo d'Alderotto, the Florentine physician, and that in the treatise de Monarchiâ, lib. i. cap. 14, he quotes a Greek word from Aristotle himself. On the other hand, he speaks of a passage in the same writer being doubtful, on account of its being differently interpreted in two different translations, a new and an old one. Convito, ii. 15. And for the word "autentin," he refers to a vocabulary compiled by Uguccione de' Bagni of Pisa, many MSS. of which have been preserved. After all, Dante's knowledge of Greek must remain as questionable as Shakspeare's of that language and of Latin.

[2] *As, to support.*] Chillingworth, cap. vi. § 54, speaks of "those crouching anticks, which seem in great buildings to labour under the weight they bear." And Lord Shaftesbury has a similar illustration in his Essay on Wit and Humour, p. 4, § 3.

CANTO XI

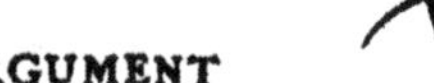

ARGUMENT

After a prayer uttered by the spirits, who were spoken of in the last Canto, Virgil inquires the way upwards, and is answered by one, who declares himself to have been Omberto, son of the Count of Santafiore. Next our Poet distinguishes Oderigi, the illuminator, who discourses on the vanity of worldly fame, and points out to him the soul of Provenzano Salvani.

"O thou Almighty Father![1] who dost make
The heavens thy dwelling, not in bounds confined,
But that, with love intenser, there thou view'st
Thy primal effluence; hallow'd be thy name:
Join, each created being, to extol
Thy might; for worthy humblest thanks and praise
Is thy blest Spirit.   May thy kingdom's peace
Come unto us; for we, unless it come,
With all our striving, thither tend in vain.
As, of their will, the angels unto thee
Tender meet sacrifice, circling thy throne
With loud hosannas; so of their's be done
By saintly men on earth.   Grant us, this day,
Our daily manna, without which he roams
Through this rough desert retrograde, who most
Toils to advance his steps.   As we to each
Pardon the evil done us, pardon thou
Benign, and of our merit take no count.
'Gainst the old adversary, prove thou not
Our virtue, easily subdued; but free

---

[1] *O thou Almighty Father.*] The first four lines are borrowed by Pulci, Morg. Magg. c. vi.   Dante, in his 'Credo,' has again versified the Lord's Prayer, if, indeed, the 'Credo' be Dante's, which some have doubted; and in the preface to Allacci's Collection it is ascribed to Antonio di Ferrara.

From his incitements, and defeat his wiles.
This last petition, dearest Lord ! is made
Not for ourselves ; since that were needless now ;
But for their sakes who after us remain.''
    Thus for themselves and us good speed imploring,
Those spirits went beneath a weight like that
We sometimes feel in dreams ; all, sore beset,
But with unequal anguish ; wearied all ;
Round the first circuit ; purging as they go
The world's gross darkness off.   In our behoof
If their vows still be offer'd, what can here
For them be vow'd and done by such, whose wills
Have root of goodness in them ?[1]   Well beseems
That we should help them wash away the stains
They carried hence ; that so, made pure and light,
They may spring upward to the starry spheres.
    " Ah ! so may mercy-temper'd justice rid
Your burdens speedily ; that ye have power
To stretch your wing, which e'en to your desire
Shall lift you ; as ye show us on which hand
Toward the ladder leads the shortest way.
And if there be more passages than one,
Instruct us of that easiest to ascend :
For this man, who comes with me, and bears yet
The charge of fleshly raiment Adam left him,
Despite his better will, but slowly mounts.''
From whom the answer came unto these words,
Which my guide spake, appear'd not ; but 'twas
        said :
" Along the bank to rightward come with us ;
And ye shall find a pass that mocks not toil
Of living man to climb : and were it not

1—— *Such whose wills*
    Have root of goodness in them.]   The Poet has before told us,
that there are no others on earth whose prayers avail to shorten the
pains of those who are in Purgatory.

That I am hinder'd by the rock, wherewith
This arrogant neck is tamed, whence needs I stoop
My visage to the ground; him, who yet lives,
Whose name thou speak'st not, him I fain would
        view;
To mark if e'er I knew him, and to crave
His pity for the fardel that I bear.
I was of Latium;[1] of a Tuscan born,
A mighty one: Aldobrandesco's name,
My sire's, I know not if ye e'er have heard.
My old blood and forefathers' gallant deeds
Made me so haughty, that I clean forgot
The common mother; and to such excess
Wax'd in my scorn of all men, that I fell,
Fell therefore; by what fate, Sienna's sons,
Each child in Campagnatico, can tell.
I am Omberto: not me, only, pride
Hath injured, but my kindred all involved
In mischief with her.   Here my lot ordains
Under this weight to groan, till I appease
God's angry justice, since I did it not
Amongst the living, here amongst the dead."
    Listening I bent my visage down: and one
(Not he who spake) twisted beneath the weight
That urged him, saw me, knew me straight, and
        call'd;
Holding his eyes with difficulty fix'd
Intent upon me, stooping as I went
Companion of their way.   "O!" I exclaim'd,
"Art thou not Oderigi?[2] art not thou

---

[1] *I was of Latium.*]   Omberto, the son of Guglielmo
Aldobrandesco, Count of Santafiore, in the territory of Sienna.
His arrogance provoked his countrymen to such a pitch of fury
against him, that he was murdered by them at Campagnatico.
[2] *Oderigi.*]   The illuminator, or miniature painter, a friend of
Giotto and Dante.

Agobbio's glory, glory of that art
Which they of Paris call the limner's skill ? "
  "Brother!" said he, "with tints, that gayer smile,
Bolognian Franco's [1] pencil lines the leaves.
His all the honour now ; my light obscured.
In truth, I had not been thus courteous to him
The whilst I lived, through eagerness of zeal
For that pre-eminence my heart was bent on.
Here, of such pride, the forfeiture is paid. [2]
Nor were I even here, if, able still
To sin, I had not turn'd me unto God.
O powers of man ! how vain your glory, nipt
E'en in its height of verdure, if an age
Less bright succeed not. [3]   Cimabue [4] thought
To lord it over painting's field ; and now
The cry is Giotto's, [5] and his name eclipsed.

[1] *Bolognian Franco.*] Franco of Bologna, who is said to have
been a pupil of Oderigi's.
   [2] *The forfeiture is paid.*]

Di tal superbia quì si paga il fio.

So in the Inferno, c. xxvii. 135.

—— in che si paga il fio.

And Ariosto, Orl. Fur. c. xxii. 59.
Prestate olà, che quì si paga il fio.

   [3] ——*If an age
   Less bright succeed not.*] If a generation of men do not follow,
among whom none exceeds or equals those who have immediately
preceded them. "Etati grosse ;" to which Volpi remarks a
similar expression in Boileau.

Villon sût le premier, dans ces siécles grossiers,
Debrouiller l'art confus de nos vieux romanciers.
Art Poétique, ch. i.

   [4] *Cimabue.*] Giovanni Cimabue, the restorer of painting, was
born at Florence, of a noble family, about 1240, and died in or after
1302. The passage in the text is an allusion to his epitaph.

Credidit ut Cimabos picturæ castra tenere,
Sic tenuit vivens : nunc tenet astra poli.

   [5] *The cry is Giotto's.*] In Giotto we have a proof at how early a
period the fine arts were encouraged in Italy. His talents were
discovered by Cimabue, while he was attending sheep for his father
in the neighbourhood of Florence, and he was afterwards patronised

Thus hath one Guido from the other [1] snatch'd
The letter'd prize: and he, perhaps, is born,[2]

by Pope Benedict XI. and Robert King of Naples; and enjoyed the society and friendship of Dante, whose likeness * he has transmitted to posterity. He died in 1336, at the age of sixty.

[1] *One Guido from the other.*] Guido Cavalcanti, the friend of our Poet (see Hell, Canto x. 59), had eclipsed the literary fame of Guido Guinicelli, of a noble family in Bologna, whom we shall meet with in the twenty-sixth Canto, and of whom frequent and honourable mention is made by our Poet in his treatise de Vulg. Eloq. Guinicelli died in 1276, as is proved by Fantuzzi, on the Bolognian writers, tom. iv. p. 345. See Mr. Mathias's Tiraboschi, tom. i. p. 110. There are more of Guinicelli's poems to be found in Allacci's Collection, than Tiraboschi, who tells us he had not seen it, supposed. From these I have selected two which appear to me singularly pathetic. It must, however, be observed that the former of them is attributed in the Vatican MS. 3213, to Cino da Pistoia, as Bottari informs us in the notes to Lettere di Fra Guittone d'Arezzo, p. 171. [Cavalcanti's poems have now been published.]

> Noi provamo ch' in questo cieco mondo
> Ciascun si vive in angosciosa doglia,
> Ch' in onni avversita ventura 'l tira.
> Beata l' alma che lassa tal pondo.
> E va nel ciel, dove è compita zoglia,
> Zoglioso cor far de corrotto e dira.
> Or dunque di chel vostro cor sospira,
> Che rallegrar si dè del suo migliore,
> Che Dio, nostro signore,
> Volse di lei, come avea l'angel detto,
> Fare il ciel perfetto.
> Per nuova cosa ogni santo la mira:
> Ed ella sta d'avante alla salute;
> Ed in ver lei parla ogni vertute.
> > *Allacci, Ediz. Napoli,* 1661, p. 378.

> By proof, in this blind mortal world, we know,
> That each one lives in grief and sore annoy;
> Such ceaseless strife of fortune we sustain.
> Blessed the soul, that leaves this weight below,
> And goes its way to heaven, where it hath joy
> Entire, without a touch of wrath or pain.
> Now then what reason hath thy heart to sigh,
> That should be glad, as for desire fulfill'd,
> That God, our Sovereign, will'd
> She, as He told His angel, should be given
> To bless and perfect heaven?
> Each saint looks on her with admiring eye;
> And she stands ever in salvation's sight;
> And every virtue bends on her its light.

[2] For note, see p. 73.

---

* [See frontispiece to this volume.]

Who shall drive either from their nest.   The noise
Of worldly fame is but a blast of wind,

> Conforto già conforto l'amor chiama,
> E pietà prega per Dio, fatti resto ;
> Or v' inchinate a sì dolce preghiera ;
> Spogliatevi di questa vesta grama,
> Da che voi sete per ragion richiesto.
> Che l'uomo per dolor more e dispera.
> Con voi vedeste poi la bella ciera.
> Se v' accogliesse morte in disperanza,
> De si grave pesanza
> Traete il vostro cor ormai per Dio,
> Che non sia cosi rio
> Ver l'alma vostra che ancora spiera
> Vederla in ciel e star nelle sue braccia,
> Dunque spene dè confortar vi piaccia.
>
> *Allacci, Ediz. Napoli*, 1661, p. 380.

> "Comfort thee, comfort thee," exclaimeth Love ;
> And Pity by thy God adjures thee " rèst : "
> Oh then incline ye to such gentle prayer ;
> Nor Reason's plea should ineffectual prove,
> Who bids ye lay aside this dismal vest :
> For man meets death through sadness and despair.
> Amongst you ye have seen a face so fair :
> Be this in mortal mourning some relief.
> And, for more balm of grief,
> Rescue thy spirit from its heavy load,
> Remembering thy God ;
> And that in heaven thou hopest again to share
> In sight of her, and with thine arms to fold :
> Hope then ; nor of this comfort quit thy hold.

To these I will add a sonnet by the same writer, from the poems
printed with the Bella Mano of Giusto de' Conti. Ediz. 1715,
p. 167.

> Io vo dal ver la mia donna laudare,
>   E rassembrarla alla rosa, ed al giglio.
>   Più che stella Diana splende, e pare,
>   Ciò che lassù è bello a lei somiglio.
> Verdi rivere a lei rassembro, l'are,
>   Tutto color di porpora, e vermiglio,
>   Oro, ed argento, e ricche gioie preclare ;
>   Medesmo amor per lei raffina miglio.
> Passa per via adorna, e sì gentile,
>   Cui bassa orgoglio, a cui dona salute,
>   E fal di nostra fe, se non la crede.
> E non le può appressare, uom che sia vile,
>   Ancor ve ne dirò maggior vertute,
> Nullo uom può mal pensar finchè la vede.

> I would from truth my lady's praise supply,
>   Resembling her to lily and to rose ;
>   Brighter than morning's lucid star she shows,
>   And fair as that which fairest is on high.

That blows from diverse points, and shifts its name,
Shifting the point it blows from.   Shalt thou more

To the blue wave, I liken her, and sky,
  All colour that with pink and crimson glows,
  Gold, silver and rich stones : nay lovelier grows
  E'en love himself, when she is standing by.
She passeth on so gracious and so mild,
  One's pride is quench'd, and one of sick is well :
  And they believe, who from the faith did err ;
And none may near her come by harm defiled.
  A mightier virtue have I yet to tell ;
  No man may think of evil, seeing her.

The two following sonnets of Guido Cavalcanti may enable the
reader to form some judgment whether Dante had sufficient reason
for preferring him to his predecessor Guinicelli.

Io temo che la mia disavventura
  Non faccia sì ch' io dico io mi dispero,
  Però ch' io sento nel cor un pensero,
  Che fa tremar la mente di paura.
E par ch' ei dica : Amor non t'assicura
  In guisa che tu possa di leggiero
  Alla tua donna sì contare il vero,
  Che morte non ti ponga in sua figura.
Della gran doglia, che l'anima sente,
  Si parte dallo core un tal sospiro
  Che va dicendo : spiritei fuggite ;
Allor null' uom, che sia pietoso, miro ;
  Che consolasse mia vita dolente,
  Dicendo : spiritei non vi partite.

Anecdota Literaria ex MSS. Codicibus eruta.
Ediz. Roma (no year), v. iii. p. 452.

I fear lest my mischance may so prevail,
  That it may make me of myself despair.
  For, my heart searching, I discover there
  A thought that makes the mind with terror quail.
It says, meseemeth, "Love shall not avail
  To strengthen thee so much, that thou shalt dare
  Tell her, thou lovest, thy passion or thy prayer,
  To save from power of death thy visage pale."
Through the dread sorrow that o'erwhelms my soul,
  There issues from my bosom such a sigh,
  As passeth, crying : "Spirits, flee away."
And then, when I am fainting in my dole,
  No man so merciful there standeth by,
  To comfort me, and answer, "Spirits, stay."

Beltà di donna, e di saccente core,
  E cavalieri armati, che sian genti,
  Cantar d'augelli, e ragionar d'amore,
  Adorni legni in mar, forti e correnti :
Aria serena, quando appar l'albore,
  E bianca neve scender senza venti,

Live in the mouths of mankind, if thy flesh
Part shrivel'd from thee, than if thou hadst died
Before the coral and the pap were left;
Or e'er some thousand years have past? and that
Is, to eternity compared, a space
Briefer than is the twinkling of an eye
To the heaven's slowest orb.   He there, who treads
So leisurely before me, far and wide
Through Tuscany resounded once; and now
Is in Sienna scarce with whispers named:
There was he sovereign, when destruction caught
The maddening rage of Florence, in that day
Proud as she now is loathsome.   Your renown
Is as the herb, whose hue doth come and go;
And his might withers it, by whom it sprang
Crude from the lap of earth."   I thus to him:

> Rivera d'acqua, e prato d'ogni fiore,
>   Oro, e argento, azurro in ornamenti.
> Ciò che può la beltate, e la valenza
>   Della mia donna in suo gentil coraggio,
>   Par che rassembra vile a chi cio guarda.
> E tanto ha più d'ogni altra conoscenza,
>   Quanto lo Ciel di questa terra è maggio,
>   A simil di natura ben non tarda.
> *La Bella Mano e Rime Antiche, Edis. Fir.* 1715, p. 128.

> Whatso is fair in lady's face or mind,
>   And gentle knights caparison'd and gay,
> Singing of sweet birds unto love inclined,
>   And gallant barks that cut the watery way;
> The white snow falling without any wind,
>   The cloudless sky at break of early day,
> The crystal stream, with flowers the meadow lined,
>   Silver, and gold, and azure for array:
> To him that sees the beauty and the worth
>   Whose power doth meet and in my lady dwell,
>   All seem as vile, their price and lustre gone.
> And, as the heaven is higher than the earth,
>   So she in knowledge doth each one excel,
>   Not slow to good in nature like her own.

[2] *He, perhaps, is born.*] Some imagine, with much probability, that Dante here augurs the greatness of his own poetical reputation. Others have absurdly fancied that he prophesies the glory of Petrarch. But Petrarch was not yet born. Lombardi doubts whether it is not spoken generally of human vicissitudes.

"True are thy sayings : to my heart they breathe
The kindly spirit of meekness, and allay
What tumours [1] rankle there.   But who is he,
Of whom thou spakest but now ? "   " This," he
    replied,
" Is Provenzano.   He is here, because
He reach'd, with grasp presumptuous, at the sway
Of all Sienna.   Thus he still hath gone,
Thus goeth never-resting, since he died.
Such is the acquittance render'd back of him,
Who, in the mortal life, too much hath dared."
I then : " If soul, that to life's verge delays
Repentance, linger in that lower space,
Nor hither mount, (unless good prayers befriend,)
Or ever [2] time, long as it lived, be past ;
How chanced admittance was vouchsafed to him ? "

    " When at his glory's topmost height," said he,
" Respect of dignity all cast aside,
Freely he fix'd him on Sienna's plain,
A suitor [3] to redeem his suffering friend,

---

[1] *What tumours.*]   Apt words have power to swage
          The tumours of a troubled mind.
                    Milton's Samson Agonistes.

[2] *Or ever.*]   This line was omitted in the former editions, as Mr.
Lyell has pointed out to me.

[3] *A suitor.*]   Provenzano Salvani humbled himself so far for
the sake of one of his friends, who was detained in captivity by
Charles I. of Sicily, as personally to supplicate the people of Sienna
to contribute the sum required by the king for his ransom : and
this act of self-abasement atoned for his general ambition and pride.
He fell in the battle of Colle in Valdelsa, wherein the Florentines
discomfited the Siennese in June, 1269. G. Villani relates some
curious particulars of his fate. "Messer Provenzano Salvani, the
lord and conductor of the army, was taken, and his head cut off
and carried through all the camp fixed upon a lance. And well
was accomplished the prophecy and revelation made to him by the
Devil by way of witchcraft, but he understood it not ; for having
compelled him to answer how he should succeed in the said
engagement, he told him lyingly : ' Thou shalt go, fight, conquer
not, die in the battle, and thy head shall be the highest in the
camp.' And he thought to have the victory, and from these words
thought to remain master of all, and noted not the fallacy, where

Who languish'd in the prison-house of Charles;
Nor, for his sake, refused through every vein
To tremble.   More I will not say; and dark,
I know, my words are; but thy neighbours soon [1]
Shall help thee to a comment on the text.
This is the work, that from these limits freed him."

CANTO XII

ARGUMENT

Dante being desired by Virgil to look down on the ground which
they are treading, observes that it is wrought over with imagery
exhibiting various instances of pride recorded in history and fable.
They leave the first cornice, and are ushered to the next by an angel
who points out the way.

WITH equal pace, as oxen in the yoke,
I, with that laden spirit, journey'd on,
Long as the mild instructor suffer'd me;
But, when he bade me quit him, and proceed,
(For "Here," said he, "behoves with sail and oars
Each man, as best he may, push on his bark,")
Upright, as one disposed for speed, I raised
My body, still in thought submissive bow'd.
    I now my leader's track not loth pursued;
And each had shown how light we fared along,
When thus he warned me: "Bend thine eyesight
        down:
For thou, to ease the way, shalt find it good
To ruminate the bed beneath thy feet."

he said 'conquer not, die.'   And therefore it is great folly to trust
such counsel as that of the Devil."   Lib. vii. cap. xxxi.
    [1] *Thy neighbours soon.*]   "Thou wilt know in the time of thy
banishment, which is near at hand, what it is to solicit favours
of others, and 'tremble through every vein,' lest they should be
refused thee."

As, in memorial of the buried, drawn
Upon earth-level tombs, the sculptured form
Of what was once, appears, (at sight whereof
Tears often stream forth, by remembrance waked,
Whose sacred stings the piteous often feel,)
So saw I there, but with more curious skill
Of portraiture o'erwrought, whate'er of space
From forth the mountain stretches.   On one part
Him I beheld, above all creatures erst
Created noblest, lightening fall from heaven,
On the other side, with bolt celestial pierced,
Briareus; cumbering earth he lay, through dint
Of mortal ice-stroke.   The Thymbræan god,[1]
With Mars,[2] I saw, and Pallas, round their sire,
Arm'd still, and gazing on the giants' limbs
Strewn o'er the ethereal field.   Nimrod I saw:
At foot of the stupendous work he stood,
As if bewilder'd, looking on the crowd
Leagued in his proud attempt on Sennaar's plain.[3]
    O Niobe! in what a trance of woe
Thee I beheld, upon that highway drawn,
Seven sons on either side thee slain.   O Saul!
How ghastly didst thou look, on thine own
      sword
Expiring, in Gilboa, from that hour
Ne'er visited with rain from heaven, or dew.
    O fond Arachne! thee I also saw,

---

[1] *The Thymbræan god.*] Apollo.

    Si modo, quem perhibes, pater est Thymbræus Apollo.
Virg. Georg. iv. 323.

[2] *Mars.*]   With such a grace,
    The giants that attempted to scale heaven,
    When they lay dead on the Phlegræan plain,
    Mars did appear to Jove.
    Beaumont and Fletcher, The Prophetess, act ii. sc. 3.

[3] *Sennaar's plain.*]   The builders such of Babel on the plain
    Of Sennaar.   *Milton, P. L.* b. iii. 467.

Half spider now, in anguish, crawling up
The unfinish'd web thou weaved'st to thy bane.
    O Rehoboam![1] here thy shape doth seem
Louring no more defiance ; but fear-smote,
With none to chase him, in his chariot whirl'd.
    Was shown beside upon the solid floor,
How dear Alcmæon[2] forced his mother rate
That ornament, in evil hour received :
How, in the temple, on Sennacherib[3] fell
His sons, and how a corpse they left him there.
Was shown the scath, and cruel mangling made
By Tomyris[4] on Cyrus, when she cried,
"Blood thou didst thirst for : take thy fill of blood."
Was shown how routed in the battle fled
The Assyrians, Holofernes[5] slain, and e'en
The relics of the carnage.   Troy I mark'd,
In ashes and in caverns.   Oh ! how fallen,
How abject, Ilion, was thy semblance there.
    What master of the pencil or the style[6]
Had traced the shades and lines, that might have
        made
The subtlest workman wonder ?   Dead, the dead ;
The living seem'd alive : with clearer view,
His eye beheld not, who beheld the truth,
Than mine what I did tread on, while I went
Low bending.   Now swell out, and with stiff necks

---

[1] *O Rehoboam*.]   1 Kings xii. 18.
[2] *Alcmæon*.]   Virg. Æn. lib. vi. 445, and Homer, Od. xi. 325.
[3] *Sennacherib*.]   2 Kings xix. 37.
[4] *Tomyris*.]   Caput Cyri amputatum in utrem humano sanguine repletum conjici Regina jubet cum hac exprobatione crudelitatis, Satia te, inquit, sanguine quem sitisti, cujusque insatiabilis semper fuisti.   Justin. lib. i. cap. 8.
[5] *Holofernes*.]   Judith xiii.
[6] *What master of the pencil or the style*.]

—— inimitable on earth
By model, or by shading pencil drawn.
                    Milton, P. L. b. iii. 509.

Pass on, ye sons of Eve! vale not your looks,
Lest they descry the evil of your path.
   I noted not (so busied was my thought)
How much we now had circled of the mount;
And of his course yet more the sun had spent;
When he, who with still wakeful caution went,
Admonish'd: "Raise thou up thy head: for know
Time is not now for slow suspense. Behold,
That way, an angel hasting towards us. Lo,
Where duly the sixth handmaid [1] doth return
From service on the day. Wear thou, in look ·
And gesture, seemly grace of reverent awe;
That gladly he may forward us aloft.
Consider that this day ne'er dawns again."
   Time's loss he had so often warn'd me 'gainst,
I could not miss the scope at which he aim'd.
   The goodly shape approach'd us, snowy white
In vesture, and with visage casting streams
Of tremulous lustre like the matin star.
His arms he open'd, then his wings; and spake:
"Onward! the steps, behold, are near; and now
The ascent is without difficulty gain'd."
   A scanty few are they, who, when they hear
Such tidings, hasten. O, ye race of men!
Though born to soar, why suffer ye a wind
So slight to baffle ye? He led us on
Where the rock parted; here, against my front,
Did beat his wings; then promised I should fare
In safety on my way. As to ascend
That steep, upon whose brow the chapel stands,[2]

---

[1] *The sixth handmaid.*] Compare Canto xxii. 116.
[2] *The chapel stands.*] The church of San Miniato in Florence,
situated on a height that overlooks the Arno, where it is crossed by
the bridge Rubaconte, so called from Messer Rubaconte da Mandella,
of Milan, chief magistrate of Florence, by whom the bridge was
founded in 1237. See G. Villani, lib. vi. cap. xxvii.

(O'er Rubaconte, looking lordly down
On the well-guided city,[1]) up the right
The impetuous rise is broken by the steps
Carved in that old and simple age, when still
The registry [2] and label rested safe;
Thus is the acclivity relieved, which here,
Precipitous, from the other circuit falls:
But, on each hand, the tall cliff presses close.

As, entering, there we turn'd, voices, in strain
Ineffable, sang: "Blessed [3] are the poor
In spirit." Ah! how far unlike to these
The straits of hell: here songs to usher us,
There shrieks of woe. We climb the holy stairs:
And lighter to myself by far I seem'd
Than on the plain before; whence thus I spake:
" Say, master, of what heavy thing have I
Been lighten'd; that scarce aught the sense of toil
Affects me journeying?" He in few replied:
" When sin's broad characters,[4] that yet remain
Upon thy temples, though well nigh effaced,
Shall be, as one is, all clean razed out:
Then shall thy feet by heartiness of will
Be so o'ercome, they not alone shall feel
No sense of labour, but delight much more
Shall wait them, urged along their upward way."

Then like to one, upon whose head is placed
Somewhat he deems not of, but from the becks
Of others, as they pass him by; his hand

---

1 *The well-guided city.*] This is said ironically of Florence.
2 *The registry.*] In allusion to certain instances of fraud committed
in Dante's time with respect to the public accounts and measures.
See Paradise, Canto xvi. 103.
3 *Blessed.*] "Blessed are the poor in spirit, for theirs is the kingdom of heaven." Matth. v. 3.
4 *Sin's broad characters.*] Of the seven P's, that denoted the same
number of sins (Peccata) whereof he was to be cleansed (see Canto ix.
100), the first had now vanished in consequence of his having past the
place where the sin of pride, the chief of them, was expiated.

Lends therefore help to assure him, searches, finds,
And well performs such office as the eye
Wants power to execute; so stretching forth
The fingers of my right hand, did I find
Six only of the letters, which his sword,
Who bare the keys, had traced upon my brow.
The leader, as he mark'd mine action, smiled.

CANTO XIII

ARGUMENT

They gain the second cornice, where the sin of envy is purged;
and having proceeded a little to the right, they hear voices uttered
by invisible spirits recounting famous examples of charity, and next
behold the shades, or souls, of the envious clad in sackcloth, and
having their eyes sewed up with an iron thread. Amongst these
Dante finds Sapia, a Siennese lady, from whom he learns the cause
of her being there.

We reach'd the summit of the scale, and stood
Upon the second buttress of that mount
Which healeth him who climbs.   A cornice there,
Like to the former, girdles round the hill;
Save that its arch, with sweep less ample, bends.
    Shadow, nor image there, is seen : all smooth
The rampart and the path, reflecting nought
But the rock's sullen hue.   "If here we wait,
For some to question," said the bard, "I fear
Our choice may haply meet too long delay."
    Then fixedly upon the sun his eyes
He fasten'd; made his right the central point
From whence to move; and turn'd the left aside.
"O pleasant light, my confidence and hope!
Conduct us thou," he cried, "on this new way,
Where now I venture; leading to the bourn

We seek. The universal world to thee
Owes warmth and lustre. If[1] no other cause
Forbid, thy beams should ever be our guide."
  Far, as is measured for a mile on earth,
In brief space had we journey'd ; such prompt will
Impell'd ; and towards us flying, now were heard
Spirits invisible, who courteously
Unto love's table bade the welcome guest.
The voice, that first flew by, call'd forth aloud,
" They have no wine," [2] so on behind us past,
Those sounds reiterating, nor yet lost
In the faint distance, when another came
Crying, " I am Orestes," [3] and alike
Wing'd its fleet way. " O father ! " I exclaim'd,
" What tongues are these ? " and as I question'd, lo !
A third exclaiming, " Love ye those have wrong'd
    you." [4]
  " This circuit," said my teacher, " knots the
    scourge [5]
For envy ; and the cords are therefore drawn
By charity's correcting hand. The curb
Is of a harsher sound ; as thou shalt hear
(If I deem rightly) ere thou reach the pass,
Where pardon sets them free. But fix thine eyes
Intently through the air ; and thou shalt see
A multitude before thee seated, each

---

  [1] *If.*] " Unless there be some urgent necessity for travelling by
night, the day-light should be preferred for that purpose."
  [2] *They have no wine.*] John ii. 3. These words of the Virgin are
referred to as an instance of charity.
  [3] *Orestes.*] Alluding to his friendship with Pylades.
  [4] *Love ye those have wrong'd you.*] " But I say unto you, Love
your enemies, bless them that curse you, do good to them that hate
you, and pray for them which despitefully use you, and persecute
you." Matth. v. 44.
  [5] *The scourge.*] " The chastisement of envy consists in hearing
examples of the opposite virtue, charity. As a curb and restraint on
this vice, you will presently hear very different sounds, those of
threatening and punishment."

  6

Along the shelving grot."   Then more than erst
I oped mine eyes; before me view'd; and saw
Shadows with garments dark as was the rock;
And when we pass'd a little forth, I heard
A crying, "Blessed Mary! pray for us,
Michael and Peter! all ye saintly host!"
    I do not think there walks on earth this day
Man so remorseless, that he had not yearn'd
With pity at the sight that next I saw.
Mine eyes a load of sorrow teem'd, when now
I stood so near them, that their semblances
Came clearly to my view.   Of sackcloth vile
Their   covering   seem'd;   and,   on   his   shoulder,
        one
Did stay another, leaning; and all lean'd
Against the cliff.   E'en thus the blind and poor,
Near the confessionals, to crave an alms,
Stand, each his head upon his fellow's sunk;
So most to stir compassion, not by sound
Of words alone, but that which moves not less,
The sight of misery.   And as never beam
Of noon-day visiteth the eyeless man,
E'en so was heaven a niggard unto these
Of his fair light: for, through the orbs of all,
A thread of wire, impiercing, knits them up,
As for the taming of a haggard hawk.
    It were a wrong, methought, to pass and look
On others, yet myself the while unseen.
To my sage counsel therefore did I turn.
He knew the meaning of the mute appeal,
Nor waited for my questioning, but said:
"Speak; and be brief, be subtile in thy words."
    On that part of the cornice, whence no rim
Engarlands its steep fall, did Virgil come;
On the other side me were the spirits, their cheeks

Bathing devout with penitential tears,
That through the dread impalement forced a way.
I turn'd me to them, and "O shades!" said I,
"Assured that to your eyes unveil'd shall shine
The lofty light, sole object of your wish,
So may heaven's grace [1] clear whatsoe'er of foam
Floats turbid on the conscience, that thenceforth
The stream of mind roll limpid from its source ;
As ye declare (for so shall ye impart
A boon I dearly prize) if any soul
Of Latium dwell among ye : and perchance
That soul may profit, if I learn so much."
    "My brother ! we are, each one, citizens
Of one true city.[2]   Any, thou wouldst say,
Who lived a stranger in Italia's land."
    So heard I answering, as appear'd a voice
That onward came some space from whence I
      stood.
    A spirit I noted, in whose look was mark'd
Expectance.   Ask ye how ?   The chin was raised
As in one reft of sight.   "Spirit," said I,
"Who for thy rise art tutoring, (if thou be
That which didst answer to me,) or by place,
Or name, disclose thyself, that I may know thee."
    "I was," it answer'd, "of Sienna : here
I cleanse away with these the evil life,

[1] *So may heaven's grace.*]

> Se tosto grazia risolva le schiume
> Di vostra coscienza, sì che chiaro
> Per esso scenda della mente il fiume.

This is a fine moral, and finely expressed.   Unless the conscience
be cleared from its impurity, which it can only thoroughly be by an
influence from above, the mind itself cannot act freely and clearly.
" If ye will do his will, ye shall know of the doctrine."   John vii. 17.

[2] —— *Citizens*
      Of one true city.]
    " For here we have no continuing city, but we seek one to come."
Heb. xiii. 14.

Soliciting with tears that He, who is,
Vouchsafe him to us.   Though Sapia [1] named,
In sapience I excell'd not; gladder far
Of other's hurt, than of the good befell me.
That thou mayst own I now deceive thee not,
Hear, if my folly were not as I speak it.
When now my years sloped waning down the
    arch,
It so bechanced, my fellow-citizens
Near Colle met their enemies in the field;
And I pray'd God to grant what He had will'd. [2]
There were they vanquish'd, and betook themselves
Unto the bitter passages of flight.
I mark'd the hunt; and waxing out of bounds
In gladness, lifted up my shameless brow,
And, like the merlin [3] cheated by a gleam,
Cried, 'It is over.   Heaven! I fear thee not.'
Upon my verge of life I wish'd for peace
With God; nor yet repentance had supplied
What I did lack of duty, were it not
The hermit Piero, [1] touch'd with charity,
In his devout oraisons thought on me.
But who art thou that question'st of our state,
Who go'st, as I believe, with lids unclosed,
And breathest in thy talk?" — "Mine eyes,"
    said I,
" May yet be here ta'en from me; but not long;

---

¹ *Sapia.*]   A lady of Sienna, who living in exile at Colle, was so
overjoyed at a defeat which her countrymen sustained near that
place, that she declared nothing more was wanting to make her die
contented.   The Latin annotator on the Monte Casino MS. says of
this lady : " fuit uxor D. Cinii de Pigezo de Senis."
    ² *And I pray'd God to grant what He had will'd.*]   That her
countrymen should be defeated in battle.
    ³ *The merlin.*]   The story of the merlin is, that having been
induced by a gleam of fine weather in the winter to escape from his
master, he was soon oppressed by the rigour of the season.
    ⁴ *The hermit Piero.*]   Piero Pettinagno, a holy hermit of Sienna.

For they have not offended grievously
With envious glances. But the woe beneath [1]
Urges my soul with more exceeding dread,
That nether load already weighs me down."

She thus: " Who then, amongst us here aloft,
Hath brought thee, if thou weenest to return?"

"He," answered I, " who standeth mute beside
    me.
I live: of me ask therefore, chosen spirit!
If thou desire I yonder yet should move
For thee my mortal feet."—"Oh!" she replied,
" This is so strange a thing, it is great sign
That God doth love thee. Therefore with thy
    prayer
Sometime assist me: and, by that I crave,
Which most thou covetest, that if thy feet
E'er tread on Tuscan soil, thou save my fame
Amongst my kindred. Them shalt thou behold
With that vain multitude,[2] who set their hope
On Telamone's haven; there to fail
Confounded, more than when the fancied stream
They sought, of Dian call'd: but they, who lead [3]
Their navies, more than ruin'd hopes shall mourn."

---

[1] *The woe beneath.*] Dante felt that he was much more subject
to the sin of pride, than to that of envy; and this is just what we
should have concluded of a mind such as his.

[2] *That vain multitude.*] The Siennese. See Hell, c. xxix. 118.
" Their acquisition of Telamone, a seaport on the confines of the
Maremma, has led them to conceive hopes of becoming a naval
power: but this scheme will prove as chimerical as their former plan
for the discovery of a subterraneous stream under their city." Why
they gave the appellation of Diana to the imagined stream, Venturi
says he leaves it to the antiquaries of Sienna to conjecture.

[3] *They, who lead.*] The Latin note to the Monte Casino MS.
informs us, that those who were to command the fleets of the
Siennese, in the event of their becoming a naval power, lost their
lives during their employment at Telamone, through the pestilent air
of the Maremma, which lies near that place.

CANTO XIV

ARGUMENT

Our Poet on this second cornice finds also the souls of Guido del Duca of Brettinoro, and Rinieri da Calboli of Romagna; the latter of whom, hearing that he comes from the banks of the Arno, inveighs against the degeneracy of all those who dwell in the cities visited by that stream; and the former, in like manner, against the inhabitants of Romagna. On leaving these, our Poets hear voices recording noted instances of envy.

" SAY,[1] who is he around our mountain winds,
Or ever death has pruned his wing for flight;
That opes his eyes, and covers them at will?"

"I know not who he is, but know thus much;
He comes not singly.   Do thou ask of him,
For thou art nearer to him; and take heed,
Accost him [2] gently, so that he may speak."

Thus on the right two spirits, bending each
Toward the other, talk'd of me; then both
Addressing me, their faces backward lean'd,
And thus the one [3] began: "O soul, who yet
Pent in the body, tendest towards the sky!
For charity, we pray thee, comfort us;

[1] *Say.*]   The two spirits who thus speak to each other are, Guido del Duca of Brettinoro, and Rinieri da Calboli of Romagna.

[2] *Accost him.*]   It is worthy of remark, that the Latin annotator on the Monte Casino MS. agrees with Landino in reading " a colo," instead of " accolo," and interprets it as he does: " Nil aliud vult auctor dicere de colo, nisi quod cum interroget ita dulciter ut respondeat (*sic*) eum ad colum, id est quod tantum respondeat auctor eis quod animus eorum remaneat in quiete et non in suspenso."   "The author means to say, that the spirit should interrogate him courteously, that he may return such an answer as shall put a *period* to their suspense."   Still I have retained my translation of the common reading generally supposed to be put by syncope for " accoglilo," " accost him."

[3] *The one.*]   Guido del Duca.

Recounting whence thou comest, and who thou art :
For thou dost make us, at the favour shown thee,
Marvel, as at a thing that ne'er hath been."

  "There stretches through the midst of Tuscany,"
I straight began, "a brooklet,[1] whose well-head
Springs up in Falterona ; with his race
Not satisfied, when he some hundred miles
Hath measured.   From his banks bring I this frame.
To tell you who I am were words mis-spent :
For yet my name scarce sounds on rumour's lip."

  "If well I do incorporate with my thought
The meaning of thy speech," said he, who first
Address'd me, " thou dost speak of Arno's wave."

  To whom the other :[2] "Why hath he conceal'd
The title of that river, as a man
Doth of some horrible thing ?"   The spirit, who
Thereof was question'd, did acquit him thus :
" I know not : but 'tis fitting well the name
Should perish of that vale ; for from the source,[3]
Where teems so plenteously the Alpine steep
Maim'd of Pelorus,[4] (that doth scarcely pass [5]
Beyond that limit,) even to the point
Where unto ocean is restored what heaven
Drains from the exhaustless store for all earth's
        streams,

---

  [1] *A brooklet.*] The Arno, that rises in Falterona, a mountain in
the Apennine.   Its course is a hundred and twenty miles, according
to G. Villani, who traces it accurately.
  [2] *The other.*] Rinieri da Calboli.
  [3] *From the source.*] "From the rise of the Arno in that 'Alpine
steep,' the Apennine, from whence Pelorus in Sicily was torn by a
convulsion of the earth, even to the point where the same river
unites its waters to the ocean, Virtue is persecuted by all."
  [4] *Maim'd of Pelorus.*] Virg. Æn. lib. iii. 414. Lucan, Phars. lib.
ii. 438.
                    —— A hill
        Torn from Pelorus.   *Milton, P. L.* b. i. 232.

  [5] *That doth scarcely pass.*] "Pelorus is in few places higher
than Falterona, where the Arno springs." Lombardi explains this
differently, and, I think, erroneously.

Throughout the space is virtue worried down,
As 't were a snake, by all, for mortal foe ;
Or through disastrous influence on the place,
Or else distortion of misguided wills
That custom goads to evil : whence in those,
The dwellers in that miserable vale,
Nature is so transform'd, it seems as they
Had shared of Circe's feeding.   'Midst brute swine,[1]
Worthier of acorns than of other food
Created for man's use, he shapeth first
His obscure way ; then, sloping onward, finds
Curs,[2] snarlers more in spite than power, from whom
He turns with scorn aside : still journeying down,
By how much more the curst and luckless foss [3]
Swells out to largeness, e'en so much it finds
Dogs turning into wolves.[4]   Descending still
Through yet more hollow eddies, next he meets
A race of foxes,[5] so replete with craft,
They do not fear that skill can master it.
Nor will I cease because my words are heard [6]
By other ears than thine.   It shall be well
For this man,[7] if he keep in memory
What from no erring spirit I reveal.
Lo! I behold thy grandson,[8] that becomes
A hunter of those wolves, upon the shore
Of the fierce stream ; and cows them all with dread.
Their flesh, yet living, sets he up to sale,

[1] *'Midst brute swine.*] The people of Casentino.
[2] *Curs.*] The Arno leaves Arezzo about four miles to the left.
[3] *Foss.*] So in his anger he terms the Arno.
[4] *Wolves.*] The Florentines.
[5] *Foxes.*] The Pisans.
[6] *My words are heard.*] It should be recollected that Guido still addresses himself to Rinieri.
[7] *For this man.*] " For Dante, who has told us that he comes from the banks of Arno."
[8] *Thy grandson.*] Fulcieri da Calboli, grandson of Rinieri da Calboli who is here spoken to. The atrocities predicted came to pass in 1302. See G. Villani, lib. viii. c. lix.

Then, like an aged beast, to slaughter dooms.
Many of life he reaves, himself of worth
And goodly estimation.   Smear'd with gore,
Mark how he issues from the rueful wood;
Leaving such havoc, that in thousand years
It spreads not to prime lustihood again."
   As one, who tidings hears of woe to come,
Changes his looks perturb'd, from whate'er part
The peril grasp him; so beheld I change
That spirit, who had turn'd to listen; struck
With sadness, soon as he had caught the word.
   His visage, and the other's speech, did raise
Desire in me to know the names of both;
Whereof, with meek entreaty, I inquired.
   The shade, who late address'd me, thus resumed :
" Thy wish imports, that I vouchsafe to do
For thy sake what thou wilt not do [1] for mine.
But, since God's will is that so largely shine
His grace in thee, I will be liberal too.
Guido of Duca know then that I am.
Envy so parch'd my blood, that had I seen
A fellow man made joyous, thou hadst mark'd
A livid paleness overspread my cheek.
Such harvest reap I of the seed I sow'd.
O man! why place [2] thy heart where there doth need
Exclusion of participants in good ?
This is Rinieri's spirit; this, the boast
And honour of the house of Calboli;
Where of his worth no heritage remains.
Nor his the only blood, that hath been stript
('Twixt Po, the mount, the Reno, and the shore [3])

---

[1] *What thou wilt not do.*]   Dante having declined telling him his name.   See v. 22.
  [2] *Why place.*]   This will be explained in the ensuing Canto.
  [3] *'Twixt Po, the mount, the Reno, and the shore.*]
The boundaries of Romagna.

Of all that truth or fancy[1] asks for bliss :
But, in those limits, such a growth has sprung
Of rank and venom'd roots, as long would mock
Slow culture's toil.   Where is good Lizio?[2] where
Manardi, Traversaro, and Carpigna?[3]
O bastard slips of old Romagna's line !
When in Bologna the low artisan,[4]
And in Faenza yon Bernardin[5] sprouts,
A gentle cyon from ignoble stem.
Wonder not, Tuscan, if thou see me weep,
When I recal to mind those once loved names,
Guido of Prata,[6] and of Azzo him[7]
That dwelt with us ;[8] Tignoso[9] and his troop,

[1] *Fancy*.] "Trastullo." Quadrio, in the notes on the second of
the Salmi Penitenziali of our author, understands this in a higher
sense, as meaning that joy which results from an easy and constant
practice of virtue. See Opere di Dante, Zatta ediz. tom. iv. part ii.
p. 193. And he is followed by Lombardi.

[2] *Lizio*.] Lizio da Valbona, whose great-nephew and namesake
is introduced into Boccaccio's Decameron, G. v. N. 4.

[3] *Manardi, Traversaro, and Carpigna*.] Arrigo Manardi of
Faenza, or, as some say, of Brettinoro ; Pier Traversaro, lord of
Ravenna ; and Guido di Carpigna of Montefeltro.

[4] *In Bologna the low artisan*.] One who had been a mechanic,
named Lambertaccio, arrived at almost supreme power in Bologna.

> Quando in Bologna un Fabro si ralligna :
> Quando in Faenza un Bernardin di Fosco.

The pointing and the marginal note of the Monte Casino MS.
entirely change the sense of these two lines. There is a mark of
interrogation added to each ; and by way of answer to both there is
written, "Quasi dicat numquam." Fabro is made a proper name, and
it is said of him : "Iste fuit Dom. Faber de Lambertaciis de Bononia" ;
and Benvenuto da Imola calls him "Nobilis Miles." I have not
ventured to alter the translation so as to make it accord with this
interpretation, as it must have been done in the face, I believe, of
nearly all the editions, and, as far as may be gathered from the silence
of Lombardi, of the MSS. also which that commentator had consulted. But those, who wish to see more on the subject, are referred
to Monti's Proposta, tom. iii. p^te 2, under the word "Rallignare."

[5] *Yon Bernardin*.] Bernardin di Fosco, a man of low origin, but
great talents, who governed at Faenza.

[6] *Prata*.] A place between Faenza and Ravenna.

[7] *Of Azzo him*.] Ugolino, of the Ubaldini family in Tuscany.

[8] *With us*.] Lombardi claims the reading, "nosco," instead of
"vosco," "with us," instead of "with you," for his favourite edition ;
but it is also in Landino's of 1488.

[9] *Tignoso*.] Federigo Tignoso of Rimini.

With Traversaro's house and Anastagio's,[1]
(Each race disherited ;) and beside these,
The ladies[2] and the knights, the toils and ease,
That witch'd us into love and courtesy ;[3]
Where now such malice reigns in recreant hearts.
O Brettinoro![4] wherefore tarriest still,

[1] *Traversaro's house and Anastagio's.*] Two noble families of Ravenna. See v. 100. She, to whom Dryden has given the name of Honoria, in the fable so admirably paraphrased from Boccaccio, was of the former : her lover and the spectre were of the Anastagi family. See Canto xxviii. 20.

[2] *The ladies, etc.*] Le donne, e i cavalier, gli affanni, e gli agi
      Che ne 'nvogliava amore e cortesia.

These two lines express the true spirit of chivalry. "Agi" is understood, by the commentators whom I have consulted, to mean, "The ease procured for others by the exertions of knight-errantry." But surely it signifies the alternation of ease with labour. Venturi is of opinion that the opening of the Orlando Furioso—

      Le donne, i cavalier, l'arme, gli amori,
      Le cortesie, l'audaci imprese io canto,

originates in this passage.

[3] *Courtesy.*] "Cortesia e onestade," etc. Convito, ii. 11. "Courtesy and honour are all one ; and because anciently virtue and good manners were usual in courts, as the contrary now is, this term was derived from thence : courtesy was as much as to say, custom of courts ; which word, if it were now taken from courts, especially those of Italy, would be no other than turpitude," "turpezza."

      —— Courtesy,
      Which oft is sooner found in lowly sheds
      With smoky rafters, than in tapstry halls
      And courts of princes, where it first was named,
      And yet is most pretended.   *Milton, Comus.*

Marino has exceeded his usual extravagance in his play on this word.

      Ma come può vero diletto? ò come
      Vera quiete altrui donar la Corte?
      Le diè la Cortesia del proprio nome
      Solo il principio, il fine ha della Morte.
                      Adone, c. ix. st. 77.

[4] *O Brettinoro.*] A beautifully situated castle in Romagna, the hospitable residence of Guido del Duca, who is here speaking. Landino relates, that there were several of this family, who, when a stranger arrived amongst them, contended with one another by whom he should be entertained ; and that in order to end this dispute, they set up a pillar with as many rings as there were fathers of families among them, a ring being assigned to each, and that according as a stranger on his arrival hung his horse's bridle on one or other of these, he became his guest to whom the ring belonged.

Since forth of thee thy family hath gone,
And many, hating evil, join'd their steps?
Well doeth he, that bids his lineage cease,
Bagnacavallo;[1] Castracaro ill,
And Conio worse,[2] who care to propagate
A race of Counties[3] from such blood as theirs.
Well shall ye also do, Pagani,[4] then
When from amongst you hies your demon child;
Not so, howe'er,[5] that thenceforth there remain
True proof of what ye were.   O Hugolin,[6]
Thou sprung of Fantolini's line! thy name
Is safe; since none is look'd for after thee
To cloud its lustre, warping from thy stock.
But, Tuscan! go thy ways; for now I take
Far more delight in weeping, than in words.
Such[7] pity for your sakes hath wrung my heart."

We knew those gentle spirits, at parting, heard
Our steps.   Their silence therefore, of our way,
Assured us.   Soon as we had quitted them,

[1] *Bagnacavallo.*] A castle between Imola and Ravenna.

[2] —— *Castracaro ill,*
And Conio worse.] Both in Romagna.

[3] *Counties.*] I have used this word here for "Counts," as it is in Shakspeare.

[4] *Pagani.*] The Pagani were lords of Faenza and Imola. One of them, Machinardo, was named *the Demon*, from his treachery. See Hell, Canto xxvii. 47, and note.

[5] *Not so, howe'er.*] "Yet your offspring will be stained with some vice, and will not afford true proof of the worth of your ancestors."

[6] *Hugolin.*] Ugolino Ubaldini, a noble and virtuous person in Faenza, who, on account of his age probably, was not likely to leave any offspring behind him. He is enumerated among the poets by Crescimbeni, and by Tiraboschi, Mr. Mathias's edit. vol. i. p. 143; and Perticari cites a beautiful little poem by him in the Apologia di Dante, parte ii. c. 27, but with so little appearance of antiquity that nothing less than the assurance of so able a critic could induce one for a moment to receive it as genuine.

[7] *Such.*] Here again the Nidobeatina edition adopted by Lombardi, and the Monte Casino MS., differ from the common reading, and both have

> Si m' ha nostra region la mente stretta.
>
> Our country's sorrow has so wrung my heart

instead of   Si m' ha vostra ragion, etc

Advancing onward, lo ! a voice, that seem'd
Like volley'd lightening, when it rives the air,
Met us, and shouted, "Whosoever finds
Will slay me;"[1] then fled from us, as the bolt
Lanced sudden from a downward-rushing cloud.
When it had given short truce unto our hearing,
Behold the other with a crash as loud
As the quick-following thunder: "Mark in me
Aglauros,[2] turn'd to rock." I, at the sound
Retreating, drew more closely to my guide.

Now in mute stillness rested all the air;
And thus he spake: "There was the galling bit,[3]
Which[4] should keep man within his boundary.
But your old enemy so baits the hook,
He drags you eager to him. Hence nor curb
Avails you, nor reclaiming call. Heaven calls,[5]
And, round about you wheeling, courts your gaze
With everlasting beauties. Yet your eye
Turns with fond doting still upon the earth.
Therefore He smites you who discerneth all."

[1] —— *Whosoever finds*
Will slay me.] The words of Cain, Gen. iv. 14.
[2] *Aglauros.*] Ovid, Met. lib. ii. fab. 12.
[3] *There was the galling bit.*] Referring to what had been before
said, Canto xiii. 35. The commentators remark the unusual word
"camo," which occurs here in the original; but they have not
observed, I believe, that Dante himself uses it in the De Monarchiâ,
lib. iii. cap. 16. For the Greek word χάμον see a fragment by S.
Petrus Alex. in Routh's Reliquiæ Sacræ, vol. iii. p. 342, and note.
[4] *Which.*] Mr. Darley has noticed the omission of this line in
the former editions.
[5] *Heaven calls.*] Or ti solleva a più beata speme,
    Mirando il ciel, che ti si volve intorno
    Immortal ed adorno.
       Petrarca, Canzone. l'vo pensando.

CANTO XV

ARGUMENT

An angel invites them to ascend the next steep. On their way
Dante suggests certain doubts, which are resolved by Virgil ; and,
when they reach the third cornice, where the sin of anger is
purged, our Poet, in a kind of waking dream, beholds remarkable
instances of patience ; and soon after they are enveloped in a dense
fog.

As much [1] as 'twixt the third hour's close and dawn,
Appeareth of heaven's sphere, that ever whirls
As restless as an infant in his play ;
So much appear'd remaining to the sun
Of his slope journey towards the western goal.
    Evening was there, and here the noon of night ;
And full upon our forehead smote the beams.
For round the mountain, circling, so our path
Had led us, that toward the sun-set now
Direct we journey'd ; when I felt a weight
Of more exceeding splendour, than before,
Press on my front.   The cause unknown, amaze
Possess'd me ! and both hands [2] against my brows
Lifting, I interposed them, as a screen,
That of its gorgeous superflux of light
Clips the diminish'd orb.   As when the ray, [3]
Striking on water or the surface clear
Of mirror, leaps unto the opposite part,

[1] *As much.*] It wanted three hours of sunset.
[2] *Both hands.*] Raising his hand to save the dazzled sense.
                         Southey's Thalaba, b. xii.
[3] *As when the ray.*]

  Sicut aquæ tremulum labris ubi lumen aēnis
  Sole repercussum, aut radiantis imagine lunæ,
  Omnia pervolitat late loca, jamque sub auras
  Erigitur, summique ferit laquearia tecti.
                         Æn. lib. viii. 25.

Compare Apoll. Rhodius, iii. 755.

Ascending at a glance,[1] e'en as it fell,
And as much[2] differs from the stone, that falls
Through equal space, (so practic skill hath shown ;)
Thus, with refracted light, before me seem'd
The ground there smitten ; whence, in sudden haste,
My sight recoil'd.   "What is this, sire beloved !
'Gainst which I strive to shield the sight in vain ?"
Cried I, "and which toward us moving seems ?"
  "Marvel not, if the family of heaven,"
He answer'd, "yet with dazzling radiance dim
Thy sense.   It is a messenger who comes,
Inviting man's ascent.   Such sights ere long,
Not grievous, shall impart to thee delight,
As thy perception is by nature wrought
Up to their pitch."   The blessed angel, soon
As we had reach'd him, hail'd us with glad
      voice :
" Here enter on a ladder far less steep
Than ye have yet encounter'd."   We forthwith
Ascending, heard behind us chanted sweet,
" Blessed the merciful,"[3] and " Happy thou,
That conquer'st."   Lonely each, my guide and I,
Pursued our upward way ; and as we went,
Some profit from his words I hoped to win,
And thus of him inquiring, framed my speech :

[1] *Ascending at a glance.*]

  Quod simul ac primum sub divo splendor aquai
  Ponitur : extemplo, cœlo stellante, serena
  Sidera respondent in aquâ radiantia mundi.
  Jamne vides igitur, quam parvo tempore imago
  Ætheris ex oris ad terrarum accidat oras.
                                  Lucret. lib. iv. 215.

[2] *And as much.*]   Lombardi, I think justly, observes that this
does not refer to the length of time which a stone is in falling to the
ground, but to the perpendicular line which it describes when
falling, as contrasted with the angle of incidence formed by light
reflected from water or from a mirror.
  [3] *Blessed the merciful.*]   Matt. v. 7.

"What meant Romagna's spirit,[1] when he spake
Of bliss exclusive, with no partner shared?"
   He straight replied: "No wonder, since he
      knows
What sorrow waits on his own worst defect,
If he chide others, that they less may mourn.
Because ye point your wishes at a mark,
Where, by communion of possessors, part
Is lessen'd, envy bloweth up men's sighs.
No fear of that might touch ye, if the love
Of higher sphere exalted your desire.
For there,[2] by how much more they call it *ours*,
So much propriety of each in good
Encreases more, and heighten'd charity
Wraps that fair cloister in a brighter flame."   .
   "Now lack I satisfaction more," said I,
"Than if thou hadst been silent at the first;
And doubt more gathers on my labouring thought.
How can it chance, that good distributed,
The many, that possess it, makes more rich,
Than if 't were shared by few?"   He answering
      thus :
"Thy mind, reverting still to things of earth,
Strikes darkness from true light.   The highest good
Unlimited, ineffable, doth so speed
To love, as beam to lucid body darts,
Giving as much of ardour as it finds.
The sempiternal effluence streams abroad,
Spreading, wherever charity extends.

   [1] *Romagna's spirit.*]   Guido del Duca, of Brettinoro, whom we
have seen in the preceding Canto.
   [2] *For there.*]   Landino has here cited, in addition to Seneca and
Boetius, the two following apposite passages from Augustine and
Saint Gregory: "Nullo modo fit minor accedente consortio
possessio bonitatis, quam tanto latius quanto concordius individua
sociorum possidet caritas."   *Augustin. de Civitate Dei.*   "Qui
facibus invidiæ carere desiderat, illam possessionem appetat, quam
numerus possidentium non angustat."

So that the more aspirants to that bliss
Are multiplied, more good is there to love,
And more is loved; as mirrors, that reflect,
Each unto other, propagated light.
If these my words avail not to allay
Thy thirsting, Beatrice thou shalt see,
Who of this want, and of all else thou hast,
Shall rid thee to the full.   Provide but thou,[1]
That from thy temples may be soon erased,
E'en as the two already, those five scars,
That, when they pain thee worst, then kindliest
    heal."
   "Thou," I had said, "content'st me;" when I
    saw
The other round was gain'd, and wondering eyes
Did keep me mute.   There suddenly I seem'd
By an extatic vision wrapt away;
And in a temple saw, methought, a crowd
Of many persons; and at the entrance stood
A dame,[2] whose sweet demeanour did express
A mother's love, who said, "Child! why hast thou
Dealt with us thus?   Behold thy sire and I
Sorrowing have sought thee;" and so held her
    peace;
And straight the vision fled.   A female next
Appear'd before me, down whose visage coursed
Those waters, that grief forces out from one
By deep resentment stung, who seem'd to say:
"If thou, Pisistratus, be lord indeed
Over this city,[3] named with such debate

---

1 *Provide but thou.*]   "Take heed that thou be healed of the five remaining sins, as thou already art of the two, namely, pride and envy."

2 *A dame.*]   Luke ii. 48.

3 *Over this city.*]   Athens, named after 'Aθήνη, Minerva, in consequence of her having produced a more valuable gift for it in the olive, than Neptune had done in the horse.

7

Of adverse gods, and whence each science sparkles,
Avenge thee of those arms, whose bold embrace
Hath clasp'd our daughter; " and to her, meseem'd,
Benign and meek, with visage undisturb'd,
Her sovran spake: " How shall we those requite [1]
Who wish us evil, if we thus condemn
The man that loves us ? "   After that I saw
A multitude, in fury burning, slay
With stones a stripling youth,[2] and shout amain
" Destroy, destroy; " and him I saw, who bow'd
Heavy with death unto the ground, yet made
His eyes, unfolded upward, gates to heaven,
Praying forgiveness of the Almighty Sire,
Amidst that cruel conflict, on his foes,
With looks that win compassion to their aim.

  Soon as my spirit, from her airy flight
Returning, sought again the things whose truth
Depends not on her shaping, I observed
She had not roved to falsehood in her dreams.

  Meanwhile the leader, who might see I moved
As one who struggles to shake off his sleep,
Exclaim'd: " What ails thee, that thou canst not
        hold
Thy footing firm ; but more than half a league
Hast travell'd with closed eyes and tottering gait,
Like to a man by wine or sleep o'ercharged ? "

  " Beloved father ! so thou deign," said I,
" To listen, I will tell thee what appear'd
Before me, when so fail'd my sinking steps."

  He thus : " Not if thy countenance were mask'd

---

  [1] *How shall we those requite.*]   The answer of Pisistratus the
tyrant to his wife, when she urged him to inflict the punishment of
death on a young man, who, inflamed with love for his daughter,
had snatched a kiss from her in public.   The story is told by
Valerius Maximus, lib. v. 1.
  [2] *A stripling youth.*]   The protomartyr Stephen.

With hundred vizards, could a thought of thine,
How small soe'er, elude me.   What thou saw'st
Was shown, that freely thou mightst ope thy heart
To the waters of peace, that flow diffused
From their eternal fountain.   I not ask'd,
What ails thee? for such cause as he doth, who
Looks only with that eye, which sees no more,
When spiritless the body lies; but ask'd,
To give fresh vigour to thy foot.   Such goads,
The slow and loitering need; that they be found
Not wanting, when their hour of watch returns."

So on we journey'd, through the evening sky
Gazing intent, far onward as our eyes,
With level view, could stretch against the bright
Vespertine ray: and lo! by slow degrees
Gathering, a fog made towards us, dark as night.
There was no room for 'scaping; and that mist
Bereft us, both of sight and the pure air.

CANTO XVI

ARGUMENT

As they proceed through the mist, they hear the voices of spirits praying. Marco Lombardo, one of these, points out to Dante the error of such as impute our actions to necessity; explains to him that man is endued with free will; and shows that much of human depravity results from the undue mixture of spiritual and temporal authority in rulers.

Hell's dunnest gloom, or night unlustrous, dark,
Of every planet 'reft, and pall'd in clouds,
Did never spread before the sight a veil
In thickness like that fog, nor to the sense
So palpable and gross.   Entering its shade,
Mine eye endured not with unclosed lids;

Which marking, near me drew the faithful guide,
Offering me his shoulder for a stay.
  As the blind man behind his leader walks,
Lest he should err, or stumble unawares
On what might harm him or perhaps destroy;
I journey'd through that bitter air and foul,
Still listening to my escort's warning voice,
"Look that from me thou part not."   Straight I
      heard
Voices, and each one seem'd to pray for peace,
And for compassion, to the Lamb of God
That taketh sins away.   Their prelude still
Was "Agnus Dei;" and through all the choir,
One voice, one measure ran, that perfect seem'd
The concord of their song.   "Are these I hear
Spirits, O master?" I exclaim'd; and he,
"Thou aim'st aright: these loose the bonds of
      wrath."
  "Now who art thou, that through our smoke
      dost cleave,
And speak'st of us, as thou[1] thyself e'en yet
Dividedst time by calends?"   So one voice
Bespake me; whence my master said, "Reply;
And ask, if upward hence the passage lead."
  "O being! who dost make thee pure, to stand
Beautiful once more in thy Maker's sight;
Along with me: and thou shalt hear and wonder."
Thus I, whereto the spirit answering spake:
"Long as 'tis lawful for me, shall my steps
Follow on thine; and since the cloudy smoke
Forbids the seeing, hearing in its stead
Shall keep us join'd."   I then forthwith began:
"Yet in my mortal swathing, I ascend
To higher regions; and am hither come

      [1] *As thou.*]   "As if thou wert still living."

Thorough the fearful agony of hell.
And, if so largely God hath doled his grace,
That, clean beside all modern precedent,
He wills me to behold his kingly state ;
From me conceal not who thou wast, ere death
Had loosed thee ; but instruct me : and instruct
If rightly to the pass I tend ; thy words
The way directing, as a safe escort."
  "I was of Lombardy, and Marco call'd : [1]
Not inexperienced of the world, that worth
I still affected, from which all have turn'd
The nerveless bow aside.   Thy course tends right
Unto the summit : " and, replying thus,
He added, "I beseech thee pray for me,
When thou shalt come aloft."   And I to him :
" Accept my faith for pledge I will perform
What thou requirest.   Yet one doubt remains,
That wrings me sorely, if I solve it not.
Singly before it urged me, doubled now
By thine opinion, when I couple that
With one elsewhere [2] declared ; each strengthening
     other.
The world indeed is even so forlorn
Of all good, as thou speak'st it, and so swarms

---

[1] *I was of Lombardy, and Marco call'd.*] A Venetian gentleman. "Lombardo," both was his sirname and denoted the country
to which he belonged. G. Villani, lib. vii. cap. cxx., terms him "a
wise and worthy courtier." Benvenuto da Imola, says Landino,
relates of him, that being imprisoned and not able to pay the price
of his ransom, he applied by letter to his friend Riccardo da Camino,
lord of Trevigi, for relief. Riccardo set on foot a contribution
among several nobles of Lombardy for the purpose ; of which when
Marco was informed, he wrote back with much indignation to
Riccardo, that he had rather die than remain under obligations to
so many benefactors. It is added that Riccardo then paid the
whole out of his own purse. Of this generous man I have occasion
to speak again in the notes to Canto viii. 71, and to Par. Canto
ix. 48.
  [2] *Elsewhere.*] He refers to what Guido del Duca had said in the
fourteenth Canto, concerning the degeneracy of his countrymen.

With every evil. Yet, beseech thee, point
The cause out to me, that myself may see,
And unto others show it : for in heaven
One places it, and one on earth below."

   Then heaving forth a deep and audible sigh,
" Brother ! " he thus began, " the world is blind ;
And thou in truth comest from it.   Ye, who live,
Do so each cause refer to heaven above,
E'en as its motion, of necessity,
Drew with it all that moves.   If this were so,[1]
Free choice in you were none ; nor justice would
There should be joy for virtue, woe for ill.
Your movements have their primal bent from
      heaven ;
Not all : yet said I all ; what then ensues ?
Light have ye still to follow evil or good,
And of the will free power, which, if it stand
Firm and unwearied in Heaven's first assay,
Conquers at last, so it be cherish'd well,

---

[1] *If this were so.*]   Mr. Crowe, in his Lewesdon Hill, has
expressed similar sentiments with much energy.

       —— Of this be sure,
Where freedom is not, there no virtue is :
If there be none, this world is all a cheat,
And the divine stability of heaven
(That assured seat for good men after death)
Is but a transient cloud, display'd so fair
To cherish virtuous hope, but at our need
Eludes the sense, and fools our honest faith,
Vanishing in a lie, etc.

So, also, Frezzi, in his Quadriregio.

    Or sappi ben che Dio ha dato il freno
      A voi di voi ; e, *se* non fosse questo,
      Libero arbitrio in voi sarebbe meno.   Lib. ii. cap. 1.

   There is much more on this subject at the conclusion of the
eighth Capitolo of this book. Compare also Origen in Genesin.
Patrum Græcor. vol. xi. p. 14, Werceburgi, 1783, 8vo, and
Tertullian, Contra Marcionem, lib. ii. p. 458, Lutetiæ, 1641, fol.
A very noble passage on the freedom of the will occurs in the first
book De Monarchiâ, beginning, "Et humanum genus, potissimum
liberum, optime se habet." "The human race, when most com-
pletely free, is in its highest state of excellence."

Triumphant over all.   To mightier force,[1]
To better nature subject, ye abide
Free, not constrain'd by that which forms in you
The reasoning mind uninfluenced of the stars.
If then the present race of mankind err,
Seek in yourselves the cause, and find it there.
Herein thou shalt confess me no false spy.
  "Forth from his plastic hand, who charm'd
      beholds
Her image ere she yet exist, the soul
Comes like a babe, that wantons sportively,[2]
Weeping and laughing in its wayward moods;
As artless, and as ignorant of aught,
Save that her Maker being one who dwells
With gladness ever, willingly she turns
To whate'er yields her joy.   Of some slight good
The flavour soon she tastes; and, snared by that,
With fondness she pursues it; if no guide
Recal, no rein direct her wandering course.
Hence it behoved, the law should be a curb;
A sovereign hence behoved, whose piercing view
Might mark at least the fortress [3] and main tower
Of the true city.   Laws indeed there are:
But who is he observes them?   None; not he,

---

1 *To mightier force.*]   "Though ye are subject to a higher
power than that of the heavenly constellations, even to the power
of the great Creator himself, yet ye are still left in the possession of
liberty.

2 *Like a babe, that wantons sportively.*]   This reminds us of the
Emperor Hadrian's verses to his departing soul.

Animula vagula blandula, etc.

3 *The fortress.*]   Justice, the most necessary virtue in the chief
magistrate, as the commentators for the most part explain it: and it
appears manifest from all our Poet says in his first book De Monarchiâ,
concerning the authority of the temporal Monarch and concerning
Justice, that they are right.   Yet Lombardi understands the law
here spoken of to be the law of God; *the sovereign*, a spiritual ruler,
and *the true city*, the society of true believers; so that *the fortress*,
according to him, denotes the principal parts of Christian duty.

Who goes before, the shepherd of the flock,
Who [1] chews the cud but doth not cleave the hoof.
Therefore the multitude, who see their guide
Strike at the very good they covet most,
Feed there and look no further.   Thus the cause
Is not corrupted nature in yourselves,
But ill-conducting, that hath turn'd the world
To evil.   Rome, that turn'd it unto good,
Was wont to boast two suns,[2] whose several beams
Cast light on either way, the world's and God's.
One since hath quench'd the other; and the
      sword
Is grafted on the crook; and, so conjoin'd,
Each must perforce decline to worse, unawed
By fear of other.   If thou doubt me, mark
The blade: each herb is judged of by its seed.
That land,[3] through which Adice and the Po
Their waters roll, was once the residence
Of courtesy and valour, ere the day [4]
That frown'd on Frederick; now secure may pass
Those limits, whosoe'er hath left, for shame,
To talk with good men, or come near their haunts.
Three aged ones are still found there, in whom

---

[1] *Who.*]   He compares the Pope, on account of the union
of the temporal with the spiritual power in his person, to an
unclean beast in the levitical law.   "The camel, because he
cheweth the cud, but divideth not the hoof; he is unclean unto
you." Levit. xi. 4.

[2] *Two suns.*]   The Emperor and the Bishop of Rome.   There
is something similar to this in the De Monarchiâ, lib. iii. cap. iv.
"They say first, according to that text in Genesis, that God made
two great lights, the greater light and the lesser, the one to rule
the day, and the other the night; then, that as the moon, which is
the lesser light, has no brightness, except as she receives it from the
sun, so neither has the temporal kingdom authority, except what it
receives from the spiritual government."   The fallacy of which
reasoning (if such it can be called) he proceeds to prove.

[3] *That land.*]   Lombardy.

[4] *Ere the day.*]   Before the Emperor Frederick II. was defeated
before Parma, in 1248.   G. Villani, lib. vi. cap. xxxv.

The old time [1] chides the new: these deem it long
Ere God restore them to a better world:
The good Gherardo; [2] of Palazzo he,
Conrad; [3] and Guido of Castello, [4] named
In Gallic phrase more fitly the plain Lombard.
On this at last conclude.   The church of Rome,
Mixing two governments that ill assort,
Hath miss'd her footing, fallen into the mire, [5]
And there herself and burden much defiled."

"O Marco!" I replied, "thine arguments
Convince me: and the cause I now discern,
Why of the heritage no portion came
To Levi's offspring.   But resolve me this:
Who that Gherardo is, that as thou say'st
Is left a sample of the perish'd race,
And for rebuke to this untoward age?"

"Either thy words," said he, "deceive, or else

1 *The old time.*] L'antica età.

—— It is silly sooth,
And dallies with the innocence of love,
Like the old age.

Shakspeare, Twelfth Night, act ii. sc. 4.

2 *The good Gherardo.*] Gherardo da Camino, of Trevigi. He is honourably mentioned in our Poet's Convito (iv. 14). "Let us suppose that Gherardo da Camino had been the grandson of the meanest hind that ever drank of the Sile or the Cagnano, and that his grandfather was not yet forgotten; who will dare to say that Gherardo da Camino was a mean man, and who will not agree with me in calling him noble? Certainly no one, however presumptuous, will deny this; for such he was, and as such let him ever be remembered." Tiraboschi supposes him to have been the same Gherardo with whom the Provençal poets were used to meet a hospitable reception. "This is probably that same Gherardo, who, together with his sons, so early as before the year 1254, gave a kind and hospitable reception to the Provençal poets." Mr. Mathias's edition, tom. i. p. 137.

3 *Conrad.*] Currado da Palazzo, a gentleman of Brescia.

4 *Guido of Castello.*] Of Reggio. All the Italians were called Lombards by the French.

5 *Fallen into the mire.*] There is a passage resembling this in the De Vulg. Eloq. lib. ii. cap. 4. "Ante omnia ergo dicimus unumquemque debere materiæ pondus propriis humeris excipere æquale, ne forte humerorum nimio gravatam virtutem in cœnum cespitare necesse sit."

Are meant to try me ; that thou, speaking Tuscan,
Appear'st not to have heard of good Gherardo ;
The sole addition that, by which I know him ;
Unless I borrow'd from his daughter Gaïa [1]
Another name to grace him.   God be with you.
I bear you company no more.   Behold
The dawn with white ray glimmering through the
    mist.
I must away—the angel comes—ere he
Appear."   He said, and would not hear me more.

CANTO XVII

ARGUMENT

The Poet issues from that thick vapour ; and soon after his fancy represents to him in lively portraiture some noted examples of anger. This imagination is dissipated by the appearance of an angel, who marshals them onward to the fourth cornice, on which the sin of gloominess or indifference is purged ; and here Virgil shows him that this vice proceeds from a defect of love, and that all love can be only of two sorts, either natural, or of the soul ; of which sorts the former is always right, but the latter may err either in respect of object or of degree.

CALL to remembrance, reader, if thou e'er
Hast on an Alpine height [2] been ta'en by cloud,

[1] *His daughter Gaïa.*]   A lady equally admired for her modesty, the beauty of her person, and the excellency of her talents.   Gaïa, says Tiraboschi, may perhaps lay claim to the praise of having been the first among the Italian ladies, by whom the vernacular poetry was cultivated.   This appears (although no one has yet named her as a poetess) from the MS. Commentary on the Commedia of Dante, by Giovanni da Serravalle, afterwards bishop of Fermo, where, commenting on Canto xvi. of the Purgatory, he says : "De istâ Gajâ filiâ dicti doni Gerardi, possent dici multæ laudes, quia fuit prudens domina, literata, magni consilii, et magnæ prudentiæ, maximæ pulchritudinis, quæ scivit bene loqui rhytmatice in vulgari." [There can be little doubt that Dante's mention of Gaïa is ironical, and that he means to imply that her reputation was a bad one.]

[2] *On an Alpine height.*]   "Nell' alpe."   Although the Alps, as

Through which thou saw'st no better than the
    mole
Doth through opacous membrane ; then, whene'er
The watery vapours dense began to melt
Into thin air, how faintly the sun's sphere
Seem'd wading through them :   so thy nimble
    thought
May image, how at first I rebeheld
The sun, that bedward now his couch o'erhung.

    Thus, with my leader's feet still equalling pace,
From forth that cloud I came, when now expired
The parting beams from off the nether shores.

    O quick and forgetive power ! that sometimes dost
So rob us of ourselves, we take no mark
Though round about us thousand trumpets clang ;
What moves thee, if the senses stir not ?   Light
Moves thee from heaven, spontaneous, self-inform'd ;
Or, likelier, gliding down with swift illapse
By will divine.   Portray'd before me came
The traces of her dire impiety,
Whose form was changed into the bird, that most
Delights itself in song : [1] and here my mind

Landino remarks, are properly those mountains which divide Italy
from France, yet from them all high mountains are in the Tuscan
language, though not in the Latin, termed Alps.   Milton uses the
word thus generally in the Samson Agonistes :

Nor breath of vernal air from snowy Alp.

And this is a sufficient answer to the charge of impropriety, which
is brought by Doctor Johnson, on the introduction of it into that
drama.   See the Rambler, No. 140.

    [1] —— *The bird, that most*
    Delights itself in song.] I cannot think with Vellutello, that
the swallow is here meant.   Dante probably alludes to the story of
Philomela, as it is found in Homer's Odyssey, b. xix. 518, rather
than as later poets have told it.   "She intended to slay the son of
her husband's brother Amphion, incited to it by the envy of his
wife, who had six children, while herself had only two, but through
mistake slew her own son Itylus, and for her punishment was
transformed by Jupiter into a nightingale."   Cowper's note on this
passage.   In speaking of the nightingale, let me observe, that while
some have considered its song as a melancholy, and others as a

Was inwardly so wrapt, it gave no place
To aught that ask'd admittance from without.
Next shower'd into my fantasy a shape
As of one crucified,[1] whose visage spake
Fell rancour, malice deep, wherein he died;
And round him Ahasuerus the great king;
Esther his bride; and Mordecai the just,
Blameless in word and deed.   As of itself
That unsubstantial coinage of the brain
Burst, like a bubble,[2] when the water fails
That fed it; in my vision straight uprose
A damsel[3] weeping loud, and cried, "O queen!
O mother! wherefore has intemperate ire
Driven thee to loathe thy being?   Not to lose
Lavinia, desperate thou hast slain thyself.

cheerful one, Chiabrera appears to have come nearest the truth, when he says, in the Alcippo, act i. sc. 1,

> Non mai si stanca d'iterar le note,
> O gioconde o dogliose,
> Al sentir dilettose.

> Unwearied still reiterates her lays,
> Jocund or sad, delightful to the ear.

See a very pleasing letter on this subject by a late illustrious statesman, *Address to the reader prefixed to Fox's History of James II. Edit.* 1808, p. xii; and a beautiful poem by Mr. Coleridge.   I know not whether the following lines by a neglected poet have yet been noticed, as showing the diversity of opinions that have prevailed respecting the song of this bird.

> —— The cheerful birds
> With sweetest notes to sing their Maker's praise,
> Among the which, the merrie nightingale
> With swete and swete, her breast against a thorn,
> Ringes out all night.   *Vallans, Tale of Two Swannes.*

[1] *One crucified.*]   Haman.   See the book of Esther, c. vii.   "In the Lunetta of Haman, we owe the sublime conception of his figure (by Michael Angelo) to this passage."   Fuseli, Lecture iii. note.

[2] *Like a bubble.*]   The earth hath bubbles, as the water has,
> And these are of them.
>> *Shakspeare, Macbeth*, act i. sc. 3.

[3] *A damsel.*]   Lavinia, mourning for her mother Amata, who, impelled by grief and indignation for the supposed death of Turnus, destroyed herself.   Æn. lib. xii. 595.

Now hast thou lost me.   I am she, whose tears
Mourn, ere I fall, a mother's timeless end."
    E'en as a sleep breaks off, if suddenly
New radiance strike upon the closed lids,
The broken slumber quivering ere it dies; [1]
Thus, from before me, sunk that imagery,
Vanishing, soon as on my face there struck
The light, outshining far our earthly beam.
As round I turn'd me to survey what place
I had arrived at, "Here ye mount:" exclaim'd
A voice, that other purpose left me none
Save will so eager to behold who spake,
I could not chuse but gaze.   As 'fore the sun,
That weighs our vision down, and veils his form
In light transcendent, thus my virtue fail'd
Unequal.   "This is Spirit from above,
Who marshals us our upward way, unsought;
And in his own light shrouds him.   As a man
Doth for himself, so now is done for us.
For whoso waits imploring, yet sees need
Of his prompt aidance, sets himself prepared
For blunt denial, ere the suit be made.
Refuse we not to lend a ready foot
At such inviting : haste we to ascend,
Before it darken : for we may not then,
Till morn again return."   So spake my guide ;
And to one ladder both address'd our steps ;
And the first stair approaching, I perceived
Near me as 't were the waving of a wing,
That fann'd my face, and whisper'd : "Blessed
    they,

---

1 *The broken slumber quivering ere it dies.*] Venturi suggests
that this bold and unusual metaphor may have been formed on that
in Virgil.

 Tempus erat quo prima quies mortalibus ægris
 Incipit, et dono divum gratissima serpit. *Æn.* lib. ii. 268.

The peace-makers:[1] they know not evil wrath."
    Now to such height above our heads were raised
The last beams, follow'd close by hooded night,
That many a star on all sides through the gloom
Shone   out.   "Why   partest   from   me,   O   my
        strength?"
So with myself I communed; for I felt
My o'ertoil'd sinews slacken.   We had reach'd
The summit, and were fix'd like to a bark
Arrived at land.   And waiting a short space,
If aught should meet mine ear in that new round,
Then to my guide I turn'd, and said: "Loved sire!
Declare what guilt is on this circle purged.
If our feet rest, no need thy speech should pause."
    He thus to me: "The love[2] of good, whate'er
Wanted of just proportion, here fulfils.
Here plies afresh the oar, that loiter'd ill.
But that thou mayst yet clearlier understand,
Give ear unto my words; and thou shalt cull
Some fruit may please thee well, from this delay.
    "Creator, nor created being, e'er,
My son," he thus began, "was without love,
Or natural,[3] or the free spirit's growth.
That hast not that to learn.   The natural still
Is without error: but the other swerves,
If on ill object bent, or through excess
Of vigour, or defect.   While e'er it seeks[4]

---

[1] *The peace-makers.*]   "Blessed are the peace-makers; for they
shall be called the children of God."   Matt. v. 9.

[2] *The love.*]   "A defect in our love towards God, or lukewarmness
in piety, is here removed."

[3] *Or natural.*]   Lombardi refers to the Convito, Canz. i. Tratt.
2, cap. 3, where this subject is diffusely treated by our Poet.

[4] *While e'er it seeks.*]   So Frezzi:

> E s'egli è ben, che d'altro ben dipenda,
>   Non s'ami quasi per se esistente,
>   Se vuoi, che quando è tolto, non t'offenda.
>   *Il Quadrir.* lib. ii. cap. 14.

The primal blessings,[1] or with measure due
The inferior,[2] no delight, that flows from it,
Partakes of ill.   But let it warp to evil,
Or with more ardour than behoves, or less,
Pursue the good ; the thing created then
Works 'gainst its Maker.   Hence thou must infer
That love is germin of each virtue in ye,
And of each act no less, that merits pain.
Now[3] since it may not be, but love intend
The welfare mainly of the thing it loves,
All from self-hatred are secure ; and since
No being can be thought to exist apart,
And independent of the first, a bar
Of equal force restrains from hating that.

"Grant the distinction just ; and it remains
The evil must be another's, which is loved.
Three ways such love is gender'd in your clay.
There is[4] who hopes (his neighbour's worth
   deprest)
Pre-eminence himself ; and covets hence,
For his own greatness, that another fall.
There is[5] who so much fears the loss of power,
Fame, favour, glory, (should his fellow mount
Above him,) and so sickens at the thought,
He loves their opposite : and there is he,[6]
Whom wrong or insult seems to gall and shame,
That he doth thirst for vengeance ; and such needs

This Capitolo, which describes the punishment of those who give
way to inordinate grief for the loss of their kindred, is marked by
much power of imagination and a sublime morality.

[1] *The primal blessings.*] Spiritual good.

[2] *The inferior.*] Temporal good.

[3] *Now.*] "It is impossible for any being, either to hate itself, or
to hate the First Cause of all, by which it exists.   We can therefore
only rejoice in the evil which befalls others."

[4] *There is.*] The proud.

[5] *There is.*] The envious.

[6] *There is he.*] The resentful.

Must dote on other's evil.   Here beneath,
This threefold love is mourn'd.[1]   Of the other sort
Be now instructed ; that which follows good,
But with disorder'd and irregular course.

   "All indistinctly apprehend a bliss,
On which the soul may rest ; the hearts of all
Yearn after it ; and to that wished bourn
All therefore strive to tend.   If ye behold,
Or seek it, with a love remiss and lax ;
This cornice, after just repenting, lays
Its penal torment on ye.   Other good
There is, where man finds not his happiness :
It is not true fruition ; not that blest
Essence, of every good the branch and root.
The love too lavishly bestow'd on this,
Along three circles[2] over us, is mourn'd.
Account of that division tripartite   .
Expect not, fitter for thine own research."

---

[1] *This threefold love is mourn'd.*]   Frezzi alludes to this
distinction.

> Superbia puote essere in tre modi ;
> Si come si dimostra dalla Musa,
> La qual hai letta, e che tu tanto lodi.
>
> *Il Quadrir.* lib. iii. cap. 2.

[2] *A long three circles.*]   According to the allegorical commentators,
as Venturi has observed, Reason is represented under the person
of Virgil, and Sense under that of Dante.   The former leaves to the
latter to discover for itself the three carnal sins—avarice, gluttony,
and libidinousness ; having already declared the nature of the
spiritual sins—pride, envy, anger, and indifference, or lukewarmness
in piety, which the Italians call *accidia*, from the Greek word
ἀκηδία, and which Chaucer vainly endeavoured to naturalise in our
language.   See the Persone's Tale.   Lombardi refers to Thomas
Aquinas, lib. i. Quest. 72, Art. 2, for the division here made by our
Poet.

CANTO XVIII

ARGUMENT

Virgil discourses further concerning the nature of love. Then a multitude of spirits rush by; two of whom in van of the rest, record instances of zeal and fervent affection, and another, who was abbot of San Zeno in Verona, declares himself to Virgil and Dante; and lastly follow other spirits, shouting forth memorable examples of the sin for which they suffer. The Poet, pursuing his meditations, falls into a dreamy slumber.

THE teacher ended,[1] and his high discourse
Concluding, earnest in my looks inquired
If I appear'd content; and I, whom still
Unsated thirst to hear him urged, was mute,
Mute outwardly, yet inwardly I said :
" Perchance my too much questioning offends."
But he, true father, mark'd the secret wish
By diffidence restrain'd ; and, speaking, gave
Me boldness thus to speak : " Master ! my sight
Gathers so lively virtue from thy beams,
That all, thy words convey, distinct is seen.
Wherefore I pray thee, father, whom this heart
Holds dearest, thou wouldst deign by proof t' un-
  fold
That love, from which, as from their source, thou
  bring'st
All good deeds and their opposite." He then :
" To what I now disclose be thy clear ken
Directed ; and thou plainly shalt behold

---

1 *The teacher ended*.] Compare Plato, Protagoras, v. iii. p. 123.
Bip. edit. Πρωταγόρας μὲν τοσαῦτα, κ.τ.λ. Apoll. Rhod. l. i. 513,
and Milton, *P. L.* b. viii. 1.

 The angel ended, and in Adam's ear
 So charming left his voice, that he awhile
 Thought him still speaking, still stood fix'd to hear.

How much those blind have err'd, who make themselves
    The guides of men.   The soul, created apt
To love, moves versatile which way soe'er
Aught pleasing prompts her, soon as she is waked
By pleasure into act.   Of substance true
Your apprehension [1] forms its counterfeit;
And, in you the ideal shape presenting,
Attracts the soul's regard.   If she, thus drawn,
Incline toward it; love is that inclining,
And a new nature knit by pleasure in ye.
Then, as the fire points up, and mounting seeks
His birth-place and his lasting seat, e'en thus
Enters the captive soul into desire,
Which is a spiritual motion, that ne'er rests
Before enjoyment of the thing it loves.
Enough to show thee, how the truth from those
Is hidden, who aver all love a thing
Praise-worthy in itself; although perhaps [2]

[1] *Your apprehension.*]   It is literally, "Your apprehensive faculty derives intension from a thing really existing, and displays that intension within you, so that it makes the soul turn to it."   The commentators labour in explaining this; but whatever sense they have elicited, may, I think, be resolved into the words of the translation in the text.

[2] *Perhaps.*]   "Our author," Venturi observes, "uses the language of the Peripatetics, which denominates the *kind* of things, as determinable by many differences, *matter*.   Love then, in kind perhaps, appears good; and it is said *perhaps*, because, strictly speaking, *in kind* there is neither good nor bad, neither praise-worthy nor blameable."   To this Lombardi adds, that what immediately follows, namely, that "every mark is not good although the wax be so," answers to this interpretation.   For the wax is precisely as the determinable matter, and the mark or impression as the determining form; and even as the wax, which is either good or at least not bad, may, by being imprinted by a bad figure, acquire the name of bad; so may love be said generally to be good or at least not bad, and acquire the name of bad by being determined to an unfit object.   "As the wax takes all shapes, and yet is wax still at the bottom; the τὸ ὑποκείμενον still is wax; so the soul transported in so many several passions of joy, fear, hope, sorrow, anger, and the like, has for its general groundwork of all this, Love."   Henry More, Discourse xvi.   This passage in the most philosophical of

Its matter seem still good.   Yet if the wax
Be good, it follows not the impression must."
  "What love is," I return'd, "thy words, O
      guide!
And my own docile mind, reveal.   Yet thence
New doubts have sprung. For, from without, if
      love
Be offer'd to us, and the spirit knows
No other footing; tend she right or wrong,
Is no desert of hers."   He answering thus:
" What reason here discovers, I have power
To show thee: that which lies beyond, expect
From Beatrice, faith not reason's task.
Spirit,[1] substantial form, with matter join'd,
Not in confusion mix'd, hath in itself
Specific virtue of that union born,
Which is not felt except it work, nor proved
But through effect, as vegetable life
By the green leaf.   From whence his intellect
Deduced its primal notices of things,
Man therefore knows not, or his appetites
Their first affections; such in you, as zeal
In bees to gather honey; at the first,
Volition, meriting nor blame nor praise.
But o'er each lower faculty supreme,
That, as she list, are summon'd to her bar,
Ye have that virtue[2] in you, whose just voice
Uttereth counsel, and whose word should keep
The threshold of assent.   Here is the source,
Whence cause of merit in you is derived;

our theologians, may serve for an answer to the objection of those
who blame Collins for not having brought in Love among the
"Passions" in his exquisite ode.
  [1] *Spirit.*] The human soul, which differs from that of brutes,
inasmuch as though united with the body it has a separate existence
of its own.
  [2] *That virtue.*] Reason.

E'en as the affections, good or ill, she takes,
Or severs,[1] winnow'd as the chaff. Those men,[2]
Who, reasoning, went to depth profoundest, mark'd
That innate freedom; and were thence induced
To leave their moral teaching to the world.
Grant then, that from necessity arise
All love that glows within you; to dismiss
Or harbour it, the power is in yourselves.
Remember, Beatrice, in her style,
Denominates free choice by eminence
The noble virtue; if in talk with thee
She touch upon that theme."   The moon, well nigh
To midnight hour belated, made the stars
Appear to wink and fade; and her broad disk
Seem'd like a crag[3] on fire, as up the vault[4]
That course she journey'd, which the sun then
    warms;
When they of Rome behold him at his set
Betwixt Sardinia and the Corsic isle.

---

[1] *Or severs.*] Lest the reader of the original should be misled, it
is right to warn him that the word "vigliare" must not be confounded with "vagliare" to winnow, and strictly means "to separate
from the straw what remains of the grain after the threshing." The
process is distinctly described in the notes on the Decameron, p. 77,
Ediz. Giunti, 1573, where this passage is referred to.

[2] *Those men.*] The great moral philosophers among the
heathens.

[3] *A crag.*] I have preferred the reading of Landino, *scheggion*,
"crag," conceiving it to be more poetical than *secchion*, "bucket,"
which is the common reading. The same cause, the vapours, which
the commentators say might give the appearance of increased magnitude to the moon, might also make her seem broken at her rise.
Lombardi explains it differently. The moon being, as he says, in
the fifth night of her wane, has exactly the figure of a brazen bucket,
round at the bottom and open at top; and, if we suppose it to be
all on fire, we shall have, besides the form of the moon, her colour
also. There is a simile in one of Fielding's novels very like this,
but so ludicrous that I am unwilling to disturb the reader's gravity by
inserting it.

[4] *Up the vault.*] The moon passed with a motion opposite to
that of the heavens, through the constellation of the Scorpion, in
which the sun is, when to those who are in Rome he appears to set
between the isles of Corsica and Sardinia.

And now the weight, that hung upon my thought,
Was lighten'd by the aid of that clear spirit,
Who raiseth Andes [1] above Mantua's name.
I therefore, when my questions had obtain'd
Solution plain and ample, stood as one
Musing in dreamy slumber; but not long
Slumber'd; for suddenly a multitude,
The steep already turning from behind,
Rush'd on.   With fury and like random rout,
As echoing on their shores at midnight heard
Ismenus and Asopus,[2] for his Thebes
If Bacchus' help were needed; so came these
Tumultuous, curving each his rapid step,
By eagerness impell'd of holy love.
  Soon they o'ertook us; with such swiftness
      moved
The mighty crowd.   Two spirits at their head
Cried, weeping, "Blessed Mary [3] sought with haste
The hilly region.   Cæsar,[4] to subdue
Ilerda, darted in Marseilles his sting,
And flew to Spain."—"Oh, tarry not: away!"
The others shouted; "let not time be lost
Through slackness of affection.   Hearty zeal
To serve reanimates celestial grace."
  "O ye! in whom intenser fervency
Haply supplies, where lukewarm erst ye fail'd,
Slow or neglectful, to absolve your part
Of good and virtuous; this man, who yet lives,

---

[1] *Andes.*]   Andes, now Pietola, made more famous than Mantua,
near which it is situated, by having been the birth-place of Virgil.
[2] *Ismenus and Asopus.*]   Rivers near Thebes.
[3] *Mary.*]   "And Mary arose in those days, and went into the
hill-country with haste, into a city of Judah; and entered into the
house of Zacharias, and saluted Elisabeth."   Luke i. 39, 40.
[4] *Cæsar.*]   See Lucan, Phars. lib. iii. and iv., and Cæsar, de
Bello Civili, lib. i.   Cæsar left Brutus to complete the siege of
Marseilles, and hastened on to the attack of Afranius and Petreius,
the generals of Pompey, at Ilerda (Lerida) in Spain.

(Credit my tale, though strange,) desires to ascend,
So morning rise to light us.   Therefore say
Which hand leads nearest to the rifted rock."
    So spake my guide; to whom a shade return'd:
" Come after us, and thou shalt find the cleft.
We may not linger: such resistless will
Speeds our unwearied course.   Vouchsafe us then
Thy pardon, if our duty seem to thee
Discourteous rudeness.   In Verona I
Was abbot [1] of San Zeno, when the hand
Of Barbarossa grasp'd Imperial sway,
That name ne'er utter'd without tears in Milan.
And there is he,[2] hath one foot in his grave,
Who for that monastery ere long shall weep,
Ruing his power misused: for that his son,
Of body ill compact, and worse in mind,
And born in evil, he hath set in place
Of its true pastor."   Whether more he spake,
Or here was mute, I know not: he had sped
E'en now so far beyond us.   Yet thus much
I heard, and in remembrance treasured it.
    He then, who never fail'd me at my need,
Cried, " Hither turn.   Lo ! two with sharp remorse
Chiding their sin."   In rear of all the troop
These shouted: " First they died,[3] to whom the sea
Open'd, or ever Jordan saw his heirs:
And they,[4] who with Æneas to the end

[1] *Abbot.*] Alberto, abbot of San Zeno in Verona, when Frederick 1.
was emperor, by whom Milan was besieged and reduced to ashes,
in 1162.

[2] *There is he.*] Alberto della Scala, Lord of Verona, who had
made his natural son abbot of San Zeno.

[3] *First they died.*] The Israelites, who on account of their dis-
obedience died before reaching the promised land.

[4] *And they.*] Those Trojans, who, wearied with their voyage,
chose rather to remain in Sicily with Acestes, than accompany
Æneas to Italy. Virg. Æn. lib. v.

Endured not suffering, for their portion chose
Life without glory."   Soon as they had fled
Past reach of sight, new thought within me rose
By others follow'd fast, and each unlike
Its fellow : till led on from thought to thought,
And pleasured with the fleeting train, mine eye
Was closed, and meditation changed to dream.

CANTO XIX

ARGUMENT

The Poet, after describing his dream, relates how, at the summoning of an angel, he ascends with Virgil to the fifth cornice, where the sin of avarice is cleansed, and where he finds Pope Adrian the fifth.

It was the hour,[1] when of diurnal heat
No reliques chafe the cold beams of the moon,
O'erpower'd by earth, or planetary sway
Of Saturn ; and the geomancer [2] sees
His Greater Fortune up the east ascend,
Where grey dawn checkers first the shadowy cone ;
When 'fore me in my dream, a woman's shape [3]

[1] *The hour.*] Near the dawn.
[2] *The geomancer.*] The geomancers, says Landino, when they divined, drew a figure consisting of sixteen marks, named from so many stars which constitute the end of Aquarius and the beginning of Pisces.   One of these they called "the greater fortune."
Chaucer has imitated this in a description of morning, (Troilus and Creseide, b. iii.) for he did not find it in his original, Boccaccio's Filostrato :—

> But when the cocke, commune astrologer,
> Gan on his brest to bete, and after crowe,
> And Lucifer the dayis messanger
> Gan for to rise, and out his bemis throwe,
> And estward rose, to him that could it knowe,
> Fortuna Major.

[3] *A woman's shape.*] Worldly happiness.   This allegory reminds us of the "Choice of Hercules."

There came, with lips that stammer'd, eyes aslant,
Distorted feet, hands maim'd, and colour pale.
  I look'd upon her: and, as sunshine cheers
Limbs numb'd by nightly cold, e'en thus my look
Unloosed her tongue; next, in brief space, her form
Decrepit raised erect, and faded face
With love's own hue [1] illumed.   Recovering speech,
She forthwith, warbling, such a strain began,
That I, how loth soe'er, could scarce have held
Attention from the song.   "I," thus she sang,
"I am the Syren, she, whom mariners
On the wide sea are wilder'd when they hear:
Such fulness of delight the listener feels.
I, from his course, Ulysses [2] by my lay
Enchanted drew.   Whoe'er frequents me once,
Parts seldom: so I charm him, and his heart
Contented knows no void."   Or ere her mouth
Was closed, to shame her, at my side appear'd
A dame [3] of semblance holy.   With stern voice
She utter'd: "Say, O Virgil! who is this?"
Which hearing, he approach'd, with eyes still bent
Toward that goodly presence: the other seized her,

[1] *Love's own hue.*]

> —— A smile that glow'd
> Celestial rosy red, love's proper hue.
> > *Milton, P. L.* b. viii. 619.

> —— facies pulcherrima tunc est,
> Quum porphyriaco variatur candida rubro.
> Quid color hic roseus sibi vult? designat amorem:
> Quippe amor est igni similis; flammasque rubentes
> Ignis habere solet.   *Palingeni Zodiacus Vitæ*, lib. xiii.

[2] *Ulysses.*]   It is not easy to determine why Ulysses, contrary to
the authority of Homer, is said to have been drawn aside from his
course by the song of the Syren.   No improbable way of accounting
for the contradiction is, to suppose that she is here represented as
purposely deviating from the truth.   Or Dante may have followed
some legend of the middle ages, in which the wanderings of Ulysses
were represented otherwise than in Homer.

[3] *A dame.*]   Philosophy, or perhaps Truth.

And, her robes tearing, open'd her before,
And show'd the belly to me, whence a smell,
Exhaling loathsome, waked me.   Round I turn'd
Mine eyes : and thus the teacher : "At the least
Three times my voice hath call'd thee.   Rise,
    begone.
Let us the opening find where thou mayst pass."
  I straightway rose.   Now day, pour'd down
    from high,
Fill'd all the circuits of the sacred mount ;
And, as we journey'd, on our shoulder smote
The early ray.   I follow'd, stooping low
My forehead, as a man, o'ercharged with thought,
Who bends him to the likeness of an arch
That midway spans the flood ; when thus I heard,
"Come, enter here," in tone so soft and mild,
As never met the ear on mortal strand.
  With swan-like wings dispred and pointing up,
Who thus had spoken marshall'd us along,
Where, each side of the solid masonry,
The sloping walls retired ; then moved his plumes,
And fanning us, affirm'd that those, who mourn,[1]
Are blessed, for that comfort shall be theirs.
  "What aileth thee, that still thou look'st to
    earth ?"
Began my leader ; while the angelic shape
A little over us his station took.
  "New vision," I replied, "hath raised in me
Surmisings strange and anxious doubts, whereon
My soul intent allows no other thought
Or room, or entrance."—"Hast thou seen," said
    he,
"That old enchantress, her, whose wiles alone

---

1 *Who mourn.*]   "Blessed are they that mourn ; for they shall be
comforted."   Matt. v. 4.

The spirits o'er us weep for?   Hast thou seen
How man may free him of her bonds?   Enough.
Let thy heels spurn the earth; [1] and thy raised ken
Fix on the lure, which heaven's eternal King
Whirls in the rolling spheres."   As on his feet
The falcon [2] first looks down, then to the sky
Turns, and forth stretches eager for the food,
That wooes him thither; so the call I heard:
So onward, far as the dividing rock
Gave way, I journey'd, till the plain was reach'd.

On the fifth circle when I stood at large,
A race appear'd before me, on the ground
All downward lying prone and weeping sore.
"My soul [3] hath cleaved to the dust," I heard
With sighs so deep, they well nigh choked the
    words.

"O ye elect of God! whose penal woes
Both hope and justice mitigate, direct
Towards the steep rising our uncertain way."

"If ye approach secure from this our doom,
Prostration, and would urge your course with speed,
See that ye still to rightward keep the brink."

So them the bard besought; and such the
    words,

---

[1] *Let thy heels spurn the earth.*]   This is a metaphor from
hawking, though less apparent than in the lines that follow.

[2] *The falcon.*]   Poi come fa 'l falcon, quando si move,
      Così Umiltà al cielo alzò la vista.
          Frezzo, Il Quadrir. lib. iv. cap. v.

Io vidi poi color tutti levare
    Inverso il cielo, come fa 'l falcone,
    Quando la preda sua prende in su l'are.   *Ibid.* cap. xiii.

One of our periodical critics has remarked, that Dante must have
loved hawking; and "that he paints his bird always to the life."
Edinburgh Review, No. lviii. p. 472.   In the same manner Mr.
Blomfield supposes that Æschylus was addicted to fishing, because
he often takes his metaphors from fishing-nets.   See that gentleman's
notes to the Persæ, Glossar. v. 430.

[3] *My soul.*]   "My soul cleaveth to the dust; quicken thou me
according to thy word."   Psalm cxix. 25.

Beyond us some short space, in answer came.
  I noted what remain'd yet hidden from them :[1]
Thence to my liege's eyes mine eyes I bent,
And he, forthwith interpreting their suit,
Beckon'd his glad assent.   Free then to act
As pleased me, I drew near, and took my stand
Over that shade whose words I late had mark'd.
And, "Spirit!" I said, "in whom repentant tears
Mature that blessed hour when thou with God
Shalt find acceptance, for a while suspend
For me that mightier care.   Say who thou wast;
Why thus ye grovel on your bellies prone;
And if, in aught, ye wish my service there,
Whence living I am come."   He answering spake :
"The cause why Heaven our back toward his cope
Reverses, shalt thou know : but me know first,
The successor of Peter,[2] and the name
And title of my lineage, from that stream[3]
That 'twixt Chiaveri and Siestri draws
His limpid waters through the lowly glen.
A month and little more by proof I learnt,
With what a weight that robe of sovereignty
Upon his shoulder rests, who from the mire
Would guard it; that each other fardel seems
But feathers in the balance.   Late, alas !
Was my conversion : but, when I became
Rome's pastor, I discerned at once the dream
And cozenage of life; saw that the heart
Rested not there, and yet no prouder height

---

  [1] *I noted what remain'd yet hidden from them.*] They were
ignorant, it appeared, whether Dante was come there to be purged
of his sins.
  [2] *The successor of Peter.*] Ottobuono, of the family of Fieschi,
Counts of Lavagna, died thirty-six days after he became pope, with
the title of Adrian v., in 1276.
  [3] *That stream.*] The river Lavagna, in the Genoese territory;
to the east of which territory are situated Siestri and Chiaveri.

Lured on the climber: wherefore, of that life
No more enamour'd, in my bosom love
Of purer being kindled.   For till then
I was a soul in misery, alienate
From God, and covetous of all earthly things;
Now, as thou seest, here punish'd for my doting.
Such cleansing from the taint of avarice,
Do spirits, converted, need.   This mount inflicts
No direr penalty.   E'en as our eyes
Fasten'd below, nor e'er to loftier clime
Were lifted;[1] thus hath justice levell'd us,
Here on the earth.   As avarice quench'd our love
Of good, without which is no working; thus
Here justice holds us prison'd, hand and foot
Chain'd down and bound, while heaven's just Lord
   shall please,
So long to tarry, motionless, outstretch'd."

My knees I stoop'd, and would have spoke; but he,
Ere my beginning, by his ear perceived
I did him reverence; and "What cause," said he,
"Hath bow'd thee thus?"—"Compunction," I
   rejoin'd,
"And inward awe of your high dignity."

"Up," he exclaim'd, "brother! upon thy feet
Arise; err not:[2] thy fellow servant I,
(Thine and all others') of one Sovran Power.
If thou hast ever mark'd those holy sounds
Of gospel truth, "nor shall be given in marriage,"[3]

---

[1] *Were lifted.*]   Rosa Morando and Lombardi are very severe on
Venturi's perplexity occasioned by the word "aderse." They have
none of them noticed Landino's reading of "aperse." Ediz. 1484.

[2] *Err not.*] "And I fell at his feet to worship him. And he
said unto me, See thou do it not: I am thy fellow servant, and of
thy brethren that have the testimony of Jesus." Rev. xix. 10.

[3] *Nor shall be given in marriage.*] "Since in this state we
neither marry nor are given in marriage, I am no longer the spouse
of the church, and therefore no longer retain my former dignity."
See Matt. xxii. 30.

Thou mayst discern the reasons of my speech.
Go thy ways now; and linger here no more.
Thy tarrying is a let unto the tears,
With which I hasten that whereof thou spakest.[1]
I have on earth a kinswoman;[2] her name
Alagia, worthy in herself, so ill
Example of our house corrupt her not:
And she is all remaineth of me there."

CANTO XX

ARGUMENT

Among those on the fifth cornice, Hugh Capet records illustrious examples of voluntary poverty and of bounty; then tells who himself is, and speaks of his descendants on the French throne; and, lastly, adds some noted instances of avarice. When he has ended, the mountain shakes, and all the spirits sing "Glory to God."

ILL strives the will, 'gainst will more wise that
        strives :
His pleasure therefore to mine own preferr'd,
I drew the sponge[3] yet thirsty from the wave.
    Onward I moved : he also onward moved,
Who led me, coasting still, wherever place
Along the rock was vacant; as a man
Walks near the battlements on narrow wall.
For those on the other part, who drop by drop
Wring out their all-infecting malady,
Too closely press the verge.   Accurst be thou,
Inveterate wolf![4] whose gorge ingluts more prey,

---

[1] *That whereof thou spakest.*] See v. 89.
[2] *A kinswoman.*] Alagia was the wife of the Marchese Moroello Malaspina, one of the Poet's protectors during his exile. See Canto viii. 133.
[3] *I drew the sponge.*] "I did not persevere in my inquiries from the spirit, though still anxious to learn more."
[4] *Wolf.*] Avarice.

Than every beast beside, yet is not fill'd ;
So bottomless thy maw.——Ye spheres of heaven !
To whom there are, as seems, who attribute
All change in mortal state, when is the day
Of his appearing,[1] for whom fate reserves
To chase her hence ?——With wary steps and slow
We pass'd ; and I attentive to the shades,
Whom piteously I heard lament and wail ;
And, 'midst the wailing, one before us heard
Cry out "O blessed Virgin ! " as a dame
In the sharp pangs of childbed ; and " How poor
Thou wast," it added, " witness that low roof
Where thou didst lay thy sacred burden down.
O good Fabricius ![2] thou didst virtue chuse
With poverty, before great wealth with vice."

The words so pleased me, that desire to know
The spirit, from whose lip they seem'd to come,
Did draw me onward.   Yet it spake the gift
Of Nicholas,[3] which on the maidens he
Bounteous bestow'd, to save their youthful prime
Unblemish'd.   "Spirit ! who dost speak of deeds

---

[1] *Of his appearing.*]   He is thought to allude to Can Grande della
Scala.   See Hell, Canto i. 98.

[2] *Fabricius.*]   So our author in the second book of the De Monarchiâ, cap. v.   "Nonne Fabricium, etc."   "Has not Fabricius
given us another example of resisting avarice, when, poor as he was,
he preserved his faith to the republic, and rejected with scorn a
great sum of gold that was offered him?   Our Poet in the sixth
book records this, when he says—

—— Parvoque potentem
Fabricium."

Compare Petrarch, Tr. della Fama, c. i.

Un Curio ed un Fabricio assai più belli
Con la lor povertà, che Mida e Crasso
Con l' oro ond' a virtù furon rubelli.

[3] *Nicholas.*]   The story of Nicholas is, that an angel having revealed to him that the father of a family was so impoverished as to
resolve on exposing the chastity of his three daughters to sale, he
threw in at the window of their house three bags of money, containing a sufficient portion for each of them.

So worthy, tell me who thou wast," I said,
" And why thou dost with single voice renew
Memorial of such praise. That boon vouchsafed
Haply shall meet reward ; if I return
To finish the short pilgrimage of life,
Still speeding to its close on restless wing."
  " I," answer'd he, " will tell thee ; not for help,
Which thence I look for ; but that in thyself
Grace so exceeding shines, before thy time
Of mortal dissolution. I was root [1]
Of that ill plant whose shade such poison sheds
O'er all the Christian land, that seldom thence
Good fruit is gather'd. Vengeance soon should come,
Had Ghent and Douay, Lille and Bruges power ; [2]
And vengeance I of heaven's great Judge implore.
Hugh Capet was I hight : from me descend
The Philips and the Louis, of whom France
Newly is govern'd : born of one, who plied
The slaughterer's trade [3] at Paris. When the race

---

[1] *Root.*] Hugh Capet, ancestor of Philip IV.

[2] *Had Ghent and Douay, Lille and Bruges power.*] These cities had lately been seized by Philip IV. The spirit is made to intimate the approaching defeat of the French army by the Flemings, in the battle of Courtrai, which happened in 1302.

[3] *The slaughterer's trade.*] This reflection on the birth of his ancestor, induced Francis I. to forbid the reading of Dante in his dominions. Hugh Capet, who came to the throne of France in 987, was, however, the grandson of Robert, who was the brother of Eudes, King of France in 888 ; and it may, therefore, well be questioned, whether by " Beccaio di Parigi' is meant literally one who carried on the trade of a butcher, at Paris, and whether the sanguinary disposition of Hugh Capet's father is not stigmatised by this opprobrious 'appellation. See Cancellieri, Osservazioni, etc. Roma, 1814, p. 6. [Dante appears to have confused Hugh Capet with his father, Hugh the Great. The tradition that the latter was the son of a butcher, though without foundation in fact, was commonly believed in the Middle Ages (see Villani, iv. 4), and was still alive in France in the fifteenth century, when it was repeated by Villon in one of his *ballades.*]

Of ancient kings had vanish'd (all save one [1]
Wrapt up in sable weeds), within my gripe
I found the reins of empire, and such powers
Of new acquirement, with full store of friends,
That soon the widow'd circlet of the crown
Was girt upon the temples of my son, [2]
He, from whose bones the anointed race begins.
Till the great dower of Provence [3] had removed
The stains, [4] that yet obscured our lowly blood,
Its sway indeed was narrow; but howe'er
It wrought no evil: there, with force and lies,
Began its rapine: after, for amends, [5]
Poitou it seized, Navarre and Gascony. [6]

[1] *All save one.*] The posterity of Charlemagne, the second race of French monarchs, had failed, with the exception of Charles of Lorraine, who is said, on account of the melancholy temper of his mind, to have always clothed himself in black. Venturi suggests that Dante may have confounded him with Childeric III., the last of the Merovingian, or first race, who was deposed and made a monk in 752.

[2] *My son.*] Hugh Capet caused his son Robert to be crowned at Orleans.

[3] *The great dower of Provence.*] Louis IX. and his brother Charles of Anjou married two of the four daughters of Raymond Berenger, Count of Provence. See Par. c. vi. 135.

[4] *The stains.*] Lombardi understands this differently from all the other commentators with whom I am acquainted. The word "vergogna" he takes in the sense of "a praise-worthy shame of doing ill;" and according to him the translation should run thus:

> The shame that yet restrain'd my race from ill.

By "Provenza" he understands the estates of Toulouse, the dowry of the only daughter of Raymond, Count of Toulouse, married to a brother of Louis IX.

[5] *For amends.*] This is ironical.

[6] *Poitou it seized, Navarre and Gascony.*] I venture to read—

> Pottì e Navarra prese e Guascogna,

instead of   Ponti e Normandia prese e Guascogna.

> Seized Ponthieu, Normandy, and Gascogny.

Landino has "Pottì," and he is probably right: for Poitou was annexed to the French crown by Philip IV. See Henault, Abrégé Chron. A.D. 1283, etc. Normandy had been united to it long before by Philip Augustus, a circumstance of which it is difficult to imagine that Dante should have been ignorant; but Philip IV., says Henault, ibid., took the title of King of Navarre: and the subjugation of Navarre is also alluded to in the Paradise, Canto xix.

To Italy came Charles ; and for amends,

140. In 1293, Philip IV. summoned Edward I. to do him homage
for the duchy of Gascogny, which he had conceived the design of
seizing.   See G. Villani, lib. viii. cap. iv.   The whole passage has
occasioned much perplexity.   I cannot withhold from my readers
the advantage of an attempt made to unravel it by the late Archdeacon Fisher, which that gentleman, though a stranger, had the
goodness to communicate to me in the following terms : " I am
encouraged to offer you an elucidation of a passage, with the interpretation of which I was never yet satisfied.   As it goes to establish
the accuracy of two very happy conjectures which you have made
at Purg. xx. 66, you will perhaps forgive me, if my notion a little
militates against your solution of the difficulty.   The passage is as
follows :—

> I' fui radice della mala pianta,
> Che la terra Cristiana tutta aduggia,
> Sì che buon frutto rado se ne schianta.
> Ma se Doagio, Guanto, Lilla, e Bruggia
> Potesser, tosto ne saria vendetta :
> Ed io la cheggio a lui, che tutto giuggia.
>
> .   .   .   .
>
> Mentre che la gran dote Provenzale
> Al sangue mio non tolse la vergogna,
> Poco valea, ma pur non facea male.
> Lì cominciò con forza e con menzogna
> La sua rapina ; e poscia, per ammenda,
> Pottì e Navarra prese, e Guascogna.

It is my persuasion that the stanzas I have copied are *one* passage,
continuous in its sense, interrupted only by a parenthesis of four
stanzas, which are introduced as necessary to the political solution
of the meaning.   Again, I think that my quoted stanzas refer to
only one person, and that Philip IV. of France.   He is depicted
by both the phrases, mala pianta, and sangue mio.   I do not find
that Louis IX. obtained any part of Provence by dowry, owing to
his marriage with the daughter of the prince of that country ; at
least nothing equivalent to the words la gran dote Provenzale.   I
suppose the stanzas quoted to depict the three great events in the
life of Philip IV.   He married, during the life of his father, the
heiress of the kingdom of Navarre, and also of the duchy of Champagne.   Philip obtained at once the sovereignty of both these
dowries, and left to his son Philip V. the title of King of France and
Navarre.   On the accession of Philip IV. to the throne, he became embroiled with the English respecting the duchy of Guienne,
which, after having changed masters frequently, was then in the
possession of Edward I.   The word Guienne included Poitou and
Gascony, and was generally the country termed by Cæsar, Aquitania.
By perfidy, and the childish ignorance of Edmund, the brother of
Edward I., Philip got possession of Guienne. . . . The duchy of
Champagne now annexed to the crown of France, lying adjacent
to that of Flanders, Philip next endeavoured to lay hands on that
fief : and failing in treacherous negotiation, he carried a cruel
and murderous war into the low-countries, and laid them desolate.
His progress was stopped by the Flemings at the battle of

9

Young Conradine,[1] an innocent victim, slew ;
And sent the angelic teacher [2] back to heaven,
Still for amends.   I see the time at hand,
That forth from France invites another Charles [3]
To make himself and kindred better known.
Unarm'd he issues, saving with that lance,
Which the arch-traitor tilted with ; [4] and that
He carries with so home a thrust, as rives
The bowels of poor Florence.   No increase

Courtrai, and he was soon after compelled to surrender Guienne to
the English king, and to make peace with his numerous enemies.
Now to these three leading epochs of Philip's life, the Poet seems
to allude.   Doagio, Guanto, Lilla e Bruggia refer to his desolating
war in Flanders ; Vendetta, to the battle of Courtrai ; la gran dote
Provenzale, to the dowry of the kingdom of Navarre and the
duchy of Champagne ; forza e menzogna, to his conduct, respecting
Guienne with its two sister provinces, as you so convincingly conjectured, Potti e Guascogna."

[1] *Young Conradine.*]   Charles of Anjou put Conradino to death
in 1268, and became King of Naples.   See Hell, Canto xxviii. 16,
and note.   Compare Fazio degli Uberti, Dittamondo, lib. ii.
cap. xxix.

[2] *The angelic teacher.*]   Thomas Aquinas.   He was reported to
have been poisoned by a physician, who wished to ingratiate himself with Charles of Anjou.   "In the year 1323, at the end of July,
by the said Pope John and by his cardinals, was canonised at
Avignon Thomas Aquinas, of the order of Saint Dominic, a master
in divinity and philosophy, a man most excellent in all science, and
who expounded the sense of Scripture better than any one since the
time of Augustine.   He lived in the time of Charles I., King of
Sicily ; and going to the council at Lyons, it is said that he was
killed by a physician of the said king, who put poison for him into
some sweetmeats, thinking to ingratiate himself with King Charles,
because he was of the lineage of the lords of Aquino, who had
rebelled against the king, and doubting lest he should be made
cardinal : whence the Church of God received great damage.   He
died at the abbey of Fossanova, in Campagna."   G. Villani, lib.
ix. cap. ccxviii.   We shall find him in the Paradise, Canto x.

[3] *Another Charles.*]   Charles of Valois, brother of Philip IV.,
was sent by Pope Boniface VIII. to settle the disturbed state of
Florence.   In consequence of the measures he adopted for that
purpose, our Poet and his friends were condemned to exile and
death.   See G. Villani, lib. viii. c. xlviii.

[4] —— *with that lance,*
    Which the arch-traitor tilted with.]

                        —— con la lancia
            Con la qual giostrò Giuda.

If I remember right, in one of the old romances, Judas is represented
tilting with our Saviour.

Of territory hence, but sin and shame
Shall be his guerdon; and so much the more
As he more lightly deems of such foul wrong.
I see the other [1] (who a prisoner late
Had stept on shore) exposing to the mart
His daughter, whom he bargains for, as do
The Corsairs for their slaves.   O avarice!
What canst thou more, who hast subdued our blood
So wholly to thyself, they feel no care
Of their own flesh?   To hide with direr guilt
Past ill and future, lo! the flower-de-luce [2]
Enters Alagna; in his Vicar Christ
Himself a captive, and his mockery
Acted again.   Lo! to his holy lip
The vinegar and gall once more applied;
And he 'twixt living robbers doom'd to bleed.
Lo! the new Pilate, of whose cruelty

---

[1] *The other.*] Charles, King of Naples, the eldest son of Charles of Anjou, having, contrary to the directions of his father, engaged with Ruggier de Lauria, the admiral of Peter of Arragon, was made prisoner, and carried into Sicily, June, 1284. He afterwards, in consideration of a large sum of money, married his daughter to Azzo VIII., Marquis of Ferrara. I take Lauria to be the hero meant by Petrarch in his Triumph of Fame,

Quel di Luria seguiva il Saladino.   Cap. ii. v. 151.

Of whom Biagioli says in a note, "Non so chi sia, e non trovo nè vivo nè morto chi mel dica." "I know not who he is, and I find no one alive or dead to tell me." Mariana, lib. xiv. cap. 10, calls Lauria "a brave captain, signalised by his former victories." See also the seventh book of G. Villani's history, and Boccaccio's Decameron, G. 5, N. 6; where he is named Ruggieri dell' Oria.

[2] *The flower-de-luce.*] Boniface VIII. was seized at Alagna in Campagna, by the order of Philip IV., in the year 1303, and soon after died of grief. G. Villani, lib. viii. cap. lxiii. "As it pleased God, the heart of Boniface being petrified with grief, through the injury he had sustained, when he came to Rome, he fell into a strange malady, for he gnawed himself as one frantic, and in this state expired." His character is strongly drawn by the annalist in the next chapter. Thus, says Landino, was verified the prophecy of Celestine respecting him, that he should enter on the popedom like a fox, reign like a lion, and die like a dog.

Such violence cannot fill the measure up,
With no decree to sanction, pushes on
Into the temple [1] his yet eager sails.
    " O sovran Master! [2] when shall I rejoice
To see the vengeance, which thy wrath, well-
        pleased,
In secret silence broods?—While daylight lasts,
So long what thou didst hear [3] of her, sole spouse
Of the Great Spirit, and on which thou turn'dst
To me for comment, is the general theme
Of all our prayers : but, when it darkens, then
A different strain we utter ; then record
Pygmalion, [4] whom his gluttonous thirst of gold
Made traitor, robber, parricide : the woes
Of Midas, which his greedy wish ensued,
Mark'd for derision to all future times :
And the fond Achan, [5] how he stole the prey,
That yet he seems by Joshua's ire pursued.
Sapphira with her husband next we blame ;
And praise the forefeet, that with furious ramp
Spurn'd Heliodorus. [6]   All the mountain round

---

[1] *Into the temple.*]   It is uncertain whether our Poet alludes
still to the event mentioned in the preceding note, or to the destruction of the Order of the Templars in 1312, but the latter appears
more probable.

[2] *O sovran Master.*]   Lombardi, who rightly corrects Venturi's
explanation of this passage, with which I will not trouble the
reader, should have acknowledged, if he was conscious of it, that
his own interpretation of it was the same as that before given by
Vellutello : "When, O Lord, shall I behold that vengeance accomplished, which being already determined in thy secret judgment,
thy retributive justice even now contemplates with delight?"

[3] *What thou didst hear.*]   See v. 21.

[4] *Pygmalion.*]   —— Ille Sychæum
        Impius ante aras, atque auri cæcus amore,
        Clam ferro incautum superat.   *Virg. Æn.* l. 1. 340.

[5] *Achan.*]   Joshua vii.

[6] *Heliodorus.*]   " For there appeared unto them an horse, with a
terrible rider upon him, and adorned with a very fair covering, and
he ran fiercely and smote at Heliodorus with his fore feet." 2
Maccabees, iii. 25.

Rings with the infamy of Thracia's·king,[1]
Who slew his Phrygian charge : and last a shout
Ascends : 'Declare, O Crassus ![2] for thou know'st,
The flavour of thy gold.'   The voice of each
Now high, now low, as each his impulse prompts,
Is led through many a pitch, acute or grave.
Therefore, not singly, I erewhile rehearsed
That blessedness we tell of in the day :
But near me, none, beside, his accent raised."

    From him we now had parted, and essay'd
With utmost efforts to surmount the way ;
When I did feel, as nodding to its fall,
The mountain tremble ; whence an icy chill
Seized on me, as on one to death convey'd.
So shook not Delos, when Latona there
Couch'd to bring forth the twin-born eyes of heaven.

    Forthwith from every side a shout arose
So vehement, that suddenly my guide
Drew near, and cried : "Doubt not, while I con-
    duct thee!"
"Glory ! " all shouted (such the sounds mine ear
Gather'd from those, who near me swell'd the
    sounds,)
"Glory in the highest be to God."   We stood
Immoveably suspended, like to those,
The shepherds, who first heard in Bethlehem's field
That song : till ceased the trembling, and the song
Was ended : then our hallow'd path resumed,
Eying the prostrate shadows, who renew'd
Their custom'd mourning.   Never in my breast

---

[1] *Thracia's king*.] Polymnestor, the murderer of Polydorus. Hell, Canto xxx. 19.
[2] *Crassus*.] Marcus Crassus, who fell miserably in the Parthian war. See Appian, Parthica.

      E vidi Ciro più di sangue avaro,
      Che Crasso d'oro, e l'uno e l'altro n'ebbe
      Tanto, che parve a ciascheduno amaro.   *Petrarca*.

Did ignorance so struggle with desire
Of knowledge, if my memory do not err,
As in that moment ; nor through haste dared I
To question, nor myself could aught discern.
So on I fared, in thoughtfulness and dread.

CANTO XXI

ARGUMENT

The two Poets are overtaken by the spirit of Statius, who, being
cleansed, is on his way to Paradise, and who explains the cause of
the mountain shaking, and of the hymn ; his joy at beholding Virgil.

THE natural thirst, ne'er quench'd but from the well[1]
Whereof the woman of Samaria craved,
Excited ; haste, along the cumber'd path,
After my guide, impell'd ; and pity moved
My bosom for the 'vengeful doom though just.
When lo! even as Luke[2] relates, that Christ
Appear'd unto the two upon their way,
New-risen from his vaulted grave ; to us
A shade appear'd, and after us approach'd,
Contemplating the crowd beneath its feet.
We were not ware of it ; so first it spake,
Saying, "God give you peace, my brethren! " then
Sudden we turn'd : and Virgil such salute,
As fitted that kind greeting, gave ; and cried :
" Peace in the blessed council be thy lot,
Awarded by that righteous court which me
To everlasting banishment exiles."

[1] *The well.*] "The woman saith unto him, Sir, give me this
water, that I thirst not." John iv. 15.
[2] *Luke.*] Chapter xxiv. 13.

"How!" he exclaim'd, nor from his speed
     meanwhile
Desisting;[1] "If that ye be spirits whom God
Vouchsafes not room above; who up the height
Has been thus far your guide?" To whom the bard:
"If thou observe the tokens,[2] which this man,
Traced by the finger of the angel, bears;
'Tis plain that in the kingdom of the just
He needs must share. But sithence she,[3] whose
     wheel
Spins day and night, for him not yet had drawn
That yarn, which on the fatal distaff piled,
Clotho apportions to each wight that breathes;
His soul, that sister is to mine and thine,
Not of herself could mount; for not like ours
Her ken: whence I, from forth the ample gulf
Of hell, was ta'en, to lead him, and will lead
Far as my lore avails. But, if thou know,
Instruct us for what cause, the mount erewhile
Thus shook, and trembled: wherefore all at once
Seem'd shouting, even from his wave-wash'd foot."
     That questioning so tallied with my wish,
The thirst did feel abatement of its edge
E'en from expectance. He forthwith replied:
"In its devotion, nought irregular
This mount can witness, or by punctual rule

---

1 —— *nor from his speed meanwhile
Desisting.*] The unintelligible reading of almost all the editions
here (but not of all, as Lombardi would lead us to suppose, except
his favourite Nidobeatina) is

     E perchè andate forte?

Vellutello has also that which is no doubt the right:

     E parte andava forte.

2 *The tokens.*] The letter P for Peccata, sins, inscribed upon his
forehead by the Angel, in order to his being cleared of them in his
passage through Purgatory to Paradise.
3 *She.*] Lachesis, one of the three fates.

Unsanction'd ; here from every change exempt,
Other than that, which heaven in itself
Doth of itself receive,[1] no influence
Can reach us.   Tempest none, shower, hail, or snow,
Hoar frost, or dewy moistness, higher falls
Than that brief scale of threefold steps : thick
    clouds,
Nor scudding rack, are ever seen : swift glance
Ne'er lightens ; nor Thaumantian [2] Iris gleams,
That yonder often shifts on each side heaven.
Vapour adust doth never mount above
The highest of the trinal stairs, whereon
Peter's vicegerent stands.   Lower perchance,
With various motion rock'd, trembles the soil :
But here, through wind in earth's deep hollow pent,
I know not how, yet never trembled : then
Trembles, when any spirit feels itself
So purified, that it may rise, or move
For rising ; and such loud acclaim ensues.
Purification, by the will alone,
Is proved, that free to change society
Seizes the soul rejoicing in her will.
Desire of bliss is present from the first ;
But strong propension hinders, to that wish [3]

---

[1] —— *that, which heaven in itself*
    Doth of itself receive.] Venturi, I think rightly, interprets
this to be light.

[2] *Thaumantian.*] Figlia di Taumante.

      Θάυμαντος θυγάτηρ.   *Hesiod, Theog.* 780.

Compare Plato, Theæt. v. ii. p. 76. Bip. edit. Virg. Æn. ix. 5, and
Spenser, Faery Queen, b. v. c. iii. st. 25.

    Fair is Thaumantias in her crystal gown.   *Drummond.*

[3] *To that wish.*] Lombardi here alters the sense by reading with
the Nidobeatina, "con tal voglia," instead of "contra voglia," and
explains it : "With the same ineffectual will, with which man was
contrary to sin, while he resolved on sinning, even with the same,
would he wish to rise from his torment in Purgatory, at the same
time that through inclination to satisfy the divine justice he yet
remains there."

By the just ordinance of heaven opposed;
Propension now as eager to fulfil
The allotted torment, as erewhile to sin.
And I, who in this punishment had lain
Five hundred years and more, but now have felt
Free wish for happier clime. Therefore thou felt'st
The mountain tremble; and the spirits devout
Heard'st, over all his limits, utter praise
To that liege Lord, whom I entreat their joy
To hasten." Thus he spake: and, since the draught
Is grateful ever as the thirst is keen,
No words may speak my fulness of content.

  "Now," said the instructor sage, " I see the net [1]
That takes ye here; and how the toils are loosed;
Why rocks the mountain, and why ye rejoice.
Vouchsafe, that from thy lips I next may learn
Who on the earth thou wast; and wherefore here,
So many an age, wert prostrate."—"In that time,
When the good Titus,[2] with Heaven's King to help,
Avenged those piteous gashes, whence the blood
By Judas sold did issue; with the name [3]
Most lasting and most honour'd, there, was I
Abundantly renown'd," the shade replied,
"Not yet with faith endued. So passing sweet
My vocal spirit; from Tolosa,[4] Rome

1 *I see the net*.] "I perceive that ye are detained here by your
wish to satisfy the divine justice."
  2 *When the good Titus*.] When it was so ordered by the divine
Providence that Titus, by the destruction of Jerusalem, should
avenge the death of our Saviour on the Jews.
  3 *The name*.] The name of Poet.
  4 *From Tolosa*.] Dante, as many others have done, confounds
Statius the poet, who was a Neapolitan, with a rhetorician of the
same name, who was of Tolosa, or Thoulouse. Thus Chaucer,
Temple of Fame, b. iii. 370.

The Tholosan, that height Stace.

And Boccaccio, as cited by Lombard :

E Stazio di Tolosa ancora caro.
Amoros. Vis. Cant. v. 34.

To herself drew me, where I merited
A myrtle garland[1] to inwreathe my brow.
Statius they name me still.   Of Thebes I sang,
And next of great Achilles; but i' the way
Fell[2] with the second burthen.   Of my flame
Those sparkles were the seeds, which I derived
From the bright fountain of celestial fire
That feeds unnumber'd lamps; the song I mean
Which sounds Æneas' wanderings: that the breast
I hung at; that the nurse, from whom my veins
Drank inspiration: whose authority
Was ever sacred with me.   To have lived
Coeval with the Mantuan, I would bide
The revolution of another sun
Beyond my stated years in banishment."
     The Mantuan, when he heard him, turn'd to
          me;
And holding silence, by his countenance
Enjoin'd me silence: but the power, which wills,
Bears not supreme control: laughter and tears
Follow so closely on the passion prompts them,
They wait not for the motions of the will
In natures most sincere.   I did but smile,[3]
As one who winks; and thereupon the shade
Broke off, and peer'd into mine eyes, where best
Our looks interpret.   "So to good event

---

[1] *A myrtle garland.*]

> Et vos, O lauri, carpam, et te, proxima myrte.
> *Virg. Ecl.* ii.

> Qual vaghezza di lauro? o qual di mirto?
> *Petrarca.*

> Yet once more, O ye laurels, and once more,
> Ye myrtles brown.   *Milton, Lycidas.*

[2] *Fell.*]   Statius lived to write only a small part of the Achilleid.
[3] *I did but smile.*]   "I smiled no more than one would do who wished by a smile to intimate his consciousness of any thing to another person."

Mayst thou conduct such great emprize," he cried,
"Say, why across thy visage beam'd, but now,
The lightning of a smile."   On either part
Now am I straiten'd; one conjures me speak,
The other to silence binds me: whence a sigh
I utter, and the sigh is heard.   "Speak on,"
The teacher cried: "and do not fear to speak;
But tell him what so earnestly he asks."
Whereon I thus: "Perchance, O ancient spirit!
Thou marvel'st at my smiling.   There is room
For yet more wonder.   He, who guides my ken
On high, he is that Mantuan, led by whom
Thou didst presume of men and gods to sing.
If other cause thou deem'dst for which I smiled,
Leave it as not the true one: and believe
Those words, thou spakest of him, indeed the
    cause."
  Now down he bent to embrace my teacher's
    feet;
But he forbade him: "Brother! do it not:
Thou art a shadow, and behold'st a shade."
He, rising, answer'd thus: "Now hast thou
    proved
The force and ardour of the love I bear thee,
When I forget we are but things of air,
And, as a substance, treat an empty shade."

CANTO XXII

ARGUMENT

Dante, Virgil, and Statius mount to the sixth cornice, where the sin of gluttony is cleansed, the two Latin Poets discoursing by the way. Turning to the right, they find a tree hung with sweet-smelling fruit, and watered by a shower that issues from the rock. Voices are heard to proceed from among the leaves, recording examples of temperance.

Now we had left the angel, who had turned
To the sixth circle our ascending step;
One gash from off my forehead razed; while
    they,
Whose wishes tend to justice, shouted forth,
" Blessed ! " [1] and ended with " I thirst : " and I,
More nimble than along the other straits,
So journey'd, that, without the sense of toil,
I follow'd upward the swift-footed shades ;
When Virgil thus began : " Let its pure flame
From virtue flow, and love can never fail
To warm another's bosom, so the light
Shine manifestly forth.   Hence, from that hour,
When, 'mongst us in the purlieus of the deep,
Came down the spirit of Aquinum's bard,[2]
Who told of thine affection, my good will
Hath been for thee of quality as strong
As ever link'd itself to one not seen.
Therefore these stairs will now seem short to me.
But tell me : and, if too secure, I loose
The rein with a friend's licence, as a friend

---

[1] *Blessed.*] " Blessed be they which do hunger and thirst after righteousness, for they shall be filled."   Matt. v. 6.
[2] *Aquinum's bard.*] Juvenal had celebrated his contemporary, Statius, Sat. vii. 82 : though some critics imagine that there is a secret derision couched under his praise.

Forgive me, and speak now as with a friend:
How chanced it covetous desire could find
Place in that bosom, 'midst such ample store
Of wisdom, as thy zeal had treasured there?"

First somewhat moved to laughter by his words,
Statius replied: "Each syllable of thine
Is a dear pledge of love. Things oft appear,
That minister false matter to our doubts,
When their true causes are removed from sight.
Thy question doth assure me, thou believest·
I was on earth a covetous man; perhaps
Because thou found'st me in that circle placed.
Know then I was too wide of avarice:
And e'en for that excess, thousands of moons
Have wax'd and waned upon my sufferings.
And were it not that I with heedful care
Noted, where thou exclaim'st as if in ire·
With human nature, 'Why,[1] thou cursed thirst
Of gold! dost not with juster measure guide
The appetite of mortals?' I had met
The fierce encounter [2] of the voluble rock.
Then was I ware that, with too ample wing,
The hands may haste to lavishment; and turn'd,
As from my other evil, so from this,
In penitence. How many from their grave
Shall with shorn locks [3] arise, who living, ay,
And at life's last extreme, of this offence,
Through ignorance, did not repent! And know,
The fault, which lies direct from any sin

---

[1] *Why.*]   Quid non mortalia pectora cogis,
        Auri sacra fames?   *Virg. Æn.* lib. iii. 57.

Venturi supposes, that Dante might have mistaken the meaning
of the word *sacra*, and construed it "holy," instead of "cursed."
But I see no necessity for having recourse to so improbable a
conjecture.

[2] *The fierce encounter.*] See Hell, Canto vii. 26.

[3] *With shorn locks.*] See Hell, Canto vii. 58.

In level opposition, here, with that,
Wastes its green rankness on one common heap.
Therefore, if I have been with those, who wail
Their avarice, to cleanse me; through reverse
Of their transgression, such hath been my lot."
    To whom the sovran of the pastoral song:
"While thou didst sing that cruel warfare waged
By the twin sorrow of Jocasta's womb,[1]
From thy discourse with Clio[2] there, it seems
As faith had not been thine; without the which,
Good deeds suffice not.   And if so, what sun
Rose on thee, or what candle pierced the dark,
That thou didst after see to hoise the sail,
And follow where the fisherman had led?"
    He answering thus: " By thee conducted first,
I enter'd the Parnassian grots, and quaff'd
Of the clear spring: illumined first by thee,
Open'd mine eyes to God.   Thou didst, as one,
Who, journeying through the darkness, bears a
        light
Behind, that profits not himself, but makes
His followers wise, when thou exclaimed'st, 'Lo!
A renovated world,[3] Justice return'd,
Times of primeval innocence restored,
And a new race descended from above.'

[1] *The twin sorrow of Jocasta's womb.*]   Eteocles and Polynices.
[2] *With Clio.*]

> Quem prius heroum Clio dabis? immodicum iræ
> Tydea? laurigeri subitos an vatis hiatus?
> > *Stat. Thebaid,* i. 42.

[3] *A renovated world.*]

> Magnus ab integro sæclorum nascitur ordo.
> Jam redit et Virgo; redeunt Saturnia regna;
> Jam nova progenies cœlo demittitur alto.
> > *Virg. Ecl.* iv. 5.

For the application of Virgil's prophecy to the incarnation, see
Natalis Alexander, Hist. Eccl. Sæc. i. Dissert. 1.   Paris, 1679,
v. i. p. 166.

Poet and Christian both to thee I owed.
That thou mayst mark more clearly what I trace,
My hand shall stretch forth to inform the lines
With livelier colouring. Soon o'er all the world,
By messengers from heaven, the true belief
Teem'd now prolific ; and that word of thine,
Accordant, to the new instructors chimed.
Induced by which agreement, I was wont
Resort to them ; and soon their sanctity
So won upon me, that, Domitian's rage
Pursuing them, I mix'd my tears with theirs ;
And, while on earth I stay'd, still succour'd them ;
And their most righteous customs made me scorn
All sects besides. Before [1] I led the Greeks,
In tuneful fiction, to the streams of Thebes,
I was baptized : but secretly, through fear,
Remain'd a Christian, and conform'd long time
To Pagan rites. Four centuries and more,
I, for that lukewarmness, was fain to pace
Round the fourth circle. Thou then, who hast raised
The covering which did hide such blessing from me,
Whilst much of this ascent is yet to climb,
Say, if thou know, where our old Terence [2] bides,
Cæcilius,[3] Plautus, Varro : [4] if condemn'd
They dwell, and in what province of the deep."

[1] *Before.*] Before I had composed the Thebaid.
[2] *Our old Terence.*] "Antico," which is found in many of the old editions, seems preferable to "amico."
[3] *Cæcilius.*] Cæcilius Statius, a Latin comic poet, of whose works some fragments only remain. Our Poet had Horace in his eye.

> Dicitur Afrani toga convenisse Menandro,
> Plautus ad exemplar Siculi properare Epicharmi,
> Vincere Cæcilius gravitate, Terentius arte.
> > *Epist.* lib. ii. 1.

[4] *Varro.*] "Quam multa pene omnia tradidit Varro." *Quintilian, Instit. Orat.* lib. xii. "Vix aperto ad philosophiam aditu, primus M. Varro veterum omnium doctissimus." *Sadolet. de liberis recte instit.* Edit. Lugd, 1533, p. 137.

"These," said my guide, "with Persius and myself,
And others many more, are with that Greek,[1]
Of mortals, the most cherish'd by the nine,
In the first ward [2] of darkness.   There oft-times,
We of that mount hold converse, on whose top
For aye our nurses live.   We have the bard
Of Pella [3] and the Teian,[4] Agatho,[5]

[1] *That Greek.*]   Homer.
[2] *In the first ward.*]   In Limbo.
[3] —— *The bard
    of Pella.*]   Euripides.
[4] *The Teian.*]   Euripide v' è nosco e Anacreonte.
The Monte Casino MS. reads "Antifonte," Antipho [which is
almost certainly right] instead of "Anacreonte."   Dante probably
knew little more of these Greek writers than the names.
[5] *Agatho.*]   Chaucer, speaking of the Daisy as a representation
of Alcestis, refers to Agaton :

> No wonder is though Jove her stellifie,
> As tellith Agaton for her goodnesse.
> *Legende of Good Women.*

And Mr. Tyrwhitt tells us that "he has nothing to say of this
writer except that one of the same name is quoted in the Prol. to
the tragedie of Cambises by Thomas Preston.   There is no reason,"
he adds, "for supposing with Gloss. Ur. that a philosopher of
Samos is meant, or any of the Agathoes of antiquity."   I am
inclined, however, to believe that Chaucer must have meant Agatho,
the dramatic writer, whose name, at least, appears to have been
familiar in the Middle Ages ; for, besides the mention of him in the
text, he is quoted by Dante in the Treatise De Monarchiâ, lib. iii.
"Deus per nuncium facere non potest, genita non esse, genita,
juxta sententiam Agathonis"   The original is to be found in
Aristotle, Ethic. Nicom. lib. vi. c. 2.

> Μόνου γὰρ αὐτοῦ καὶ θεὸς στερίσκεται
> Ἀγένητα ποιεῖν ἄσσ' ἂν ᾖ πεπραγμένα.

Agatho is mentioned by Xenophon in his Symposium, by Plato in
the Protagoras, and in the Banquet, a favourite book with our
author, and by Aristotle in his Art of Poetry, where the following
remarkable passage occurs respecting him, from which I will leave
it to the reader to decide whether it is possible that the allusion in
Chaucer might have arisen: ἐν ἐνίαις μὲν ἓν ἢ δύο τῶν γνωρίμων ἐστὶν
ὀνομάτων, τὰ δὲ ἄλλα πεποιημένα· ἐν ἐνίαις δὲ οὐδέν· οἷον ἐν τῷ Ἀγά-
θωνος Ἄνθει. ὁμοίως γὰρ ἐν τούτῳ τά τε πράγματα καὶ τὰ ὀνόματα
πεποίηται, καὶ οὐδὲν ἧττον εὐφραίνει.   Edit. 1794, p. 33.   "There are,
however, some tragedies, in which one or two of the names are
historical, and the rest feigned ; there are even some, in which none
of the names are historical ; such is Agatho's tragedy called *The
Flower*; for in that all is invention, both incidents and names ;
and yet it pleases." *Aristotle's Treatise on Poetry*, by Thomas
Twining, 8vo Edit. 1812, vol. i. p. 128.

Simonides, and many a Grecian else
Ingarlanded with laurel.   Of thy train,[1]
Antigone is there, Deïphile,
Argia, and as sorrowful as erst
Ismene, and who show'd Langia's wave :[2]
Deïdamia with her sisters there,
And blind Tiresias' daughter,[3] and the bride
Sea-born of Peleus."[4]   Either poet now
Was silent ; and no longer by the ascent
Or the steep walls obstructed, round them cast
Inquiring eyes.   Four handmaids[5] of the day
Had finish'd now their office, and the fifth
Was at the chariot-beam, directing still
Its flamy point aloof ; when thus my guide :
" Methinks, it well behoves us to the brink
Bend the right shoulder, circuiting the mount,
As we have ever used."   So custom there
Was usher to the road ; the which we chose
Less doubtful, as that worthy shade[6] complied.

   They on before me went : I sole pursued,
Listening their speech, that to my thoughts convey'd

---

[1] *Of thy train.*] " Of those celebrated in thy Poem."
[2] *Who show'd Langia's wave.*] Hypsipile.   See note to Canto
xxvi. v. 87.
[3] *Tiresias' daughter.*]   Dante, as some have thought, had forgotten that he had placed Manto, the daughter of Tiresias, among
the sorcerers.   See Hell, Canto xx.   Vellutello endeavours, rather
awkwardly, to reconcile the apparent inconsistency, by observing,
that although she was placed there as a sinner, yet, as one of famous
memory, she had also a place among the worthies in Limbo.
Lombardi, or rather the Della Crusca academicians, excuse our
author better, by observing that Tiresias had a daughter named
Daphne.   See Diodorus Siculus, lib. iv. § 66.   I have here to
acknowledge a communication made to me by the learned writer of
an anonymous letter, who observes that Manto and Daphne are
only different names for the same person; and that Servius, in his
Commentary on the Æneid, x. 198, says, that some make Manto
the prophetess to be a daughter of Hercules.
[4] —— *The bride*
   Sea-born of Peleus.]   Thetis.
[5] *Four handmaids.*]   Compare Canto xii. v. 74.
[6] *That worthy shade.*]   Statius.

10

Mysterious lessons of sweet poesy.
But soon they ceased ; for midway of the road
A tree we found, with goodly fruitage hung,
And pleasant to the smell : and as a fir,
Upward from bough to bough, less ample spreads ;
So downward this less ample spread ; [1] that none,
Methinks, aloft may climb.   Upon the side,
That closed our path, a liquid crystal fell
From the steep rock, and through the sprays above
Stream'd showering.   With associate step the bards
Drew near the plant ; and, from amidst the leaves,
A voice was heard : " Ye shall be chary of me ; "
And after added : " Mary took more thought [2]
For joy and honour of the nuptial feast,
Than for herself, who answers now for you.
The women of old Rome [3] were satisfied
With water for their beverage.   Daniel [4] fed

[1] *Downward this less ample spread.*]   The early commentators understand that this tree had its root upward and the boughs downward ; and this opinion, however derided by their successors, is not a little countenanced by the imitation of Frezzi, who lived so near the time of our Poet.

> Su dentro al cielo avea la sua radice,
> E giù inverso terra i rami spande.
> > *Il Quadrir.* lib. iv. cap. 1.

> —— It had in heaven
> Its root above, and downward to the earth
> Stretch'd forth the branches.

[2] *Mary took more thought.*]   " The blessed Virgin, who answers for you now in heaven, when she said to Jesus, at the marriage in Cana of Galilee, ' they have no wine,' regarded not the gratification of her own taste, but the honour of the nuptial banquet."

[3] *The women of old Rome.*]   See Valerius Maximus, l. ii. c. 1.

[4] *Daniel.*]   " Then said Daniel to Melzar, whom the prince of the eunuchs had set over Daniel, Hananiah, Michael, and Azariah, Prove thy servants, I beseech thee, ten days ; and let them give us pulse to eat, and water to drink."   Daniel i. 11, 12.   " Thus Melzar took away the portion of their meat, and the wine that they should drink : and gave them pulse.   As for these four children, God gave them knowledge and skill in all learning and wisdom : and Daniel had understanding in all visions and dreams."   *Ibid.* 16, 17.

On pulse, and wisdom gain'd.   The primal age
Was beautiful as gold : and hunger then
Made acorns tasteful ; thirst, each rivulet
Run nectar.   Honey and locusts were the food,
Whereon the Baptist in the wilderness
Fed, and that eminence of glory reach'd
And greatness, which the Evangelist records."

CANTO XXIII

ARGUMENT

They are overtaken by the spirit of Forese, who had been a friend of our Poet's on earth, and who now inveighs bitterly against the immodest dress of their countrywomen at Florence.

On the green leaf mine eyes were fix'd, like his
Who throws away his days in idle chase
Of the diminutive birds, when thus I heard
The more than father warn me : " Son ! our time
Asks thriftier using.   Linger not : away."
Thereat my face and steps at once I turn'd
Toward the sages, by whose converse cheer'd
I journey'd on, and felt no toil : and lo !
A sound of weeping, and a song : " My lips,[1]
O Lord ! " and these so mingled, it gave birth
To pleasure and to pain.   " O Sire beloved !
Say what is this I hear."   Thus I inquired.
" Spirits," said he, " who, as they go, perchance,
Their debt of duty pay."   As on their road
The thoughtful pilgrims, overtaking some
Not known unto them, turn to them, and look,
But stay not ; thus, approaching from behind

---

[1] *My lips.*] "O Lord, open thou my lips ; and my mouth shall show forth thy praise."   Psalm li. 15.

With speedier motion, eyed us, as they pass'd,
A crowd of spirits, silent and devout.
The eyes [1] of each were dark and hollow; pale
Their visage, and so lean withal, the bones
Stood staring through the skin.   I do not think
Thus dry and meagre Erisicthon show'd,
When pinch'd by sharp-set famine to the quick.

   " Lo ! " to myself I mused, " the race, who lost
Jerusalem, when Mary [2] with dire beak
Prey'd on her child."   The sockets seem'd as rings, [3]
From which the gems were dropt.   Who reads
        the name [4]
Of man upon his forehead, there the M
Had traced most plainly.   Who would deem, that
        scent
Of water and an apple could have proved
Powerful to generate such pining want,
Not knowing how it wrought?   While now I stood,
Wondering what thus could waste them, (for the
        cause

[1] *The eyes.*]   Compare Ovid, Metam. lib. viii. 801.

  Hirtus erat crinis ; cava lumina, pallor in ore :

   . . . . . .

  Dura cutis, per quam spectari viscera possent :
  Ossa sub incurvis exstabant arida lumbis.

[2] *When Mary.*]   Josephus, de Bello Jud. lib. vii. c. xxi. p. 954.
Ed. Genev. fol. 1611.   The shocking story is well known.

[3] *Rings.*]   Senza fior prato o senza gemma anello.
      Petrarca, Son. Lasciata hai, morte.

  O ring of which the rubie is outfall.
      Chaucer, Troilus and Creseide, b. v.

   —— in this habit
  Met I my father with his bleeding rings,
  Their precious stones new lost.
      Shakspeare, Lear, act v. sc. 3.

[4] *Who reads the name.*]   " He who pretends to distinguish the
letters which form OMO in the features of the human face, might
easily have traced out the M on their emaciated countenances."
The temples, nose, and forehead, are supposed to represent this
letter ; and the eyes the two O's placed within each side of it.

Of their gaunt hollowness and scaly rind
Appear'd not,) lo! a spirit turn'd his eyes
In their deep-sunken cells, and fasten'd them
On me, then cried with vehemence aloud : .
" What grace is this vouchsafed me ? " By his
    looks
I ne'er had recognised him : but the voice
Brought to my knowledge what his cheer conceal'd.
Remembrance of his altered lineaments
Was kindled from that spark ; and I agnized
The visage of Forese.[1] " Ah! respect
This wan and leprous-wither'd skin," thus he
Suppliant implored, " this macerated flesh.
Speak to me truly of thyself. And who
Are those twain spirits, that escort thee there ?
Be it not said thou scorn'st to talk with me."
  " That face of thine," I answer'd him, " which
    dead
I once bewail'd, disposes me not less
For weeping, when I see it thus transform'd.
Say then, by Heaven, what blasts ye thus? The
    whilst
I wonder, ask not speech from me : unapt
Is he to speak, whom other will employs."
  He thus : " The water and the plant, we pass'd,
With power are gifted, by the eternal will
Infused ; the which so pines me. Every spirit,
Whose song bewails his gluttony indulged
Too grossly, here in hunger and in thirst
Is purified. The odour, which the fruit,

---

[1] *Forese*.] One of the brothers of Piccarda ; he who is again
spoken of in the next Canto, and introduced in the Paradise, Canto
iii. Cionacci, in his Storia della Beata Umiliana, Parte iv. cap. i., is
referred to by Lombardi, in order to show that Forese was also the
brother of Corso Donati, our author's political enemy. See
next Canto, v. 81. Tiraboschi, after Crescimbeni, enumerates him
among the Tuscan poets. Stor. della Poes. It. v. i. p. 139.

And spray that showers upon the verdure, breathe,
Inflames us with desire to feed and drink.
Nor once alone, encompassing our route,
We come to add fresh fuel to the pain :
Pain, said I ? solace rather : for that will,
To the tree, leads us, by which Christ was led
To call on Eli, joyful, when he paid
Our ransom from his vein."   I answering thus :
" Forese ! from that day, in which the world
For better life thou changedst, not five years
Have circled.   If the power [1] of sinning more
Were first concluded in thee, ere thou knew'st
That kindly grief which re-espouses us
To God, how hither art thou come so soon ?
I thought to find thee lower,[2] there, where time
Is recompense for time."   He straight replied :
" To drink up the sweet wormwood of affliction
I have been brought thus early, by the tears
Stream'd down my Nella's [3] cheeks.   Her prayers
    devout,
Her sighs have drawn me from the coast, where oft
Expectance lingers ; and have set me free
From the other circles.   In the sight of God
So much the dearer is my widow prized,
She whom I loved so fondly, as she ranks
More singly eminent for virtuous deeds.
The tract, most barbarous of Sardinia's isle,[4]
Hath dames more chaste, and modester by far,
Than that wherein I left her.   O sweet brother !

[1] *If the power.*] " If thou didst delay thy repentance to the last,
when thou hadst lost the power of sinning, how happens it thou art
arrived here so early ?"

[2] *Lower.*] In the Ante-Purgatory. See Canto ii.

[3] *My Nella.*] The wife of Forese.

[4] *The tract, most barbarous of Sardinia's isle.*] The *Barbagia* is
a part of Sardinia, to which that name was given, on account of the
uncivilised state of its inhabitants, who are said to have gone nearly
naked.

What wouldst thou have me say?[1] A time to
    come
Stands full within my view, to which this hour
Shall not be counted of an ancient date,
When from the pulpit shall be loudly warn'd
The unblushing dames of Florence,[2] lest they
    bare
Unkerchief'd bosoms to the common gaze.
What savage women hath the world e'er seen,
What Saracens,[3] for whom there needed scourge
Of spiritual or other discipline,
To force them walk with covering on their limbs?
But did they see, the shameless ones, what Heaven
Wafts on swift wing toward them while I speak,
Their mouths were oped for howling: thcy shall
    taste
Of sorrow (unless foresight cheat me here)
Or e'er the cheek of him be clothed with down,
Who is now rock'd with lullaby[4] asleep.
Ah! now, my brother, hide thyself no more:

---

[1] *What wouldst thou have me say?*] The interrogative, which Lombardi would dismiss from this place, as unmeaning and superfluous, appears to me to be the natural result of a deep feeling, and to prepare us for the invective that follows.

[2] *The unblushing dames of Florence.*] Landino's note exhibits a curious instance of the changeableness of his countrywomen. He even goes beyond the acrimony of the original. "In those days," says the commentator, "no less than in ours, the Florentine ladies exposed the neck and bosom, a dress, no doubt, more suitable to a harlot than a matron. But, as they changed soon after, insomuch that they wore collars up to the chin, covering the whole of the neck and throat, so have I hopes they will change again; not indeed so much from motives of decency, as through that fickleness, which pervades every action of their lives."

[3] *Saracens.*] "This word, during the middle ages, was indiscriminately applied to Pagans and Mahometans; in short, to all nations (except the Jews) who did not profess Christianity." Mr. Ellis's Specimens of Early English Metrical Romances, vol. i. p. 196 (a note). Lond. 8vo, 1805.

[4] *With lullaby.*] Colui che mo si consola non nanna.
"Nanna" is said to have been the sound with which the Florentine women hushed their children to sleep.

Thou seest [1] how not I alone, but all,
Gaze, where thou veil'st the intercepted sun."
    Whence I replied : " If thou recal to mind
What we were once together, even yet
Remembrance of those days may grieve thee sore.
That I forsook that life, was due to him
Who there precedes me, some few evenings past,
When she was round, who shines with sister lamp
To his that glisters yonder," and I show'd
The sun.   " 'Tis he, who through profoundest
    night
Of the true dead has brought me, with this flesh
As true, that follows.   From that gloom the aid
Of his sure comfort drew me on to climb,
And, climbing, wind along this mountain-steep,
Which rectifies in you whate'er the world
Made crooked and depraved.   I have his word,
That he will bear me company as far
As till I come where Beatrice dwells :
But there must leave me.   Virgil is that spirit,
Who thus hath promised," and I pointed to him :
" The other is that shade, for whom so late
Your realm, as he arose, exulting, shook
Through every pendent cliff and rocky bound."

    [1] *Thou seest.*]   Thou seest how we wonder that thou art here in
a living body.

CANTO XXIV

ARGUMENT

Forese points out several others by name who are here, like himself, purifying themselves from the vice of gluttony; and amongst the rest, Buonaggiunta of Lucca, with whom our Poet converses. Forese then predicts the violent end of Dante's political enemy, Corso Donati; and, when he has quitted them, the Poet, in company with Statius and Virgil, arrives at another tree, from whence issue voices that record ancient examples of gluttony; and proceeding forwards, they are directed by an angel which way to ascend to the next cornice of the mountain.

Our journey was not slacken'd by our talk,
Nor yet our talk by journeying.   Still we spake,
And urged our travel stoutly, like a ship
When the wind sits astern.   The shadowy forms,
That seem'd things dead and dead again, drew in
At their deep-delved orbs rare wonder of me,
Perceiving I had life; and I my words
Continued, and thus spake: "He journeys [1] up
Perhaps more tardily than else he would,
For others' sake.   But tell me, if thou know'st,
Where is Piccarda? [2]   Tell me, if I see
Any of mark, among this multitude
Who eye me thus."—"My sister (she for whom,
'Twixt beautiful and good, [3] I cannot say
Which name was fitter) wears e'en now her crown,
And triumphs in Olympus."   Saying this,

[1] *He journeys.*] The soul of Statius perhaps proceeds more slowly, in order that he may enjoy as long as possible the company of Virgil.

[2] *Piccarda.*] See Paradise, Canto iii.

[3] *'Twixt beautiful and good.*]

—— Tra bella e onesta
Qual fu più, lasciò in dubbio.
Petrarca, Son. Ripensando a quel.

He added : "Since spare diet [1] hath so worn
Our semblance out, 'tis lawful here to name
Each one.   This," and his finger then he raised,
"Is Buonaggiunta,[2]—Buonaggiunta, he

[1] *Diet.*] Dieta.
> And dieted with fasting every day.
> > *Spenser, F. Q.* b. i. c. i. st. 26.
> Spare fast that oft with gods doth diet.
> > *Milton, Il Penseroso.*

[2] *Buonaggiunta.*] Buonaggiunta Urbiciani, of Lucca. "There is a canzone by this poet, printed in the collection made by the Giunti, (p. 209,) and a sonnet to Guido Guinicelli in that made by Corbinelli, (p. 169,) from which we collect that he lived not about 1230, as Quadrio supposes, (t. ii. p. 159,) but towards the end of the thirteenth century. Concerning other poems by Buonaggiunta, that are preserved in MS. in some libraries, Crescimbeni may be consulted." Tiraboschi, Mr. Mathias's ed. v. i. p. 115. Three of these, a canzone, a sonnet, and a ballata, have been published in the Anecdota Literaria ex MSS. Codicibus eruta, 8vo, Roma, (no year,) v. iii. p. 453. He is thus mentioned by our author in his Treatise de Vulg. Eloq. lib. i. cap. xiii. "Next let us come to the Tuscans, who, made senseless by their folly, arrogantly assume to themselves the title of a vernacular diction, more excellent than the rest ; nor are the vulgar alone misled by this wild opinion, but many famous men have maintained it, as Guittone d'Arezzo, who never addicted himself to the polished style of the court, Buonaggiunta of Lucca, Gallo of Pisa, Mino Mocato of Sienna, and Brunetto of Florence, whose compositions, if there shall be leisure for examining them, will be found not to be in the diction of the court, but in that of their respective cities." As a specimen of Buonaggiunta's manner, the reader will take the following Sonnet from Corbinelli's Collection added to the Bella Mano :—

> Qual uomo è in su la rota per Ventura,
> > Non si rallegri, perchè sia innalzato ;
> > Che quando più si mostra chiara, e pura,
> > Allor si gira, ed hallo disbassato.
> E nullo prato ha sì fresca verdura,
> > Che li suoi fiori non cangino stato ;
> > E questo saccio, che avvien per natura ;
> > Più grave cade, chi piu è montato.
> Non si dee uomo troppo rallegrare
> > Di gran grandezza, nè tenere spene ;
> > Che egli è gran doglia, allegrezza fallire:
> Anzi si debbe molto umiliare ;
> > Non far soperchio, perchè aggia gran bene ;
> > Che ogni monte a valle dee venire.
> > > *La Bella Mano e Rime Antiche, ediz. Firenze,* 1715, p. 170.

> What man is raised on Fortune's wheel aloft,
> > Let him not triumph in his bliss elate ;
> For when she smiles with visage fair and soft,
> > Then whirls she round, reversing his estate.

Of Lucca: and that face beyond him, pierced
Unto a leaner fineness than the rest,
Had keeping of the church; he was of Tours,[1]
And purges by wan abstinence away
Bolsena's eels and cups of muscadel."[2]
  He show'd me many others, one by one:
And all, as they were named, seem'd well content;
For no dark gesture I discern'd in any.
I saw, through hunger, Ubaldino[3] grind
His teeth on emptiness; and Boniface,[4]
That waved the crozier[5] o'er a numerous flock:

> Fresh was the verdure in the sunny croft,
>   Yet soon the wither'd flowerets met their fate;
> And things exalted most, as chanceth oft,
>   Fall from on high to earth with ruin great.
> Therefore ought none too greatly to rejoice
>   In greatness, nor too fast his hope to hold:
>   For one, that triumphs, great pain is to fail.
> But lowly meekness is the wiser choice;
>   And he must down, that is too proud and bold:
>   For every mountain stoopeth to the vale.

[1] *He was of Tours.*] Simon of Tours became Pope with the title
of Martin IV. in 1281, and died in 1285.

[2] *Bolsena's eels and cups of muscadel.*] The Nidobeatina edition
and the Monte Casino MS. agree in reading

L'anguille di Bolsena in la vernaccia;

from which it would seem, that Martin the Fourth refined so much
on epicurism as to have his eels killed by being put into the wine
called vernaccia, in order to heighten their flavour. The Latin
annotator on the MS. relates, that the following epitaph was
inscribed on the sepulchre of the pope:

Gaudent anguillæ, quod mortuus hic jacet ille,
    Qui quasi morte reas excoriabat eas.

[3] *Ubaldino.*] Ubaldino degli Ubaldini, of Pila, in the Florentine
territory.

[4] *Boniface.*] Archbishop of Ravenna. By Venturi he is called
Bonifazio de' Fieschi, a Genoese; by Vellutello, the son of the
above-mentioned Ubaldini; and by Landino, Francioso, a Frenchman.

[5] *Crozier.*] It is uncertain whether the word "rocco," in the
original, means a "crozier" or a "bishop's rochet," that is, his
episcopal gown. In support of the latter interpretation Lombardi
cites Du Fresne's Glossary, article Roccus. "Rochettum hodie
vocant vestem linteam episcoporum . . . quasi parvum roccum;"
and explains the verse,

Che pasturò col rocco molte genti:

" who, from the revenues of his bishoprick, supported in luxury a

I saw the Marquis,[1] who had time erewhile
To swill at Forli with less drought ; yet so,
Was one ne'er sated.   I howe'er, like him
That, gazing 'midst a crowd, singles out one,
So singled him of Lucca ; for methought
Was none amongst them took such note of me.
Somewhat I heard him whisper of Gentucca :[2]
The sound was indistinct, and murmur'd there,[3]
Where justice, that so strips them, fix'd her sting.

   " Spirit ! " said I, " it seems as thou wouldst fain
Speak with me.   Let me hear thee.   Mutual wish
To converse prompts, which let us both indulge."

   He, answering, straight began : " Woman is
      born,
Whose brow no wimple shades yet,[4] that shall
      make
My city please thee, blame it as they may.[5]
Go then with this forewarning.   If aught false
My whisper too implied, the event shall tell.
But say, if of a truth I see the man
Of that new lay the inventor, which begins
With ' Ladies, ye that con the lore of love.' "[6]
   To whom I thus : " Count of me but as one,

large train of dependants."   If the reader wishes to learn more on
the subject, he is referred to Monti's Proposta, under the word
" Rocco."

   [1] *The Marquis.*]   The Marchese de' Rigogliosi, of Forli.   When
his butler told him it was commonly reported in the city that he did
nothing but drink, he is said to have answered : " And do you tell
them that I am always thirsty."

   [2] *Gentucca.*]   Of this lady it is thought that our Poet became
enamoured during his exile.   See note to Canto xxxi. 56.

   [3] *There.*]   In the throat, the part in which they felt the torment
inflicted by the divine justice.

   [4] *Whose brow no wimple shades yet.*]   " Who has not yet
assumed the dress of a woman."

   [5] *Blame it as they may.*]   See Hell, Canto xxi. 39.

   [6] *Ladies, ye that con the lore of love.*]

          Donne ch' avete intelletto d'amore.

The first verse of a canzone in our author's Vita Nuova.

Who am the scribe of love ; that, when he breathes,
Take up my pen, and, as he dictates, write."
  "Brother !" said he, "the hindrance, which once held
The notary,[1] with Guittone[2] and myself,

[1] *The notary.*] Jacopo da Lentino, called the Notary, a poet of these times. He was probably an Apulian : for Dante, (De Vulg. Eloq. lib. i. cap. 12,) quoting a verse which belongs to a canzone of his, published by the Giunti, without mentioning the writer's name, terms him one of "the illustrious Apulians," præfulgentes Apuli. See Tiraboschi, Mr. Mathias's edit. vol. i. p. 137. Crescimbeni (lib. i. Della Volg. Poes. p. 72, 4to ed. 1698) gives an extract from one of his poems, printed in Allacci's Collection, to show that the whimsical compositions called "Ariette," are not of modern invention. His poems have been collected among the Poeti del primo secolo della Lingua Italiana, 2 vol. 8vo. Firenze, 1816. They extend from p. 249 to p. 319 of the first volume.

[2] *Guittone.*] Fra Guittone, of Arezzo, holds a distinguished place in Italian literature, as, besides his poems printed in the Collection of the Giunti, he has left a collection of letters, forty in number, which afford the earliest specimen of that kind of writing in the language. They were published at Rome in 1743, with learned illustrations by Giovanni Bottari. He was also the first who gave to the sonnet its regular and legitimate form, a species of composition in which not only his own countrymen, but many of the best poets in all the cultivated languages of modern Europe, have since so much delighted. Guittone, a native of Arezzo, was the son of Viva di Michele. He was of the order of the "Frati Godenti," of which an account may be seen in the notes to Hell, Canto xxiii. In the year 1293 he founded a monastery of the order of Camaldoli, in Florence, and died in the following year. Tiraboschi, *ibid.* p. 119. Dante, in the Treatise de Vulg. Eloq. lib. i. cap. 13, (see note to v. 20, above,) and lib. ii. cap. 6, blames him for preferring the plebeian to the more courtly style; and Petrarch twice places him in the company of our Poet: Triumph of Love, cap. iv. and Son. Par. Sec. "Sennuccio mio." The eighth book in the collection of the old poets published by the Giunti in 1527 consists of sonnets and canzoni by Guittone. They are marked by a peculiar solemnity of manner, of which the ensuing sonnet will afford a proof and an example.

    Gran piacer Signor mio, e gran desire
      Harei d' essere avanti al divin trono,
      Dove si prenderà pace e perdono
      Di suo ben fatto e d'ogni suo fallire ;
    E gran piacer harei hor di sentire
      Quella sonante tromba e quel gran suono,
      E d'udir dire : hora venuti sono,
      A chi dar pace, a chi crudel martire.
    Questo tutto vorrei caro signore ;
      Perchè fia scritto a ciaschedun nel volto
      Quel chè già tenne ascoso dentro al core :

Short of that new and sweeter style [1] I hear,
Is now disclosed : I see how ye your plumes
Stretch, as the inditer guides them ; which, no question,
Ours did not.   He that seeks a grace beyond,
Sees not the distance parts one style from other."
And, as contented, here he held his peace.
    Like as the birds,[2] that winter near the Nile,
In squared regiment direct their course,
Then stretch themselves in file for speedier flight ;
Thus all the tribe of spirits, as they turn'd
Their visage, faster fled, nimble alike
Through leanness and desire.   And as a man,
Tired with the motion of a trotting steed,[3]
Slacks pace, and stays behind his company,
Till his o'erbreathed lungs keep temperate time ;

Allhor vedrete a la mia fronte avvolto
    Un brieve, che dirà ; che 'l crudo amore
    Per voi me prese, e mai non m' ha disciolto.

Great joy it were to me to join the throng,
    That thy celestial throne, O Lord, surround,
    Where perfect peace and pardon shall be found,
    Peace for good doings, pardon for the wrong :
Great joy to hear the vault of heaven prolong
    That everlasting trumpet's mighty sound,
    That shall to each award their final bound,
    Wailing to these, to those the blissful song.
All this, dear Lord, were welcome to my soul.
    For on his brow then every one shall bear
    Inscribed, what late was hidden in the heart ;
And round my forehead wreathed a letter'd scroll
    Shall in this tenor my sad fate declare :
    " Love's bondman I from him might never part."
    Bottari doubts whether some of the sonnets attributed to Guittone
in the Rime Antiche are by that writer.   See his notes to Lettere di
Fra Guittone, p. 135.
    [1] *That new and sweeter style.*]   He means the style introduced
in our Poet's time.
    [2] *The birds.*]   Hell, Canto v. 46.   Euripides, Helena, 1495, and
Statius, Theb. lib. v. 12.
    [3] *Tired with the motion of a trotting steed.*]   I have followed
Venturi's explanation of this passage.   Others understand

            —— di trottare è lasso

of the fatigue produced by running.

E'en so Forese let that holy crew
Proceed, behind them lingering at my side,
And saying : " When shall I again behold thee ? "
  " How long my life may last," said I, " I know
    not.
This know, how soon soever I return,
My wishes will before me have arrived :
Sithence the place,[1] where I am set to live,
Is, day by day, more scoop'd of all its good ;
And dismal ruin seems to threaten it."
  "Go now," he cried: "lo! he,[2] whose guilt
    is most,
Passes before my vision, dragg'd at heels
Of an infuriate beast.   Toward the vale,
Where guilt hath no redemption, on it speeds,
Each step increasing swiftness on the last ;
Until a blow it strikes, that leaveth him
A corse most vilely shatter'd. No long space
Those wheels have yet. to roll," (therewith his
    eyes
Look'd up to heaven), " ere thou shalt plainly see
That which my words may not more plainly tell.
I quit thee : time is precious here : I lose
Too much, thus measuring my pace with thine."
  As from a troop of well rank'd chivalry,

1 *The place.*]   Florence.
2 *He.*]   Corso Donati was suspected of aiming at the sovereignty
of Florence.   To escape the fury of his fellow-citizens, he fled away
on horseback, but falling, was overtaken and slain, A.D. 1308.
The contemporary annalist, after relating at length the circumstances of his fate, adds, "that he was one of the wisest and most
valorous knights, the best speaker, the most expert statesman, the
most renowned and enterprising man of his age in Italy, a comely
knight and of graceful carriage, but very worldly, and in his time
had formed many conspiracies in Florence, and entered into many
scandalous practices for the sake of attaining state and lordship."
G. Villani, lib. viii. cap. xcvi.   The character of Corso is forcibly
drawn by another of his contemporaries, Dino Compagni, lib. iii.
Muratori, Rer. Ital. Script. tom. ix. p. 523.   Guittone d'Arezzo's
seventh letter is addressed to him.   It is in verse.

One knight, more enterprising than the rest,
Pricks forth at gallop, eager to display
His prowess in the first encounter proved;
So parted he from us, with lengthen'd strides;
And left me on the way with those twain spirits,
Who were such mighty marshals of the world.

When he beyond us had so fled, mine eyes
No nearer reach'd him, than my thought his words;
The branches of another fruit, thick hung,
And blooming fresh, appear'd.   E'en as our steps
Turn'd thither; not far off, it rose to view.
Beneath it were a multitude, that raised
Their hands, and shouted forth I know not what
Unto the boughs; like greedy and fond brats,
That beg, and answer none obtain from him,
Of whom they beg; but more to draw them on,
He, at arm's length, the object of their wish
Above them holds aloft, and hides it not.

At length, as undeceived, they went their way:
And we approach the tree, whom vows and tears
Sue to in vain; the mighty tree.   "Pass on,
And come not near.   Stands higher up the wood,
Whereof Eve tasted: and from it was ta'en
This plant."   Such sounds from midst the thickets
      came.
Whence I, with either bard, close to the side
That rose, pass'd forth beyond.   "Remember,"
      next
We heard, "those unblest creatures of the clouds,[1]
How they their twyfold bosoms, overgorged,
Opposed in fight to Theseus: call to mind
The Hebrews,[2] how, effeminate, they stoop'd

---

[1] *Creatures of the clouds.*] The Centaurs.   Ovid, Met. lib. xii.
fab. 4.
[2] *The Hebrews.*] Judges vii.

To ease their thirst; whence Gideon's ranks were
    thinn'd,
As he to Madian [1] march'd adown the hills."
  Thus near one border coasting, still we heard
The sins of gluttony, with woe erewhile
Reguerdon'd. Then along the lonely path,
Once more at large, full thousand paces on
We travell'd, each contemplative and mute.
  "Why pensive journey so ye three alone?"
Thus suddenly a voice exclaim'd: whereat
I shook, as doth a scared and paltry beast;
Then raised my head, to look from whence it came.
  Was ne'er, in furnace, glass, or metal, seen
So bright and glowing red, as was the shape
I now beheld. "If ye desire to mount,"
He cried; "here must ye turn. This way he
    goes,
Who goes in quest of peace." His countenance
Had dazzled me; and to my guides I faced
Backward, like one who walks as sound directs.
  As when, to harbinger the dawn, springs up
On freshen'd wing the air of May, and breathes
Of fragrance, all impregn'd with herb and flowers;
E'en such a wind I felt upon my front
Blow gently, and the moving of a wing
Perceived, that, moving, shed ambrosial smell;
And then a voice: "Blessed are they, whom grace
Doth so illume, that appetite in them
Exhaleth no inordinate desire,
Still hungering as the rule of temperance wills."

1 *To Madian.*] The matchless Gideon in pursuit
    Of Madian and her vanquisht kings.
             Milton, Samson Agonistes.

CANTO XXV

ARGUMENT

Virgil and Statius resolve some doubts that have arisen in the
mind of Dante from what he had just seen. They all arrive on the
seventh and last cornice, where the sin of incontinence is purged in
fire ; and the spirits of those suffering therein are heard to record
illustrious instances of chastity.

It was an hour, when he who climbs, had need
To walk uncrippled : for the sun [1] had now
To Taurus the meridian circle left,
And to the Scorpion left the night.   As one,
That makes no pause, but presses on his road,
Whate'er betide him, if some urgent need
Impel ; so enter'd we [2] upon our way,
One before other ; for, but singly, none
That steep and narrow scale admits to climb.

E'en as the young stork lifteth up his wing
Through wish to fly, yet ventures not to quit
The nest, and drops it ; so in me desire
Of questioning my guide arose, and fell,
Arriving even to the act that marks
A man prepared for speech.   Him all our haste
Restrain'd not ; but thus spake the sire beloved :

---

[1] *The sun.*]   The sun had passed the meridian two hours, and
that meridian was now occupied by the constellation of Taurus, to
which as the Scorpion is opposite, the latter constellation was
consequently at the meridian of night.

[2] *So enter'd we.*]   Davanti a me andava la mia guida :
  E poi io dietro per una via stretta
  Seguendo lei come mia scorta fida.
     Fressi, Il Quadrir. lib. ii. cap. 3.

The good prelate of Foligno has followed our Poet so closely
throughout this Capitolo, that it would be necessary to transcribe
almost the whole of it in order to show how much he has copied.
These verses of his own may well be applied to him on the occasion.

" Fear not to speed the shaft,[1] that on thy lip
Stands trembling for its flight."   Encouraged thus,
I straight began : " How there can leanness come,[2]
Where is no want of nourishment to feed ?"

  "If thou," he answer'd, "hadst remember'd thee,
How Meleager[3] with the wasting brand
Wasted alike, by equal fires consumed ;
This would not trouble thee : and hadst thou thought,
How in the mirror[4] your reflected form
With mimic motion vibrates ; what now seems
Hard, had appear'd no harder than the pulp
Of summer-fruit mature.   But that thy will
In certainty may find its full repose,
Lo Statius here ! on him I call, and pray
That he would now be healer of thy wound."

  "If, in thy presence, I unfold to him
The secrets of heaven's vengeance, let me plead
Thine own injunction to exculpate me."
So Statius answer'd, and forthwith began :

1 *Fear not to speed the shaft*.] " Fear not to utter the words
that are already at the tip of thy tongue."

Πολλὰ μὲν ἀρτιεπὴς
Γλῶσσα μοι τοξεύματ' ἔχει περὶ κείνων
Κελαδῆσαι   *Pindar*, Isthm. v. 60.

Full many a shaft of sounding rhyme
Stands trembling on my lip
Their glory to declare.

2 *How there can leanness come*.] " How can spirits, that need
not corporeal nourishment, be subject to leanness ?" This question
gives rise to the following explanation of Statius respecting the
formation of the human body from the first, its junction with the
soul, and the passage of the latter to another world.

3 *Meleager*.] Virgil reminds Dante that, as Meleager was
wasted away by the decree of the fates, and not through want of
blood ; so by the divine appointment, there may be leanness where
there is no need of nourishment.

4 *In the mirror*.] As the reflexion of a form in a mirror is
modified in agreement with the modification of the form itself ; so
the soul, separated from the earthly body, impresses the image or
ghost of that body with its own affections.

"Attend my words, O son, and in thy mind
Receive them; so shall they be light to clear
The doubt thou offer'st.   Blood, concocted well,
Which by the thirsty veins is ne'er imbibed,
And rests as food superfluous, to be ta'en
From the replenish'd table, in the heart
Derives effectual virtue, that informs
The several human limbs, as being that
Which passes through the veins itself to make
    them.
Yet more concocted it descends, where shame
Forbids to mention: and from thence distils
In natural vessels on another's blood.
There each unite together; one disposed
To endure, to act the other, through that power
Derived from whence it came;[1] and being met,
It 'gins to work, coagulating first;
Then vivifies what its own substance made
Consist.   With animation now indued,
The active virtue (differing from a plant
No further, than that this is on the way,
And at its limit that) continues yet
To operate, that now it moves, and feels,
As sea-sponge[2] clinging to the rock: and there
Assumes the organic powers its seed convey'd.
This is the moment, son! at which the virtue,
That from the generating heart proceeds,
Is pliant and expansive; for each limb
Is in the heart by forgeful nature plann'd.
How babe[3] of animal becomes, remains

---

[1] *From whence it came.*]   "From the heart," as Lombardi
rightly interprets it.

[2] *As sea-sponge.*]   The fœtus is in this stage a zoophyte.

[3] *Babe.*]   By "fante," which is here rendered "babe," is meant
"the human creature."   "The creature that is distinguished from
others by its faculty of speech," just as Homer calls men,

γενεαὶ μερόπων ἀνθρώπων

For thy considering.   At this point, more wise,
Than thou, has err'd,[1] making the soul dis-
    join'd
From passive intellect, because he saw
No organ for the latter's use assign'd.
    "Open' thy bosom to the truth that comes.
Know, soon as in the embryo, to the brain
Articulation is complete, then turns,
The primal Mover with a smile of joy
On such great work of nature ; and imbreathes
New spirit replete with virtue, that what here
Active it finds, to its own substance draws ;
And forms an individual soul, that lives,
And feels, and bends reflective on itself.
And that thou less mayst marvel at the word,
Mark the sun's heat ;[2] how that to wine doth
        change,
Mix'd with the moisture filter'd through the vine.
    "When Lachesis hath spun the thread,[3] the
        soul
Takes with her both the human and divine,
Memory, intelligence, and will, in act
Far keener than before ; the other powers
Inactive all and mute.   No pause allow'd,

---

[1]   —— *More wise,*
    Than thou, has err'd.] Averroes is said to be here meant.
Venturi refers to his commentary on Arisotle, De Anim. lib. iii.
cap. 5, for the opinion that there is only one universal intellect or
mind pervading every individual of the human race.   Much of the
knowledge displayed by our Poet in the present Canto, appears to
have been derived from the medical work of Averroes called the
Colliget, lib. ii. f. 10.   Ven. 1490, fol.
    [2] *Mark the sun's heat.*] Redi and Tiraboschi (Mr. Mathias's
ed. v. ii. p. 36) have considered this as an anticipation of a profound
discovery of Galileo's in natural philosophy ; but it is in reality
taken from a passage in Cicero "de Senectute," where, speaking of
the grape, he says, " quæ, et succo terræ et calore solis augescens,
primo est peracerba gustatu, deinde maturata dulcescit."
    [3] *When Lachesis hath spun the thread.*] When a man's life on
earth is at an end.

In wondrous sort self-moving, to one strand
Of those, where the departed roam, she falls :
Here learns her destined path.   Soon as the place
Receives her, round the plastic virtue beams,
Distinct as in the living limbs before :
And as the air, when saturate with showers,
The casual beam refracting, decks itself
With many a hue ; so here the ambient air
Weareth that form, which influence of the soul
Imprints on it : and like the flame, that where
The fire moves, thither follows ; so, henceforth,
The new form on the spirit follows still :
Hence hath it semblance, and is shadow call'd,
With each sense, even to the sight, endued :
Hence speech is ours, hence laughter, tears, and
    sighs,
Which thou mayst oft have witness'd on the
    mount.
The obedient shadow fails not to present
Whatever varying passion moves within us.
And this the cause of what thou marvell'st at."
    Now the last flexure of our way we reach'd ;
And to the right hand turning other care
Awaits us.   Here the rocky precipice
Hurls forth redundant flames ; and from the rim
A blast up-blown, with forcible rebuff
Driveth them back, sequester'd from its bound.
    Behoved us, one by one, along the side,
That border'd on the void, to pass ; and I
Fear'd on one hand the fire, on the other fear'd
Headlong to fall : when thus the instructor
    warn'd ;
" Strict rein must in this place direct the eyes.
A little swerving and the way is lost."
    Then from the bosom of the burning mass,

"O God of mercy!"[1] heard I sung, and felt
No less desire to turn.   And when I saw
Spirits along the flame proceeding, I
Between their footsteps and mine own was fain
To share by turns my view.   At the hymn's close
They shouted loud, "I do not know a man;"[2]
Then in low voice again took up the strain;
Which once more ended, "To the wood," they
    cried,
"Ran Dian, and drave forth Callisto[3] stung
With Cytherea's poison:" then return'd
Unto their song; then many a pair extoll'd,
Who lived in virtue chastely and the bands
Of wedded love.   Nor from that task, I ween,
Surcease they; whileso'er the scorching fire
Enclasps them.   Of such skill appliance needs,
To medicine the wound that healeth last.[4]

[1] *"O God of mercy."*]   "Summæ Deus clementiæ."   The
beginning of the hymn sung on the Sabbath at matins, as it stands
in the ancient breviaries; for in the modern it is "summæ parens
clementiæ." *Lombardi.*

[2] *I do not know a man.*]   Luke i. 34.

[3] *Callisto.*]   See Ovid, Met. lib. ii. fab. 5.

[4] *The wound that healeth last.*]   The marginal note in the
Monte Casino MS. on this passage is: "id est ultima litera quæ
denotat ultimum peccatum mortale;" and the editor remarks, that
Dante in these last two verses admonishes himself, and in himself all
those guilty of carnal sin, in what manner the wound, inflicted by it,
and expressed by the last P on his forehead, may be healed.

CANTO XXVI

ARGUMENT

The spirits wonder at seeing the shadow cast by the body of Dante on the flame as he passes it. This moves one of them to address him. It proves to be Guido Guinicelli, the Italian poet, who points out to him the spirit of Arnault Daniel, the Provençal, with whom he also speaks.

WHILE singly thus along the rim we walk'd,
Oft the good master warn'd me: "Look thou well.
Avail it that I caution thee." The sun
Now all the western clime irradiate changed
From azure tinct to white; and, as I pass'd,
My passing shadow made the umber'd flame
Burn ruddier. At so strange a sight I mark'd
That many a spirit marvell'd on his way.
    This bred occasion first to speak of me.
" He seems," said they, " no insubstantial frame: "
Then, to obtain what certainty they might,
Stretch'd towards me, careful not to overpass
The burning pale. "O thou! who followest
The others, haply not more slow than they,
But moved by reverence; answer me, who burn
In thirst and fire: nor I alone, but these
All for thine answer do more thirst, than doth
Indian or Æthiop for the cooling stream.
Tell us, how is it that thou makest thyself
A wall against the sun, as thou not yet
Into the inextricable toils of death
Hadst enter'd?" Thus spake one: and I had
    straight
Declared me, if attention had not turn'd
To new appearance. Meeting these, there came,

Midway the burning path, a crowd, on whom
Earnestly gazing, from each part I view
The shadows all press forward, severally
Each snatch a hasty kiss, and then away.
E'en so the emmets, 'mid their dusky troops,
Peer closely one at other, to spy out
Their mutual road perchance, and how they thrive.
  That friendly greeting parted, ere dispatch
Of the first onward step, from either tribe
Loud clamour rises : those, who newly come,
Shout, " Sodom and Gomorrah ! " these, " The cow
Pasiphae enter'd, that the beast she woo'd
Might rush unto her luxury." Then as cranes,
That part towards the Riphæan mountains fly,
Part towards the Lybic sands, these to avoid
The ice, and those the sun ; so hasteth off
One crowd, advances the other ; and resume
Their first song, weeping, and their several shout.[1]
  Again drew near my side the very same,
Who had erewhile besought me ; and their looks
Mark'd eagerness to listen. I, who twice
Their will had noted, spake : "O spirits ! secure,
Whene'er the time may be, of peaceful end ;
My limbs, nor crude, nor in mature old age,
Have I left yonder : here they bear me, fed
With blood, and sinew-strung. That I no more
May live in blindness, hence I tend aloft.
There is a dame on high, who wins for us
This grace, by which my mortal through your realm
I bear. But may your utmost wish soon meet
Such full fruition, that the orb of heaven,
Fullest of love, and of most ample space,

---

[1] *Their first song, weeping, and their several shout.*] See the last Canto, v. 118, and v. 123.

Receive you; as ye tell (upon my page
Henceforth to stand recorded) who ye are;
And what this multitude, that at your backs
Have past behind us."   As one, mountain-bred,
Rugged and clownish, if some city's walls
He chance to enter, round him stares agape,
Confounded and struck dumb; e'en such appear'd
Each spirit.   But when rid of that amaze,
(Not long the inmate of a noble heart,[1])
He, who before had question'd, thus resum'd:
"O blessed! who, for death preparing, takest
Experience of our limits, in thy bark;
Their crime, who not with us proceed, was that
For which, as he did triumph, Cæsar[2] heard
The shout of 'queen,' to taunt him.   Hence their
    cry
Of 'Sodom,' as they parted; to rebuke
Themselves, and aid the burning by their shame.
Our sinning was Hermaphrodite: but we,

[1]   —— *Amaze,*
(Not long the inmate of a noble heart.)]

        —— stupore
Lo qual negli alti cor tosto s'attuta.

Thus Speroni: —— lo stupore
Lo qual dagli alti cor tosto si parte.   *Canace.*

He does not say that wonder is not natural to a lofty mind, for it is the very principle of knowledge (μάλα γὰρ φιλοσόφου τοῦτο τὸ πάθος, τὸ θαυμάζειν, οὐ γὰρ ἄλλη ἀρχὴ φιλοσοφίας ἢ αὐτή. *Plato, Theæt.* Edit. Bipont. tom. ii. p. 76), but that it is not of long continuance in such a mind.   On this subject it is well said by Doctor Horsley: "Wonder, connected with a principle of rational curiosity, is the source of all knowledge and discovery, and it is a principle even of piety: but wonder, which ends in wonder, and is satisfied with wonder, is the quality of an idiot."   Sermons, vol. i. p. 227. Compare Aristotle, Metaph. lib. i. p. 335.   Edit. Sylb.   The above passage from Plato is adduced by Clemens Alexand. Strom. lib. ii. sect. 9.

[2] *Cæsar.*]   For the opprobrium cast on Cæsar's effeminacy, see Suetonius, Julius Cæsar, c. 49.   [Dante's authority for this incident was probably not Suetonius but the *Magnæ Derivationes* of Uguccione da Pisa, whose version (given under the word *triumphus*) exactly agrees with that of Dante.]

Because the law of human kind we broke,
Following like beasts our vile concupiscence,
Hence parting from them, to our own disgrace
Record the name of her, by whom the beast
In bestial tire was acted. Now our deeds
Thou know'st, and how we sinn'd. If thou by
    name
Wouldst haply know us, time permits not now
To tell so much, nor can I. Of myself
Learn what thou wishest. Guinicelli[1] I ;
Who having truly sorrow'd ere my last,
Already cleanse me." With such pious joy,
As the two sons upon their mother gazed
From sad Lycurgus [2] rescued ; such my joy
(Save that I more repress'd it) when I heard
From his own lips the name of him pronounced,
Who was a father to me, and to those
My betters, who have ever used the sweet
And pleasant rhymes of love. So nought I heard,
Nor spake ; but long time thoughtfully I went
Gazing on him ; and, only for the fire,
Approach'd not nearer. When my eyes were fed
By looking on him ; with such solemn pledge,
As forces credence, I devoted me
Unto his service wholly. In reply
He thus bespake me : " What from thee I hear
Is graved so deeply on my mind, the waves

---

[1] *Guinicelli.*] See note to Canto xi. 96.
[2] *Lycurgus.*] Statius, Theb. lib. iv. and v. Hypsipile had left
her infant charge, the son of Lycurgus, on a bank, where it was
destroyed by a serpent, when she went to show the Argive army
the river of Langia : and, on her escaping the effects of Lycurgus's
resentment, the joy her own children felt at the sight of her was
such, as our Poet felt on beholding his predecessor Guinicelli.
The incidents are beautifully described in Statius, and seem to have
made an impression on Dante, for he before (Canto xxii. 110)
characterises Hypsipile as her—

    Who show'd Langia's wave.

Of Lethe shall not wash it off, nor make
A whit less lively.   But as now thy oath
Has seal'd the truth, declare what cause impels
That love, which both thy looks and speech bewray."

   " Those dulcet lays," I answer'd ; " which, as long
As of our tongue the beauty does not fade,
Shall make us love the very ink that traced them."

   "Brother !" he cried, and pointed at the shade
Before him, "there is one, whose mother speech
Doth owe to him a fairer ornament.
He [1] in love ditties, and the tales of prose,

[1] *He.*]   The united testimony of Dante, and of Petrarch, places
Arnault Daniel at the head of the Provençal poets.

> —— poi v'era un drappello
> Di portamenti e di volgari strani :
> Fra tutti il primo Arnaldo Daniello
> Gran maestro d'amor ch' a la sua terra
> Ancor fa anor col suo dir nuovo e bello.
> *Petrarca, Trionfo d'Amora,* c. iv.

He was born of poor but noble parents, at the castle of Ribeyrac
in Périgord, and spent some time in England at the court of
Richard Cœur-de-Lion.   Our Poet frequently cites him in the work
De Vulgari Eloquio.   In the second chapter of the second book, he
is instanced as one "who had treated of love;" and in the tenth
chapter, he is said to have used in almost all his canzoni a particular
kind of stanza, the sestine, which Dante had followed in one of his
own canzoni, beginning,

> Al poco giorno ed al gran cerchio d'ombra.

This stanza is termed by Gray, "both in sense and sound, a very
mean composition."   Gray's Works, 4to, Lond. 1814, vol. ii. p. 23.
According to Crescimbeni, (Della Volg. Poes. lib. i. p. 7, ed. 1698,)
he died in 1189.   Arnault Daniel was not soon forgotten; for Ausias
March, a Catalonian, who was himself distinguished as a Provençal
poet in the middle of the fifteenth century, makes honourable
mention of him in some verses, which are quoted by Bastero in his
Crusca Provenzale, Ediz. Roma, 1724, p. 75.

> Envers alguns aço miracle par ;
> Mas sin's membram d'en Arnau Daniel
> E de aquels que la terra los es vel,
> Sabrem Amor vers nos que pot donar.
>
> To some this seems a miracle to be ;
> But if we Arnault Daniel call to mind,
> And those beside, whom earthly veil doth bind,
> We then the mighty power of love shall see.

Since this note was written, M. Raynouard has made us better

Without a rival stands; and lets the fools
Talk on, who think the songster of Limoges [1]
O'ertops him.   Rumour and the popular voice

acquainted with the writings and history of the Provençal poets. [The poems of Arnault Daniel have now been published, with an account of his life, by Canello (Halle, 1883).]

[1] *The songster of Limoges.*]   Giraud de Borneil, of Essideuil, a castle in Limoges.   He was a Troubadour, much admired and caressed in his day, and appears to have been in favour with the monarchs of Castile, Leon, Navarre, and Arragon.   Giraud is mentioned by Dante in a remarkable passage of the De Vulg. Eloq. lib. ii. cap. 2.   "As man is endowed with a triple soul, vegetable, animal, and rational, so he walks in a triple path.   Inasmuch as he is vegetable, he seeks utility, in which he has a common nature with plants; inasmuch as he is animal, he seeks for pleasure, in which he participates with brutes; inasmuch as he is rational, he seeks for honour, in which he is either alone, or is associated with the angels. Whatever we do, appears to be done through these three principles, etc."—"With respect to utility, we shall find on a minute inquiry that the primary object with all who seek it, is safety; with regard to pleasure, love is entitled to the first place; and as to honour, no one will hesitate in assigning the same pre-eminence to virtue. These three then, safety, love, virtue, appear to be three great subjects, which ought to be treated with most grandeur; that is, those things which chiefly pertain to these, as courage in arms, ardency of love, and the direction of the will: concerning which alone we shall find on inquiry that illustrious men have composed their poems in the vernacular tongues; Bertrand de Born, of arms; Arnault Daniel, of love; Giraud de Borneil, of rectitude; Cino da Pistoia, of love; his friend," (by whom he means himself,) "of rectitude; but I find no Italian as yet who has treated of arms." Giraud is again quoted in the sixth chapter of this book.   The following notice respecting him is found in Gray's posthumous Works, 4to, Lond. 1814, vol. ii. p. 23.   "The canzone is of very ancient date, the invention of it being ascribed to Girard de Borneil of the school of Provence, who died in 1178.   He was of Limoges, and was called *Il Maestro de' Trovatori.*"   That he was distinguished by this title (a circumstance that, perhaps, induced Dante to vindicate the superior claims of Arnault Daniel) is mentioned by Bastero in his Crusca Provenzale, Ediz. Roma, p. 84, where we find the following list of his MSS. poems preserved in the Vatican, and in the library of S. Lorenzo at Florence.   "Una tenzone col Re d'Aragona; e un Serventese contra Cardaillac, e diverse Canzoni massimamente tre pel ricuperamento del S. Sepolcro, o di Terra Santa, ed alcune col titolo di Canterete, cioè picciole cantari, ovvero canzonette."   The light which these and similar writings might cast, not only on the events, but still more on the manners of a most interesting period of history, would surely, without taking into the account any merit they may possess as poetical compositions, render them objects well deserving of more curiosity than they appear to have hitherto excited in the public mind.   Many of his poems are still remaining in MS.   He died *circ.* 1220.   Some of his poems have been published by Raynouard, Poésies des Troubadours, tom. iii. p. 304, etc.

They look·to, more than truth ; and so confirm
Opinion, ere by art or reason taught.
Thus many of the elder time cried up
Guittone,[1] giving him the prize, till truth
By strength of numbers vanquish'd.   If thou own
So ample privilege, as to have gain'd
Free entrance to the cloister, whereof Christ
Is Abbot of the college ; say to him
One paternoster for me, far as needs [2]
For dwellers in this world, where power to sin
No longer tempts us."   Haply to make way
For one that follow'd next, when that was said,
He vanish'd through the fire, as through the
        wave
A fish, that glances diving to the deep.
  I, to the spirit he had shown me, drew
A little onward, and besought his name,
For which my heart, I said, kept gracious room.
He frankly thus began : " Thy courtesy [3]

[1] *Guittone.*]   See Canto xxiv. 56.
[2] *Far as needs.*]   See Canto xi. 23.
[3] *Thy courtesy.*]   Arnault is here made to speak in his own
tongue, the Provençal.   According to Dante, (De Vulg. Eloq. lib. i.
c. 8,) the Provençal was one language with the Spanish.   What he
says on this subject is so curious, that the reader will perhaps not be
displeased if I give an abstract of it.   He first makes three great
divisions of the European languages.   " One of these extends from the
mouths of the Danube, or the lake of Mæotis, to the western limits
of England, and is bounded by the limits of the French and Italians,
and by the ocean.   One idiom obtained over the whole of this space :
but was afterwards subdivided into the Sclavonian, Hungarian,
Teutonic, Saxon, English, and the vernacular tongues of several
other people, one sign remaining to all, that they use the affirmative
io (our English *ay*).   The whole of Europe, beginning from the
Hungarian limits and stretching towards the east, has a second
idiom, which reaches still further than the end of Europe, into Asia.
This is the Greek.   In all that remains of Europe, there is a third
idiom, subdivided into three dialects, which may be severally distinguished by the use of the affirmatives, *oc*, *oïl*, and *si* ; the first
spoken by the Spaniards, the next by the French, the third by the
Latins (or Italians).   The first occupy the western part of southern
Europe, beginning from the limits of the Genoese.   The third occupy the
eastern part from the said limits, as far, that is, as to the promontory
of Italy, where the Adriatic sea begins, and to Sicily.   The second

So wins on me, I have nor power nor will
To hide me.   I am Arnault; and with songs,

are in a manner northern, with respect to these, for they have the
Germans to the east and north, on the west they are bounded by
the English sea and the mountains of Arragon, and on the south
by the people of Provence and the declivity of the Apennine."
Ibid. c. x.   "Each of these three," he observes, "has its own claims
to distinction.   The excellency of the French language consists in
its being best adapted, on account of its facility and agreeableness,
to prose narration (quicquid redactum, sive inventum est ad vulgare
prosaicum, suum est;) and he instances the books compiled on the
gests of the Trojans and Romans, and the delightful Adventures of
King Arthur, with many other histories and works of instruction.   The
Spanish or (Provençal) may boast of its having produced such as first
cultivated in this, as in a more perfect and sweet language, the
vernacular poetry : among whom are Pierre d'Auvergne, and others
more ancient.   The privileges of the Latin, or Italian, are two ; first,
that it may reckon for its own those writers who have adopted a
more sweet and subtile style of poetry, in the number of whom are
Cino da Pistoia and his friend ; and the next, that its writers seem
to adhere to certain general rules of grammar, and in so doing give
it, in the opinion of the intelligent, a very weighty pretension to
preference."   Since the last edition of this book, it has appeared
that Mr. Gray understood by the words "Grammaticæ, quæ
communis est ;" "the Latin or mother-tongue," and not, as I have
rendered them, "general rules of grammar."   In this latter sense,
however, the word "Grammatica" has been used twice before in
the Treatise de Vulg. Eloq., though it is certainly afterwards
applied in the sense in which Gray took it.   See the edition of
Gray's Works, for which we are so much indebted to Mr. Mathias,
4to, London, 1814, vol. ii. p. 35.   We learn from our author's Vita
Nuova (§ 25) that there were no poetic compositions in the Provençal
or Italian, more than one hundred and fifty years before the Vita
Nuova was written ; and that the first who wrote in the vernacular
languages, wrote to make himself understood by a lady.   M.
Raynouard supposed the text of all the editions to be miserably
corrupted in this place, and took much pains to restore it.   I will
add the passage as that learned writer concluded it to have come
from the hand of Dante :—

> "Tan m'abellis vostre cortes deman,
>   Ch' ieu non me puesc ni m voil a vos cobrire ;
>   Jeu sui Arnautz, che plor e vai cantan ;
>   Consiros, vei la passada follor,
>   E vei jauzen lo joi qu'esper denan ;
>   Aras vos prec, per aquella valor
>   Que us guida al som sens freich e sens calina,
>   Sovegna vos atenprar ma dolor.

"Tant me plaît votre courtoise demande, — que je ne puis ni ne me
veux à vous cacher ;—je suis Arnaud, qui pleure et va chantant ;—
soucieux, je vois la passée folie,—et vois joyeux le bonheur, que
j'espère à l'avenir ;—maintenant je vous prie, par cette vertu—qui
vous guide au sommet, sans froid et sans chaud ; qu'il souvienne à
vous de soulager ma douleur.   Il n'est pas un des nombreux

Sorely waymenting for my folly past,
Thorough this ford of fire I wade, and see .
The day, I hope for, smiling in my view.
I pray ye by the worth that guides ye up
Unto the summit of the scale, in time
Remember ye my sufferings."   With such words
He disappear'd in the refining flame.

CANTO XXVII

ARGUMENT.

An angel sends them forward through the fire to the last ascent, which leads to the terrestrial Paradise, situated on the summit of the mountain.   They have not proceeded many steps on their way upward, when the fall of night hinders them from going further ; and our Poet, who has lain down with Virgil and Statius to rest, beholds in a dream two females, figuring the active and contemplative life. With the return of morning, they reach the height ; and here Virgil gives Dante full liberty to use his own pleasure and judgment in the choice of his way, till he shall meet with Beatrice.

Now was the sun[1] so station'd, as when first
His early radiance quivers on the heights,
Where stream'd his Maker's blood ; while Libra
    hangs

manuscrits de la Divina Commedia, pas une des éditions multipliées qui en ont été données, qui ne présente dans les vers que Dante prête au troubadour Arnaud Daniel, un texte défiguré et devenu, de copie en copie, presque inintelligible.   Cependant j'ai pensé qu'il n'était pas impossible de rétablir le texte de ces vers, en comparant avec soin. dans les manuscrits de Dante que possèdent les dépôts publics de Paris, toutes les variantes qu'ils pouvaient fournir, et en les choisissant d'après les régles grammaticales et les notions lexico-graphiques de la langue des troubadours.   Mon espoir n'a point été trompè, et sans aucun secours conjectural, sans aucun déplace-ment ni changement de mots, je suis parvenu, par le simple choix des variantes, à retrouver le texte primitif, tel qu'il a dú être produit par Dante."   Raynouard, Lexique Roman, tom. i. p. xlii. 8°.   Par. 1830.
    [1] *The sun.*]   At Jerusalem it was dawn, in Spain midnight, and in India noonday, while it was sunset in Purgatory.

Above Hesperian Ebro; and new fires,
Meridian, flash on Ganges' yellow tide.
  So day was sinking, when the angel of God
Appear'd before us.   Joy was in his mien.
Forth of the flame he stood upon the brink;
And with a voice, whose lively clearness far
Surpass'd our human, " Blessed [1] are the pure
In heart," he sang: then near him as we came,
"Go ye not further, holy spirits! " he cried,
" Ere the fire pierce you: enter in; and list
Attentive to the song ye hear from thence."
  I, when I heard his saying, was as one
Laid in the grave.[2]   My hands together clasp'd,
And upward stretching, on the fire I look'd;
And busy fancy conjured up the forms
Erewhile beheld alive consumed in flames.
  The escorting spirits turn'd with gentle looks
Toward me; and the Mantuan spake: " My son,
Here torment thou mayst feel, but canst not death.
Remember thee, remember thee, if I
Safe e'en on Geryon brought thee; now I come
More near to God, wilt thou not trust me now?
Of this be sure; though in its womb that flame
A thousand years contain'd thee, from thy head

[1] *Blessed.*]   Matt. v. 8.
[2] —— *As one*
  Laid in the grave.]   Quale è colui che nella fossa è messo.

Lombardi understands this of a man who is taken to execution in
the manner described in Hell, c. xix. 52.   " Colui," he thinks, cannot be properly applied to a corse.   Yet Boccaccio's imitation
confirms the opinion of the other commentators :—

  Essa era tale, a guardarla nel viso,
  Qual donna morta alla fossa portata.
                    Il Filostrato, p. v. st. 83.

which Chaucer has thus translated :—

  She was right soche to sene in her visage,
  As is that wight that men on bere ybinde.
                    Troilus and Creseide, b. iv.

No hair should perish.   If thou doubt my truth,
Approach; and with thy hands thy vesture's hem
Stretch forth, and for thyself confirm belief.
Lay now all fear, oh! lay all fear aside.
Turn hither, and come onward undismay'd."
  I still, though conscience urged, no step advanced.
  When still he saw me fix'd and obstinate,
Somewhat disturb'd he cried: " Mark now, my son,
From Beatrice thou art by this wall
Divided."   As at Thisbe's name the eye
Of Pyramus was open'd, (when life ebb'd
Fast from his veins,) and took one parting glance,
While vermeil dyed the mulberry;[1] thus I turn'd
To my sage guide, relenting, when I heard
The name that springs for ever in my breast.
  He shook his forehead; and, " How long," he said,
"Linger we now?" then smiled, as one would smile
Upon a child that eyes the fruit and yields.
Into the fire before me then he walk'd;
And Statius, who erewhile no little space
Had parted us, he pray'd to come behind.
  I would have cast me into molten glass
To cool me, when I enter'd; so intense
Raged the conflagrant mass.   The sire beloved,
To comfort me, as he proceeded, still
Of Beatrice talk'd.   " Her eyes," saith he,
" E'en now I seem to view."   From the other side
A voice, that sang, did guide us; and the voice
Following, with heedful ear, we issued forth,
There where the path led upward.   " Come, "[2] we heard,
    we heard,

---

[1] *While vermeil dyed the mulberry.*] Ovid, Metam. lib. iv. 125.
[2] *Come.*] Matt. xxv. 34.

"Come, blessed of my Father."   Such the sounds,
That hail'd us from within a light, which shone
So radiant, I could not endure the view.
"The sun," it added, "hastes: and evening comes.
Delay not: ere the western sky is hung
With blackness, strive ye for the pass."   Our way
Upright within the rock arose, and faced
Such part of heaven, that from before my steps
The beams were shrouded of the sinking sun.

    Nor many stairs were overpast, when now
By fading of the shadow we perceived
The sun behind us couch'd; and ere one face
Of darkness o'er its measureless expanse
Involved the horizon, and the night her lot
Held individual, each of us had made
A stair his pallet; not that will, but power,
Had fail'd us, by the nature of that mount
Forbidden further travel.   As the goats,
That late have skipt and wanton'd rapidly
Upon the craggy cliffs, ere they had ta'en
Their supper on the herb, now silent lie
And ruminate beneath the umbrage brown,
While noon-day rages; and the goatherd leans
Upon his staff, and leaning watches them:
And as the swain, that lodges out all night
In quiet by his flock, lest beast of prey
Disperse them: even so all three abode,
I as a goat, and as the shepherds they,
Close pent on either side by shelving rock.

    A little glimpse of sky was seen above;
Yet by that little I beheld the stars,
In magnitude and lustre shining forth
With more than wonted glory.   As I lay,
Gazing on them, and in that fit of musing,
Sleep overcame me, sleep, that bringeth oft

Tidings of future hap.   About the hour,
As I believe, when Venus from the east
First lighten'd on the mountain, she whose orb
Seems alway glowing with the fire of love,
A lady young and beautiful, I dream'd,
Was passing o'er a lea; and, as she came,
Methought I saw her ever and anon
Bending to cull the flowers; and thus she sang:
" Know ye, whoever of my name would ask,
That I am Leah:[1] for my brow to weave
A garland, these fair hands unwearied ply.
To please me[2] at the crystal mirror, here
I deck me.   But my sister Rachel, she[3]
Before her glass abides the livelong day,
Her radiant eyes beholding, charm'd no less,
Than I with this delightful task.   Her joy
In contemplation, as in labour mine."

    And now as glimmering dawn appear'd, that breaks
More welcome to the pilgrim still, as he
Sojourns less distant on his homeward way,
Darkness from all sides fled, and with it fled
My slumber; whence I rose, and saw my guide
Already risen.   " That delicious fruit,
Which through so many a branch the zealous care
Of mortals roams in quest of, shall this day
Appease thy hunger."   Such the words I heard
From Virgil's lip; and never greeting heard,
So pleasant as the sounds.   Within me straight

---

[1] *I am Leah.*] By Leah is understood the active life, as Rachel
figures the contemplative.   Michel Angelo has made these allegorical personages the subject of two statues on the monument of
Julius II. in the church of S. Pietro in Vincolo.   See Mr. Duppa's
Life of Michel Angelo, Sculpture viii. and x. and p. 247.

[2] *To please me.*] " For the sake of that enjoyment which I shall
have in beholding my God face to face, I thus exercise myself in
good works."

[3] *She.*] " Her delight is in admiring in her mirror, that is, in the
Supreme Being, the light, or knowledge, that He vouchsafes her."

Desire so grew upon desire to mount,
Thenceforward at each step I felt the wings
Increasing for my flight. When we had run
O'er all the ladder to its topmost round,
As there we stood, on me the Mantuan fix'd
His eyes, and thus he spake : "Both fires, my son,
The temporal and eternal, thou hast seen ;
And art arrived, where of itself my ken
No further reaches. I, with skill and art,
Thus far have drawn thee. Now thy pleasure take
For guide. Thou hast o'ercome the steeper way,
O'ercome the straiter. Lo ! the sun, that darts
His beam upon thy forehead : lo ! the herb,[1]
The arborets and flowers, which of itself
This land pours forth profuse. Till those bright eyes[2]
With gladness come, which, weeping, made me haste
To succour thee, thou mayst or seat thee down,
Or wander where thou wilt. Expect no more
Sanction of warning voice or sign from me,
Free of thy own arbitrement to chuse,
Discreet, judicious. To distrust thy sense
Were henceforth error. I invest thee then
With crown and mitre, sovereign o'er thyself."

[1] *Lo ! the herb.*] "In alium campum transit amœnissimum.—Ipse vero campus splendidus, suavis ac decorus quantæ magnitudinis, quantæ gloriæ, quantæque sit pulchritudinis, nulla lingua, nullusque sermo, potest enarrare : plenus est enim omni jucunditate, et gaudio, et lætitia. Ibi liliorum, et rosarum odor, ibi odoramentorum omnium redolet fragrantia, ibi mannæ, omniumque eternarum deliciarum redundat abundantia. In hujus campi medio paradisus est." Alberici Visio, § 20.
[2] *Those bright eyes.*] The eyes of Beatrice.

CANTO XXVIII

ARGUMENT

Dante wanders through the forest of the terrestrial Paradise, till he is stopped by a stream, on the other side of which he beholds a fair lady, culling flowers. He speaks to her; and she, in reply, explains to him certain things touching the nature of that place, and tells that the water, which flows between them, is here called Lethe, and in another place has the name of Eunoe.

THROUGH that celestial forest, whose thick shade
With lively greenness the new-springing day
Attemper'd, eager now to roam, and search
Its limits round, forthwith I left the bank;
Along the champain leisurely my way
Pursuing, o'er the ground, that on all sides
Delicious odour breathed.   A pleasant air,[1]
That intermitted never, never veer'd,
Smote on my temples, gently, as a wind
Of softest influence: at which the sprays,
Obedient all, lean'd trembling to that part[2]
Where first the holy mountain casts his shade;
Yet were not so disorder'd, but that still

---

[1] *A pleasant air.*]

> Cantan fra i rami gli augelletti vaghi,
> Azzurri, e bianchi, e verdi, e rossi, e gialli;
> Mormoranti ruscelli, e cheti laghi
> Di limpidezza vincono i cristalli.
> Una dolc' aura, che ti par che vaghi
> A un modo sempre, e dal suo stil non falli,
> Facea sì l'aria tremolar d'intorno,
> Che non potea nojar calor del giorno.
> *Ariosto, Orl. Fur.* c. xxxiv. st. 50.

> Therewith a winde, unnethe it might be less,
> Made in the levis grene a noise soft,
> Accordant to the foulis song on loft.
> *Chaucer, The Assemble of Foules.*

[2] *To that part.*] The west.

Upon their top the feather'd quiristers[1]
Applied their wonted art, and with full joy
Welcomed those hours of prime, and warbled
    shrill
Amid the leaves, that to their jocund lays
Kept tenour; even as from branch to branch,
Along the piny forests on the shore
Of Chiassi,[2] rolls the gathering melody,
When Eolus hath from his cavern loosed
The dripping south. Already had my steps,
Though slow, so far into that ancient wood
Transported me, I could not ken the place
Where I had enter'd; when, behold! my path
Was bounded by a rill, which, to the left,
With little rippling waters bent the grass
That issued from its brink. On earth no wave,
How clean soe'er, that would not seem to have
Some mixture in itself, compared with this,
Transpicuous clear; yet darkly on it roll'd,
Darkly beneath perpetual gloom, which ne'er
Admits or sun or moon-light there to shine.

  My feet advanced not; but my wondering eyes
Pass'd onward, o'er the streamlet, to survey
The tender may-bloom, flush'd through many a
    hue,
In prodigal variety: and there,
As object, rising suddenly to view,
That from our bosom every thought beside

---

1 *The feather'd quiristers.*] Imitated by Boccaccio, Fiammetta, lib. iv. "Odi i queruli uccelli," etc.—"Hear the querulous birds plaining with sweet songs, and the boughs trembling and moved by a gentle wind, as it were keeping tenour to their notes.

2 *Chiassi.*] This is the wood, where the scene of Boccaccio's sublimest story (taken entirely from Elinand, as I learn in the notes to the Decameron, Ediz. Giunti, 1573, p. 62) is laid. See Dec. G. 5, N. 8, and Dryden's Theodore and Honoria. Our Poet perhaps wandered in it during his abode with Guido Novello da Polenta.

With the rare marvel chases, I beheld
A lady [1] all alone, who, singing, went,
And culling flower from flower, wherewith her
    way
Was all o'er painted. "Lady beautiful!
Thou, who (if looks, that use to speak the heart,
Are worthy of our trust) with love's own beam
Dost warm thee," thus to her my speech I
    framed;
"Ah! please thee hither towards the streamlet
    bend
Thy steps so near, that I may list thy song.
Beholding thee and this fair place, methinks,
I call to mind where wander'd and how look'd
Proserpine, in that season, when her child
The mother lost, and she the bloomy spring."

    As when a lady, turning in the dance,
Doth foot it featly, and advances scarce
One step before the other to the ground;
Over the yellow and vermilion flowers
Thus turn'd she at my suit, most maiden-like
Valing her sober eyes; and came so near,
That I distinctly caught the dulcet sound.
Arriving where the limpid waters now
Laved the green swerd, her eyes she deign'd to
    raise,
That shot such splendour on me, as I ween

<hr>

[1] *A lady*.] Most of the commentators suppose, that by this lady, who in the last Canto is called Matilda, is to be understood the Countess Matilda, who endowed the holy see with the estates called the Patrimony of St. Peter, and died in 1115. See G. Villani, lib. iv. cap. xx. But it seems more probable that she should be intended for an allegorical personage. Venturi accordingly supposes that she represents the active life. But, as Lombardi justly observes, we have had that already shadowed forth in the character of Leah; and he therefore suggests, that by Matilda may be understood that affection which we ought to bear towards the holy church, and for which the lady above mentioned was so remarkable.

Ne'er glanced from Cytherea's, when her son
Had sped his keenest weapon to her heart.
Upon the opposite bank she stood and smiled;
As through her graceful fingers shifted still
The intermingling dyes, which without seed
That lofty land unbosoms.   By the stream
Three paces only were we sunder'd: yet,
The Hellespont, where Xerxes pass'd it o'er,
(A curb for ever to the pride of man,[1])
Was by Leander not more hateful held
For floating, with inhospitable wave,
'Twixt Sestus and Abydos, than by me
That flood, because it gave no passage thence.
   " Strangers ye come; and haply in this place,
That cradled human nature in her birth,
Wondering, ye not without suspicion view
My smiles: but that sweet strain of psalmody,
' Thou, Lord! hast made me glad,' [2] will give ye
     light,
Which may uncloud your minds.   And thou, who
     stand'st
The foremost, and didst make thy suit to me,
Say if aught else thou wish to hear: for I
Came prompt to answer every doubt of thine."
   She spake; and I replied: "I know not how [3]
To reconcile this wave, and rustling sound
Of forest leaves, with what I late have heard
Of opposite report."   She answering thus:
" I will unfold the cause, whence that proceeds,
Which makes thee wonder; and so purge the cloud

---

[1] *A curb for ever to the pride of man.*]   Because Xerxes had
been so humbled, when he was compelled to repass the Hellespont
in one small bark, after having a little before crossed with a pro-
digious army, in the hopes of subduing Greece.
   [2] *Thou, Lord! hast made me glad.*]   Psalm xcii. 4.
   [3] *I know not how.*]   See Canto xxi. 45.

That hath enwrapt thee.   The First Good, whose
    joy
Is only in himself, created man,
For happiness; and gave this goodly place,
His pledge and earnest of eternal peace.
Favour'd thus highly, through his own defect
He fell; and here made short sojourn; he fell,
And, for the bitterness of sorrow, changed
Laughter unblamed and ever-new delight.
That vapours none, exhaled from earth beneath,
Or from the waters, (which, wherever heat
Attracts them, follow,) might ascend thus far
To vex man's peaceful state, this mountain rose
So high toward the heaven, nor fears the rage
Of elements contending; [1] from that part
Exempted, where the gate his limit bars.
Because the circumambient air, throughout,
With its first impulse circles still, unless
Aught interpose to check or thwart its course;
Upon the summit, which on every side
To visitation of the impassive air
Is open, doth that motion strike, and makes
Beneath its sway the umbrageous wood resound:
And in the shaken plant such power resides,
That it impregnates with its efficacy
The voyaging breeze, upon whose subtle plume
That, wafted, flies abroad; and the other land, [2]
Receiving, (as 'tis worthy in itself,

[1] *Of elements contending*.]   In the Dittamondo of Fazio degli
Uberti, l. i. cap. xi., there is a description of the terrestrial
Paradise, in which the poet has had Dante before him.

[2] *The other land*.]   The continent, inhabited by the living, and
separated from Purgatory by the ocean, is affected (and that
diversely, according to the nature of the soil, or the climate) by a
virtue, or efficacy, conveyed to it by the winds from plants growing
in the terrestrial Paradise, which is situated on the summit of
Purgatory; and this is the cause why some plants are found on
earth without any apparent seed to produce them.

Or in the clime, that warms it,) doth conceive ;
And from its womb produces many a tree
Of various virtue.   This when thou hast heard,
The marvel ceases, if in yonder earth
Some plant, without apparent seed, be found
To fix its fibrous stem.   And further learn,
That with prolific foison of all seeds
This holy plain is fill'd, and in itself
Bears fruit that ne'er was pluck'd on other soil.
  "The water, thou behold'st, springs not from vein,
Restored by vapour, that the cold converts ;
As stream that intermittently repairs
And spends his pulse of life ; but issues forth
From fountain, solid, undecaying, sure :
And, by the will omnific, full supply
Feeds whatsoe'er on either side it pours ;
On this, devolved with power to take away
Remembrance of offence ; on that, to bring
Remembrance back of every good deed done.
From whence its name of Lethe on this part ;
On the other, Eunoe : both of which must first
Be tasted, ere it work ; the last exceeding
All flavours else.   Albeit thy thirst may now
Be well contented, if I here break off,
No more revealing ; yet a corollary
I freely give beside : nor deem my words
Less grateful to thee, if they somewhat pass
The stretch of promise.   They, whose verse of yore
The golden age recorded and its bliss,
On the Parnassian mountain,[1] of this place
Perhaps had dream'd.   Here was man guiltless ; here

---

[1] *On the Parnassian mountain.*]
    In bicipiti somniasse Parnasso.   *Persius, Prol.*

Perpetual spring,[1] and every fruit; and this
The far-famed nectar." Turning to the bards,
When she had ceased, I noted in their looks
A smile at her conclusion; then my face
Again directed to the lovely dame.

CANTO XXIX

ARGUMENT

The lady, who in a following Canto is called Matilda, moves along the side of the stream in a contrary direction to the current, and Dante keeps equal pace with her on the opposite bank. A marvellous sight, preceded by music, appears in view.

SINGING,[2] as if enamour'd, she resumed
And closed the song, with "Blessed they[3] whose
    sins
Are cover'd." Like the wood-nymphs then, that
    tripp'd
Singly across the sylvan shadows; one
Eager to view, and one to escape the sun;
So moved she on, against the current, up
The verdant rivage. I, her mincing step
Observing, with as tardy step pursued.
    Between us not an hundred paces trod,
The bank, on each side bending equally,
Gave me to face the orient. Nor our way

---

[1] *Perpetual spring.*]

> Ver erat æternum, placidique tepentibus auris
> Mulcebant zephyri natos sine semine flores.
>
> . . . .
>
> Flumina jam lactis, jam flumina nectaris ibant.
> *Ovid, Metam.* lib. i. v. 111.

[2] *Singing.*] Cantava come fosse innamorata.
    Guido Cavalcanti, Poeti del primo secolo, v. 2, p. 233.

Blessed they.] Psalm xxxii. 1.

Far onward brought us, when to me at once
She turn'd, and cried: "My brother! look, and
  hearken."
And lo! a sudden lustre ran across
Through the great forest on all parts, so bright,
I doubted whether lightning were abroad;
But that, expiring ever in the spleen
That doth unfold it, and this during still,
And waxing still in splendour, made me question
What it might be: and a sweet melody
Ran through the luminous air.   Then did I chide,
With warrantable zeal, the hardihood
Of our first parent; for that there, where earth
Stood in obedience to the heavens, she only,
Woman, the creature of an hour, endured not
Restraint of any veil, which had she borne
Devoutly, joys, ineffable as these,
Had from the first, and long time since, been mine.

  While, through that wilderness of primy sweets
That never fade, suspense I walk'd, and yet
Expectant of beatitude more high;
Before us, like a blazing fire, the air
Under the green boughs glow'd; and, for a song,
Distinct the sound of melody was heard.

  O ye thrice holy virgins! for your sakes
If e'er I suffer'd hunger, cold, and watching,
Occasion calls on me to crave your bounty.
Now through my breast let Helicon his stream
Pour copious, and Urania[1] with her choir
Arise to aid me; while the verse unfolds
Things, that do almost mock the grasp of thought.

---

[1] *Urania.*] Landino observes, that intending to sing of heavenly
things, he rightly invokes Urania. Thus Milton:

> Descend from Heaven, Urania, by that name
> If rightly thou art call'd.   *P. L.* b. vii. 1.

Onward a space, what seem'd seven trees of gold
The intervening distance to mine eye
Falsely presented ; but, when I was come
So near them, that no lineament was lost
Of those, with which a doubtful object, seen
Remotely, plays on the misdeeming sense ;
Then did the faculty, that ministers
Discourse to reason, these for tapers of gold [1]
Distinguish ; and i' the singing trace the sound
"Hosanna."   Above, their beauteous garniture
Flamed with more ample lustre, than the moon
Through cloudless sky at midnight, in her noon.

I turn'd me, full of wonder, to my guide ;
And he did answer with a countenance
Charged with no less amazement : whence my view
Reverted to those lofty things, which came
So slowly moving towards us, that the bride [2]
Would have outstript them on her bridal day.

The lady call'd aloud : "Why thus yet burns
Affection in thee for these living lights,
And dost not look on that which follows them ? "

I straightway mark'd a tribe behind them walk,
As if attendant on their leaders, clothed
With raiment of such whiteness, as on earth
Was never.   On my left, the watery gleam
Borrow'd, and gave me back, when there I look'd,
As in a mirror, my left side portray'd.

---

[1] *Tapers of gold.*] See Rev. i. 12. The commentators are not
agreed whether the seven sacraments of the Church, or the seven
gifts of the Spirit are intended. In his Convito (iv. 21), our author
says : "Because these gifts proceed from ineffable charity, and
divine charity is appropriated to the Holy Spirit, hence, also, it is
that they are called gifts of the Holy Spirit, the which, as Isaiah
distinguishes them, are seven."

[2] *The bride.*] E come va per via sposa novella
    A passi rari, e porta gli occhi bassi
    Con faccia vergognosa, e non favella.
       Frezzi, Il Quadrir. lib. i. cap. 16.

When I had chosen on the river's edge
Such station, that the distance of the stream
Alone did separate me; there I stay'd
My steps for clearer prospect, and beheld
The flames go onward, leaving,[1] as they went,
The air behind them painted as with trail
Of liveliest pencils;[2] so distinct were mark'd
All those seven listed colours,[3] whence the sun
Maketh his bow, and Cynthia her zone.
These streaming gonfalons did flow beyond
My vision; and ten paces,[4] as I guess,
Parted the outermost. Beneath a sky
So beautiful, came four and twenty elders,[5]
By two and two, with flower-de-luces crown'd.

[1] *Leaving.*] Lasciando dietro a se l'aer dipinto.
        Che lascia dietro a se l'aria dipinta.
    Mr. Mathias's Ode to Mr. Nichols, Gray's Works,
                            vol. i. p. 532.

[2] *Pencils.*] Since this translation was made, Perticari has affixed
another sense to the word, "pennelli," which he interprets
"pennons" or "streamers." Monti, in his Proposta, highly
applauds the discovery. The conjecture loses something of its
probability, if we read the whole passage, not as Monti gives it,
but as it stands in Landino's edition of 1484.

        Et vidi le fiamelle andar davante
            lasciando drieto a se laire dipinto
            che di tratti pennegli havea sembiante
        Siche li sopra rimanea distinto
            di sette liste tutte in que colori
            onde fa larcho el sole & delia elcinto.

[3] *Listed colours.*] Di sette liste tutte in quei colori, etc.

                —— a bow
        Conspicuous with three listed colours gay.
                        Milton, P. L. b. xi. 865.

[4] *Ten paces.*] For an explanation of the allegorical meaning of
this mysterious procession, Venturi refers those, "who would see in
the dark," to the commentaries of Landino, Vellutello, and others;
and adds, that it is evident the Poet has accommodated to his own
fancy many sacred images in the Apocalypse. In Vasari's Life of
Giotto, we learn that Dante recommended that book to his friend,
as affording fit subjects for his pencil.
[5] *Four and twenty elders.*] "Upon the seats I saw four and
twenty elders sitting." Rev. iv. 4.

All sang one song : " Blessed be thou [1] among
The daughters of Adam ! and thy loveliness
Blessed for ever ! "   After that the flowers,
And the fresh herblets, on the opposite brink,
Were free from that elected race ; as light
In heaven doth second light, came after them
Four [2] animals, each crown'd with verdurous leaf.
With six wings each was plumed ; the plumage full
Of eyes ; and the eyes of Argus would be such,
Were they endued with life.   Reader ! more rhymes
I will not waste in shadowing forth their form :
For other need so straitens, that in this
I may not give my bounty room.   But read
Ezekiel ; [3] for he paints them, from the north
How he beheld them come by Chebar's flood,
In whirlwind, cloud, and fire ; and even such
As thou shalt find them character'd by him,
Here were they ; save as to the pennons : there,
From him departing, John [4] accords with me.
   The space, surrounded by the four, enclosed

[1] *Blessed be thou.*] " Blessed art thou among women, and blessed
is the fruit of thy womb."   Luke i. 42.
   [2] *Four.*]   The four evangelists.
   [3] *Ezekiel.*]   " And I looked, and behold, a whirlwind came out
of the north, a great cloud, and a fire infolding itself, and a brightness was about it, and out of the midst thereof as the colour of
amber, out of the midst of the fire.   Also out of the midst thereof
came the likeness of four living creatures.   And this was their
appearance ; they had the likeness of a man.   And every one had
four faces, and every one had four wings."   Ezekiel i. 4, 5, 6.
   [4] *John.*]   " And the four beasts had each of them six wings about
him."   Rev. iv. 8.   " Aliter senas alas propter senarii numeri
perfectionem positum arbitror ; quia in sexta ætate, id est
adveniente plenitudine temporum, hæc Apostolus peracta com-
memorat ; in novissimo enim animali conclusit omnia."   Primasii,
Augustini discipuli, Episcopi Comment. lib. quinque in Apocal.
Ed. Basil. 1544.   " With this interpretation it is very consonant that
Ezekiel discovered in these animals only four wings, because his
prophecy does not extend beyond the fourth age ; beyond that is
the end of the synagogue and the calling of the Gentiles : whereas
Dante beholding them in the sixth age, saw them with six wings,
as did Saint John."   Lombardi.

A car triumphal :[1] on two wheels it came,
Drawn at a Gryphon's [2] neck ; and he above
Stretch'd either wing uplifted, 'tween the midst
And the three listed hues, on each side, three ;
So that the wings did cleave or injure none ;
And out of sight they rose.   The members, far
As he was bird, were golden ; white the rest,
With vermeil intervein'd.   So beautiful [3]
A car, in Rome, ne'er graced Augustus' pomp,
Or Africanus' : e'en the sun's itself
Were poor to this ; that chariot of the sun,
Erroneous, which in blazing ruin fell
At Tellus' prayer [4] devout, by the just doom
Mysterious of all-seeing Jove.   Three nymphs,[5]
At the right wheel, came circling in smooth dance :
The one so ruddy, that her form had scarce
Been known within a furnace of clear flame ;
The next did look, as if the flesh and bones
Were emerald ; snow new-fallen seem'd the third.
Now seem'd the white to lead, the ruddy now ;
And from her song who led, the others took

[1] *A car triumphal.*]   Either the Christian church, or perhaps the Papal chair.
[2] *Gryphon.*]   Under the gryphon, an imaginary creature, the fore-part of which is an eagle, and the hinder a lion, is shadowed forth the union of the divine and the human nature in Jesus Christ.

[3] *So beautiful.*]   E certo quando Roma più onore
Di carro trionfale a Scipione
Fece, non fu cotal, nè di splendore
Passato fu da quello, il qual Fetone
Abbandonò per soverchio tremore.
            Boccaccio, Teseide, lib. ix. st. 31.

Thus in the Quadriregio, lib. i. cap. 5.

        Mai vide Roma carro trionfante
        Quanto era questo bel, ne vedrà unquanco.

[4] *Tellus' prayer.*]   Ovid, Met. lib. ii. v. 279.
[5] *Three nymphs.*]   The three evangelical virtues : the first Charity, the next Hope, and the third Faith.   Faith may be produced by charity, or charity by faith, but the inducements to hope must arise either from one or other of these.

13

Their measure, swift or slow.   At the other wheel,
A band quaternion,[1] each in purple clad,
Advanced with festal step, as, of them, one
The rest conducted ;[2] one, upon whose front
Three eyes were seen.   In rear of all this group,
Two old men[3] I beheld, dissimilar
In raiment, but in port and gesture like,
Solid and mainly grave ; of whom, the one
Did show himself some favour'd counsellor
Of the great Coan,[4] him, whom nature made
To serve the costliest creature of her tribe :
His fellow mark'd an opposite intent ;
Bearing a sword, whose glitterance and keen edge,
E'en as I viewed it with the flood between,
Appall'd me.   Next, four others[5] I beheld
Of humble seeming : and, behind them all,
One single old man,[6] sleeping as he came,

[1] *A band quaternion.*]   The four moral or cardinal virtues, of whom Prudence directs the others.

[2]   —— *One*
The rest conducted.]   Prudence, described with three eyes, because she regards the past, the present, and the future.

[3] *Two old men.*]   Saint Luke, the physician, characterised as the writer of the Acts of the Apostles, and Saint Paul, represented with a sword, on account, as it should seem, of the power of his style.

[4] *Of the great Coan.*]   Hippocrates, "whom nature made for the benefit of her favourite creature, man."

[5] *Four others.*]   "The commentators," says Venturi, "suppose these four to be the four evangelists ; but I should rather take them to be four principal doctors of the church."   Yet both Landino and Vellutello expressly call them the authors of the epistles, James, Peter, John, and Jude.

[6] *One single old man.*]   As some say, Saint John, under the character of the author of the Apocalypse.   But, in the poem attributed to Giacopo, the son of our Poet, which in some MSS. and in one of the earliest editions, accompanies the original of this work, and is descriptive of its plan, this old man is said to be Moses.

> E'l vecchio, ch' era dietro a tutti loro,
> Fu Moyse.

> And the old man, who was behind them all,
> Was Moses.

See No. 3459 of the Harl. MSS. in the British Museum.

With a shrewd visage.   And these seven, each
Like the first troop were habited ; but wore
No braid of lilies on their temples wreathed.
Rather, with roses and each vermeil flower,
A sight, but little distant, might have sworn,
That they were all on fire [1] above their brow.

    Whenas the car was o'er against me, straight
Was heard a thundering, at whose voice it seem'd
The chosen multitude were stay'd ; for there,
With the first ensigns, made they solemn halt.

CANTO XXX

ARGUMENT

Beatrice descends from heaven, and rebukes the Poet.

Soon as that polar light,[2] fair ornament
Of the first heaven, which hath never known
Setting nor rising, nor the shadowy veil
Of other cloud than sin, to duty there
Each one convoying, as that lower doth
The steersman to his port, stood firmly fix'd ;
Forthwith the saintly tribe, who in the van
Between the Gryphon and its radiance came,
Did turn them to the car, as to their rest :
And one, as if commission'd from above,
In holy chant thrice shouted forth aloud ;

---

[1] *All on fire.*]   So Giles Fletcher,

> The wood's late wintry head
> With flaming primroses set all on fire.
>   *Christ's Triumph after Death.*

[2] *That polar light.*]   The seven candlesticks of gold, which he
calls the polar light of heaven itself, because they perform the same
office for Christians that the polar star does for mariners, in guiding
them to their port

" Come,[1] spouse ! from Libanus : " and all the rest
Took up the song.—At the last audit, so
The blest shall rise, from forth his cavern each
Uplifting lightly his new-vested flesh ;
As, on the sacred litter, at the voice
Authoritative of that elder, sprang
A hundred ministers and messengers
Of life eternal.   " Blessed [2] thou, who comest ! "
And, " Oh ! " they cried, " from full hands [3]
    scatter ye
Unwithering lilies : " and, so saying, cast
Flowers over head and round them on all sides.
    I have beheld, ere now, at break of day,
The eastern clime all roseate ; and the sky
Opposed, one deep and beautiful serene ;
And the sun's face so shaded, and with mists
Attemper'd, at his rising, that the eye
Long while endured the sight : thus, in a cloud
Of flowers,[4] that from those hands angelic rose,
And down within and outside of the car
Fell showering, in white veil with olive wreathed,
A virgin in my view appear'd, beneath
Green mantle, robed in hue of living flame :

[1] *Come.*] " Come with me from Lebanon, my spouse, with me, from Lebanon."   Song of Solomon iv. 8.
[2] *Blessed.*]   " Blessed is he that cometh in the name of the Lord."   Matt. xxi. 9.
[3] *From full hands.*]   Manibus date lilia plenis.
                            Virg. Æn. lib. vi. 884.
[4] —— *In a cloud*
    Of flowers.]   Dentro una nuvola di fiori.

               —— ninguntque rosarum.
    Floribus, umbrantes matrem, etc.   *Lucretius,* lib. ii.
Thus Milton :
              —— Eve separate he spies,
    Veil'd in a cloud of fragrance, where she stood.
                     P. L. b. ix. v. 425.
And Thomson, in his Invocation to Spring :
             —— veil'd in a shower
    Of shadowing roses, on our plains descend.

And [1] o'er my spirit, that so long a time
Had from her presence felt no shuddering dread,
Albeit mine eyes discern'd her not, there moved
A hidden virtue from her, at whose touch
The power of ancient love [2] was strong within me.
    No sooner on my vision streaming, smote
The heavenly influence, which, years past, and e'en
In childhood, thrill'd me, than towards Virgil I
Turn'd me to leftward; panting, like a babe,
That flees for refuge to his mother's breast,
If aught have terrified or work'd him woe:
And would have cried, "There is no dram of
    blood,
That doth not quiver in me.   The old flame [3]
Throws out clear tokens of reviving fire."
But Virgil had bereaved us of himself;

[1] *And.*]   In the first edition it stood thus:

> And o'er my spirit, that in former days
> Within her presence had abode so long,
> No shuddering terror crept.   Mine eyes no more
> Had knowledge of her ; yet there moved from her
> A hidden virtue, at whose touch awaked, etc.,

and this was a translation of the common reading, which has "con la sua presenza," instead of "che alla sua presenza," and a full stop instead of a comma after "infranto."   As I have little doubt but that the reading of the Nidobeatina edition and that of many MSS. is right in this instance, I have altered the version as it now stands in the text, which still perhaps needs some explanation.   His spirit, which had been so long unawed by the presence of Beatrice (for she had been ten years dead) now felt, through a secret influence proceeding from her, its ancient love revived, though his sight had not yet distinguished her.

[2] *The power of ancient love.*]

> D'antico amor sentì la gran potenza.
> Io sento sì d'amor la gran possanza.
> > *Dante, Canzone* vi.

> Sveglia d'antico amor la gran possanza.
> > *Mr. Mathias's Ode to Mr. Nichols, Gray's Works,*
> > 4to, 1814, vol. i. p. 532.

[3] *The old flame.*]   Agnosco veteris vestigia flammæ.
> > *Virg. Æn.* lib. iv. 23.

> Conosco i segni dell' antico fuoco.
> > *Giusto de' Conti, La Bella Mano.*

Virgil, my best-loved father ; Virgil, he
To whom I gave me up for safety : nor [1]
All, our prime mother lost, avail'd to save
My undew'd cheeks from blur of soiling tears.
    "Dante ! weep not that Virgil leaves thee ; nay,
Weep thou not yet : behoves thee feel the edge
Of other sword ; and thou shalt weep for that."
    As to the prow or stern, some admiral
Paces the deck, inspiriting his crew,
When 'mid the sail-yards all hands ply aloof ;
Thus, on the left side of the car, I saw
(Turning me at the sound of mine own name,
Which here I am compell'd to register)
The virgin station'd, who before appear'd
Veil'd in that festive shower angelical.
    Towards me, across the stream, she bent her
        eyes ;
Though from her brow the veil descending, bound
With foliage of Minerva, suffer'd not
That I beheld her clearly : then with act
Full royal, still insulting o'er her thrall,
Added, as one who, speaking, keepeth back
The bitterest saying, to conclude the speech :
"Observe me well.   I am, in sooth, I am
Beatrice.   What ! and hast thou deign'd at last
Approach the mountain ?   Knewest not, O man !
Thy happiness is here ?"   Down fell mine eyes
On the clear fount ; but there, myself espying,
Recoil'd, and   sought   the   greenswerd ;   such   a
        weight
Of shame was on my forehead.   With a mien
Of that stern majesty, which doth surround
A mother's presence to her awe-struck child,

---

[1] *Nor.*] "Not all the beauties of the terrestrial Paradise in
which I was, were sufficient to allay my grief."

She look'd; a flavour of such bitterness
Was mingled in her pity.   There her words
Brake off; and suddenly the angels sang,
"In thee, O gracious Lord! my hope hath
      been:"
But [1] went no further than, "Thou, Lord! hast
      set
My feet in ample room."   As snow, that lies,
Amidst the living rafters [2] on the back
Of Italy, congeal'd, when drifted high
And closely piled by rough Sclavonian blasts;
Breathe but the land whereon no shadow falls, [3]
And straightway melting it distils away,
Like a fire-wasted taper: thus was I,
Without a sigh or tear, or ever these
Did sing, that, with the chiming of heaven's
      sphere,
Still in their warbling chime: but when the strain
Of dulcet symphony express'd for me
Their soft compassion, more than could the words,
"Virgin! why so consumest him?" then, the ice [4]
Congeal'd about my bosom, turn'd itself
To spirit and water; and with anguish forth
Gush'd, through the lips and eyelids, from the
      heart.

[1] *But.*] They sang the thirty-first Psalm, to the end of the eighth verse. What follows in that Psalm would not have suited the place or the occasion.

[2] *The living rafters.*] "Vive travi." The leafless woods on the Apennine.

Fraxineæque trabes.   *Virg. Æn.* lib. vi. 181.

      and

Trabibusque obscurus acernis.   *Ibid.* lib. ix. 87.

[3] *The land whereon no shadow falls.*] "When the wind blows from off Africa, where, at the time of the equinox, bodies, being under the equator, cast little or no shadow; or, in other words, when the wind is south."

[4] *The ice.*] Milton has transferred this conceit, though scarcely worth the pains of removing, into one of his Italian poems, Son. v.

Upon the chariot's same edge [1] still she stood,
Immoveable ; and thus address'd her words
To those bright semblances with pity touch'd :
" Ye in the eternal day your vigils keep ;
So that nor night nor slumber, with close stealth,
Conveys from you a single step, in all
The goings on of time : thence, with more heed
I shape mine answer, for his ear intended,
Who there stands weeping ; that the sorrow now
May equal the transgression.   Not alone
Through operation of the mighty orbs,
That mark each seed to some predestined aim,
As with aspect or fortunate or ill
The constellations meet ; but through benign
Largess of heavenly graces, which rain down
From such a height as mocks our vision, this man
Was, in the freshness of his being,[2] such,
So gifted virtually, that in him
All better habits wonderously had thrived.
The more of kindly strength is in the soil,
So much doth evil seed and lack of culture
Mar it the more, and make it run to wildness.
These looks sometime upheld him ; for I show'd
My youthful eyes, and led him by their light
In upright walking.   Soon as I had reach'd
The threshold of my second age,[3] and changed
My mortal for immortal ; then he left me,

---

[1] *Same edge.*]   The Nidobeatina edition, and many MSS., here
read "*detta* coscia," instead of "destra," or "dritta coscia ;" and
it is probable from what has gone before, that the former is the
right reading.   See v. 60.

[2] *In the freshness of his being.*]   Nella sua vita nuova.
Some suppose our Poet alludes to the work so called, written in his
youth.

[3] *The threshold of my second age.*]   In the Convito (iv. 24), our
Poet makes a division of human life into four ages, the first of
which lasts till the twenty-fifth year.   Beatrice, therefore, passed
from this life to a better, about that period.

And gave himself to others.   When from flesh
To spirit I had risen, and increase
Of beauty and of virtue circled me,
I was less dear to him, and valued less.
His steps were turn'd into deceitful ways,
Following false images of good, that make
No promise perfect.   Nor avail'd me aught
To sue for inspirations, with the which,
I, both in dreams of night, and otherwise,
Did call him back ; of them, so little reck'd him.
Such depth he fell, that all device was short
Of his preserving, save that he should view
The children of perdition.   To this end
I visited the purlieus of the dead :
And one, who hath conducted him thus high,
Received my supplications urged with weeping.
It were a breaking of God's high decree,
If Lethe should be past, and such food [1] tasted,
Without the cost of some repentant tear."

CANTO XXXI 

ARGUMENT

Beatrice continues her reprehension of Dante, who confesses his
error, and falls to the ground : coming to himself again, he is by
Matilda drawn through the waters of Lethe, and presented first to
the four virgins who figure the cardinal virtues ; these in their turn
lead him to the Gryphon, a symbol of our Saviour ; and the three
virgins, representing the evangelical virtues, intercede for him with
Beatrice, that she would display to him her second beauty.

"O thou ! " her words she thus without delay
Resuming, turn'd their point on me, to whom

[1] *Such food.*]   The oblivion of sins.

They, with but lateral edge,[1] seem'd harsh before:
" Say thou, who stand'st beyond the holy stream,
If this be true.   A charge, so grievous, needs
Thine own avowal."   On my faculty
Such strange amazement hung, the voice expired
Imperfect, ere its organs gave it birth.
    A little space refraining, then she spake:
" What dost thou muse on?   Answer me.   The
        wave
On thy remembrances of evil yet
Hath done no injury."   A mingled sense
Of fear and of confusion, from my lips
Did such a " Yea " produce, as needed help
Of vision to interpret.   As when breaks,
In act to be discharged, a cross-bow bent
Beyond its pitch, both nerve and bow o'erstretch'd ;
The flagging weapon feebly hits the mark :
Thus, tears and sighs forth gushing, did I burst,
Beneath the heavy load : and thus my voice
Was slacken'd on its way.   She straight began :
" When my desire invited thee to love
The good, which sets a bound to our aspirings ;
What bar of thwarting foss or linked chain
Did meet thee, that thou so shouldst quit the hope
Of further progress ? or what bait of ease,
Or promise of allurement, led thee on
Elsewhere, that thou elsewhere shouldst rather
        wait ? "
    A bitter sigh I drew, then scarce found voice
To answer ; hardly to these sounds my lips
Gave utterance, wailing : " Thy fair looks with-
        drawn,

---

[1] *With but lateral edge.*]   The words of Beatrice, when not
addressed directly to himself, but spoken to the angel of him, Dante
had thought sufficiently harsh.

Things present, with deceitful pleasures, turn'd
My steps aside."   She answering spake : " Hadst
    thou
Been silent, or denied what thou avow'st,
Thou hadst not hid thy sin the more ; such eye
Observes it.   But whene'er the sinner's cheek
Breaks forth into the precious-streaming tears
Of self-accusing, in our court the wheel
Of justice doth run counter to the edge.[1]
Howe'er, that thou mayst profit by thy shame
For errors past, and that henceforth more strength
May arm thee, when thou hear'st the Syren-voice ;
Lay thou aside the motive to this grief,
And lend attentive ear, while I unfold
How opposite a way my buried flesh
Should have impell'd thee.   Never didst thou spy,
In art or nature, aught so passing sweet,
As were the limbs that in their beauteous frame
Enclosed me, and are scatter'd now in dust.
If sweetest thing thus fail'd thee with my death,
What, afterward, of mortal, should thy wish
Have tempted ? When thou first hadst felt the
    dart
Of perishable things, in my departing
For better realms, thy wing thou shouldst have
    pruned
To follow me ; and never stoop'd again,
To 'bide a second blow, for a slight girl,[2]

---

[1] *Counter to the edge.*] " The weapons of divine justice are
blunted by the confession and sorrow of the offender."

[2] *For a slight girl.*] " Daniello and Venturi say that this alludes
to Gentucca of Lucca, mentioned in the twenty-fourth Canto.
They did not, however, observe that Buonaggiunta there gives us
to understand that Dante knew not if Gentucca were then in the
world, and that Beatrice is now reprehending him for past and not
for future errors." Thus Lombardi. Pelli (Memor. p. 57) acquaints
us that Corbinelli, in the Life of Dante, added to the edition of the
De Vulg. Eloq., says the name of this lady was " Pargoletta."

Or other gaud as transient and as vain.
The new and inexperienced bird[1] awaits,
Twice it may be, or thrice, the fowler's aim;
But in the sight of one whose plumes are full,
In vain the net is spread, the arrow wing'd."
  I stood, as children silent and ashamed
Stand, listening, with their eyes upon the earth,
Acknowledging their fault, and self-condemn'd.
And she resumed: "If, but to hear, thus pains
      thee;
Raise thou thy beard, and lo! what sight shall
      do."
  With less reluctance yields a sturdy holm,
Rent from its fibres by a blast, that blows
From off the pole, or from Iarbas' land,[2]
Than I at her behest my visage raised:
And thus the face denoting by the beard,[3]
I mark'd the secret sting her words convey'd.
  No sooner lifted I mine aspect up,

But the intimation, as Pelli justly remarks, can scarcely be deemed
authentic. The annotator on the Monte Casino MS. gives a very
different turn to the allusion. "Quæ proca fuit, etc." "This
was either a mistress; or else it is put for the poetic art, as when
he says in a certain song :

> Io mi son pargoletta bella e nuova
>   E son venuta,

which rebuke of Beatrice's may be delivered in the person of many
theologians, dissuading from poetry and other worldly sciences; a
rebuke that should be directed against those who read the poets to
gratify their own inclination, and not for the sake of instruction,
that they may defeat the errors of the Gentiles." It remains to be
considered whether our Poet's marriage with Gemma de' Donati,
and the difficulties in which that engagement involved him, may
not be the object of Beatrice's displeasure.
  [1] *Bird.*] "Surely in vain the net is spread in the sight of any
bird." Prov. i. 17.
  [2] *From Iarbas' land.*] The south.
  [3] *The beard.*] "I perceived, that when she desired me to raise
my beard, instead of telling me to lift up my head, a severe reflection was implied on my want of that wisdom which should
accompany the age of manhood."

Than I perceived[1] those primal creatures cease
Their flowery sprinkling ; and mine eyes beheld
(Yet unassured and wavering in their view)
Beatrice ; she, who towards the mystic shape,
That joins two natures in one form, had turn'd :
And, even under shadow of her veil,
And parted by the verdant rill that flow'd
Between, in loveliness she seem'd as much
Her former self surpassing, as on earth
All others she surpass'd.   Remorseful goads
Shot sudden through me.   Each thing else, the
    more
Its love had late beguiled me, now the more
Was loathsome.   On my heart so keenly smote
The bitter consciousness, that on the ground
O'erpower'd I fell : and what my state was then,
She knows, who was the cause.   When now my
    strength
Flow'd back, returning outward from the heart,
The lady,[2] whom alone I first had seen,
I found above me.   "Loose me not," she. cried :
"Loose not thy hold : " and lo ! had dragg'd me
    high
As to my neck into the stream ; while she,
Still as she drew me after, swept along,
Swift as a shuttle, bounding o'er the wave.
    The blessed shore approaching, then was heard

---

[1] *Than I peceived.*]   I had before translated this differently, and
in agreement with those editions, which read,

> Posarsi quelle belle creature
> Da loro apparsion.

> instead of   Posarsi quelle prime creature
> Da loro aspersion.

for which reading I am indebted to Lombardi, who derives it from
the Nidobeatina edition. By the "primal creatures" are meant
the angels, who were scattering the flowers on Beatrice.
[2] *The lady.*]   Matilda.

So sweetly, "Tu asperges me,"[1] that I
May not remember, much less tell the sound.
    The beauteous dame, her arms expanding, clasp'd
My temples, and immerged me where 'twas fit
The wave should drench me: and, thence raising
        up,
Within the fourfold dance of lovely nymphs
Presented me so laved; and with their arm
They each did cover me.   "Here are we nymphs,
And in the heaven are stars.[2]   Or ever earth
Was visited of Beatrice, we,
Appointed for her handmaids, tended on her.
We to her eyes will lead thee: but the light
Of gladness, that is in them, well to scan,
Those yonder three,[3] of deeper ken than ours,
Thy sight shall quicken."   Thus began their song:
And then they led me to the Gryphon's breast,
Where, turn'd toward us, Beatrice stood.
" Spare not thy vision.   We have station'd thee
Before the emeralds,[4] whence love, erewhile,
Hath drawn his weapons on thee."   As they spake,
A thousand fervent wishes riveted

[1] *Tu asperges me.*]   "Purge me with hyssop, and I shall be
clean; wash me, and I shall be whiter than snow." Ps. li. 7.
Sung by the choir, while the priest is sprinkling the people with
holy water.

[2] *And in the heaven are stars.*]   See Canto i. 24.

[3] *Those yonder three.*]   Faith, hope, and charity.

[4] *The emeralds.*]   The eyes of Beatrice.   The author of Illustrations of Shakspeare, 8vo, 1807, vol. ii. p. 193, has referred to old
writers, by whom the epithet green is given to eyes, as by the early
French poets, and by Shakspeare, Romeo and Juliet, act iii. sc. 5.

    —— an eagle, madam,
    Hath not so green, so quick, so fair an eye.

Mr. Douce's conjecture, that eyes of this colour are much less
common now than formerly, is not so probable as that writers, and
especially poets, should at times be somewhat loose and general in
applying terms expressive of colour, whereof an instance may be
seen in some ingenious remarks by Mr. Blomfield on the word
κυάνεος. Æschyli Persæ. Edit. 1814, Glossar. p. 107.

Mine eyes upon her beaming eyes, that stood,
Still fix'd toward the Gryphon, motionless.
As the sun strikes a mirror, even thus
Within those orbs the twyfold being shone;
For ever varying, in one figure now
Reflected, now in other. Reader! muse
How wondrous in my sight it seem'd, to mark
A thing, albeit stedfast in itself,
Yet in its imaged semblance mutable.
    Full of amaze, and joyous, while my soul
Fed on the viand, whereof still desire
Grows with satiety; the other three,
With gesture that declared a loftier line,
Advanced: to their own carol, on they came
Dancing, in festive ring angelical.
    "Turn, Beatrice!" was their song: "Oh! turn
Thy saintly sight on this thy faithful one,
Who, to behold thee, many a wearisome pace
Hath measured. Gracious at our prayer, vouchsafe
Unveil to him thy cheeks; that he may mark
Thy second beauty, now conceal'd." O splendour!
O sacred light eternal! who is he,
So pale with musing in Pierian shades,
Or with that fount so lavishly imbued,
Whose spirit should not fail him in the essay
To represent thee such as thou didst seem,
When under cope of the still-chiming heaven
Thou gavest to open air thy charms reveal'd?

CANTO XXXII

ARGUMENT

Dante is warned not to gaze too fixedly on Beatrice.   The procession moves on, accompanied by Matilda, Statius, and Dante, till they
reach an exceeding lofty tree, where divers strange chances befall.

MINE eyes with such an eager coveting
Were bent to rid them of their ten years' thirst,[1]
No other sense was waking : and e'en they
Were fenced on either side from heed of aught ;
So tangled, in its custom'd toils, that smile
Of saintly brightness drew me to itself :
When forcibly, toward the left, my sight
The sacred virgins turn'd ; for from their lips
I heard the warning sounds : " Too fix'd a gaze ! "[2]
    Awhile my vision labour'd ; as when late
Upon the o'erstrained eyes the sun hath smote :
But soon,[3] to lesser object, as the view
Was now recover'd, (lesser in respect
To that excess of sensible, whence late
I had perforce been sunder'd,) on their right
I mark'd that glorious army wheel, and turn,
Against the sun and sevenfold lights, their front.
As when, their bucklers for protection raised,
A well-ranged troop, with portly banners curl'd,
Wheel circling, ere the whole can change their ground,

---

[1] *Their ten years' thirst.*]   Beatrice had been dead ten years.

[2] *Too fix'd a gaze.*]   The allegorical interpretation of Vellutello,
whether it be considered as justly inferrible from the text or not,
conveys so useful a lesson, that it deserves our notice.   " The
understanding is sometimes so intently engaged in contemplating the
light of divine truth in the Scriptures, that it becomes dazzled, and
is made less capable of attaining such knowledge, than if it had
sought after it with greater moderation."

[3] *But soon.*]   As soon as his sight was recovered, so as to bear the
view of that glorious procession, which splendid as it was, was yet
less so than Beatrice, by whom his vision had been overpowered, etc.

E'en thus the goodly regiment of heaven,
Proceeding, all did pass us ere the car
Had sloped his beam.   Attendant at the wheels
The damsels turn'd ; and on the Gryphon moved
The sacred burden, with a pace so smooth,
No feather on him trembled.   The fair dame,
Who through the wave had drawn me, companied
By Statius and myself, pursued the wheel,
Whose orbit, rolling, mark'd a lesser arch.
     Through the high wood, now void, (the more
          her blame,
Who by the serpent was beguiled,) I pass'd,
With step in cadence to the harmony
Angelic.   Onward had we moved, as far,
Perchance, as arrow at three several flights
Full wing'd had sped, when from her station down
Descended Beatrice.   With one voice
All murmur'd "Adam ; " circling next a plant [1]
Despoiled of flowers and leaf, on every bough.
Its tresses,[2] spreading more as more they rose,
Were such, as 'midst their forest wilds, for height,
The Indians [3] might have gazed at.   "Blessed thou,

[1] *A plant.*] Lombardi has conjectured, with much probability,
that this tree is not (as preceding commentators had supposed)
merely intended to represent the tree of knowledge of good and evil,
but that the Roman empire is figured by it. Among the maxims
maintained by our Poet, as the same commentator observes, were
these : that one monarchy had been willed by Providence, and was
necessary for universal peace ; and that this monarchy, by right of
justice and by the divine ordinance, belonged to the Roman people
only. His treatise de Monarchiâ was written indeed to inculcate
these maxims, and to prove that the temporal monarchy depends
immediately on God, and should be kept as distinct as possible from
the authority of the pope.

[2] *Its tresses.*] "I saw, and behold, a tree in the midst of the
earth, and the height thereof was great." Daniel iv. 10.

[3] *The Indians.*]
          —— Quos oceano proprior gerit India lucos.
                         Virg. Georg. lib. ii. 122.
          —— Such as at this day to Indians known.
                         Milton, P. L. b. ix. 1102.

14

Gryphon ![1] whose beak hath never pluck'd that tree
Pleasant to taste : for hence the appetite
Was warp'd to evil."   Round the stately trunk
Thus shouted forth the rest, to whom return'd
The animal twice-gender'd : " Yea ! for so
The generation of the just are saved."
And turning to the chariot-pole, to foot
He drew it of the widow'd branch, and bound
There, left unto the stock [2] whereon it grew.

As when large floods of radiance [3] from above
Stream, with that radiance mingled, which ascends
Next after setting of the scaly sign,
Our plants then burgein, and each wears anew
His wonted colours, ere the sun have yoked
Beneath another star his flamy steeds ;
Thus putting forth a hue more faint than rose,
And deeper than the violet, was renew'd
The plant, erewhile in all its branches bare.
Unearthly was the hymn, which then arose.
I understood it not, nor to the end
Endured the harmony.   Had I the skill
To pencil forth how closed the unpitying eyes [4]
Slumbering, when Syrinx warbled, (eyes that paid

[1]   ——*Blessed thou,*
Gryphon !] Our Saviour's submission to the Roman empire appears to be intended, and particularly his injunction, " to render unto Cæsar the things that are Cæsar's."

[2] *There, left unto the stock.*] Dante here seems, I think, to intimate what he has attempted to prove at the conclusion of the second book de Monarchiâ ; namely, that our Saviour, by his suffering under the sentence, not of Herod, but of Pilate, who was the delegate of the Roman emperor, acknowledged and confirmed the supremacy of that emperor over the whole world ; for if, as he argues, all mankind were become sinners through the sin of Adam, no punishment, that was inflicted by one who had a right of jurisdiction over less than the whole human race, could have been sufficient to satisfy for the sins of all men. See note to Paradise, c. vi. 89.

[3] *When large floods of radiance.*]   When the sun enters into Aries, the constellation next to that of the Fish.

[4] *The unpitying eyes.*] See Ovid, Met. lib. i. 689.

So dearly for their watching,) then, like painter,
That with a model paints, I might design
The manner of my falling into sleep.
But feign who will the slumber cunningly,
I pass it by to when I waked; and tell,
How suddenly a flash of splendour rent
The curtain of my sleep, and one cries out,
"Arise: what dost thou?" As the chosen
    three,
On Tabor's mount, admitted to behold
The blossoming of that fair tree,[1] whose fruit
Is coveted of angels, and doth make
Perpetual feast in heaven; to themselves
Returning, at the word whence deeper sleeps [2]
Were broken, they their tribe diminish'd saw;
Both Moses and Elias gone, and changed
The stole their master wore; thus to myself
Returning, over me beheld I stand
The piteous one,[3] who, cross the stream, had
    brought
My steps. "And where," all doubting, I
    exclaim'd,
"Is Beatrice?"—"See her," she replied,
"Beneath the fresh leaf, seated on its root.
Behold the associate choir, that circles her.
The others, with a melody more sweet
And more profound, journeying to higher realms,
Upon the Gryphon tend." If there her words
Were closed, I know not; but mine eyes had now
Ta'en view of her, by whom all other thoughts

---

1 *The blossoming of that fair tree.*] Our Saviour's transfigura-
tion. "As the apple-tree among the trees of the wood, so is my
beloved among the sons." Solomon's Song ii. 3.
  2 *Deeper sleeps.*] The sleep of death, in the instance of the ruler
of the Synagogue's daughter and of Lazarus.
  3 *The piteous one.*] Matilda.

Were barr'd admittance.   On the very ground
Alone she sat, as she had there been left
A guard upon the wain, which I beheld
Bound to the twyform beast.   The seven nymphs
Did make themselves a cloister round about her ;
And, in their hands, upheld those lights[1] secure
From blast septentrion and the gusty south.
  " A little while thou shalt be forester here ;
And citizen shalt be, for ever with me,
Of that true Rome,[2] wherein Christ dwells a Roman.
To profit the misguided world, keep now
Thine eyes upon the car ; and what thou seest,
Take heed thou write, returning to that place." [3]
  Thus Beatrice : at whose feet inclined
Devout, at her behest, my thought and eyes
I, as she bade, directed.   Never fire,
With so swift motion, forth a stormy cloud
Leap'd downward from the welkin's furthest
       bound,
As I beheld the bird of Jove[4] descend
Down through the tree ; and, as he rush'd, the rind
Disparting crush beneath him ; buds much more,
And leaflets.   On the car, with all his might
He struck ; whence, staggering, like a ship it
       reel'd,
At random driven, to starboard now, o'ercome,
And now to larboard, by the vaulting waves.
  Next, springing up into the chariot's womb,
A fox[5] I saw, with hunger seeming pined

[1] *Those lights.*]   The tapers of gold.
[2] *Of that true Rome.*]   Of heaven.
[3] *To that place.*]   To the earth.
[4] *The bird of Jove.*]   This, which is imitated from Ezekiel
xvii. 3, 4, is typical of the persecutions which the church sustained
from the Roman emperors.
[5] *A fox.*]   By the fox probably is respresented the treachery of
the heretics.

Of all good food.   But, for his ugly sins
The saintly maid rebuking him, away
Scampering he turn'd, fast as his hide - bound
    corpse
Would bear him.   Next, from whence before he
    came,
I saw the eagle dart into the hull
O' the car, and leave it with his feathers lined : [1]
And then a voice, like that which issues forth
From heart with sorrow rived, did issue forth
From heaven, and, " O poor bark of mine ! " it
    cried,
" How badly art thou freighted."   Then it
    seem'd
That the earth open'd, between either wheel ;
And I beheld a dragon [2] issue thence,
That through the chariot fix'd his forked train ;
And like a wasp, that draggeth back the sting,
So drawing forth his baleful train, he dragg'd
Part of the bottom forth ; and went his way,
Exulting.   What remain'd, as lively turf
With green herb, so did clothe itself with
    plumes, [3]
Which haply had, with purpose chaste and kind,
Been offer'd ; and therewith were clothed the
    wheels,
Both one and other, and the beam, so quickly,
A sigh were not breathed sooner.   Thus trans-
    form'd,
The holy structure, through its several parts,

---

[1] *With his feathers lined.*]   In allusion to the donations made
by Constantine to the Church.

[2] *A dragon.*]   Probably Mahomet ; for what Lombardi offers to
the contrary is far from satisfactory.

[3] *With plumes.*]   The increase of wealth and temporal dominion,
which followed the supposed gift of Constantine.

Did put forth heads ;[1] three on the beam, and one
On every side : the first like oxen horn'd ;
But with a single horn upon their front,
The four.   Like monster, sight hath never seen.
O'er it[2] methought there sat, secure as rock
On mountain's lofty top, a shameless whore,
Whose ken roved loosely round her.   At her
      side,
As 't were that none might bear her off, I saw
A giant stand ; and ever and anon
They mingled kisses.   But, her lustful eyes
Chancing on me to wander, that fell minion
Scourged her from head to foot all o'er ; then full
Of jealousy, and fierce with rage, unloosed
The monster, and dragg'd on,[3] so far across
The forest, that from me its shades alone
Shielded the harlot and the new-form'd brute.

[1] *Heads.*]   By the seven heads, it is supposed with sufficient
probability, are meant the seven capital sins : by the three with
two horns, pride, anger, and avarice, injurious both to man himself and to his neighbour : by the four with one horn, gluttony,
gloominess, concupiscence, and envy, hurtful, at least in their
primary effects, chiefly to him who is guilty of them.   Vellutello
refers to Rev. xvii.   Landino, who is followed by Lombardi, understands the seven heads to signify the seven sacraments, and the ten
horns the ten commandments.   Compare Hell, c. xix. 112.

[2] *O'er it.*]   The harlot is thought to represent the state of the
church under Boniface viii., and the giant to figure Philip iv. of
France.

[3] *Dragg'd on.*]   The removal of the Pope's residence from Rome
to Avignon is pointed at.

CANTO XXXIII

ARGUMENT

After a hymn sung, Beatrice leaves the tree, and takes with her
the seven virgins, Matilda, Statius, and Dante. She then darkly
predicts to our Poets some future events. Lastly, the whole band
arrive at the fountain, from whence the two streams, Lethe and
Eunoe, separating, flow different ways; and Matilda, at the desire
of Beatrice, causes our Poet to drink of the latter stream.

"The heathen,[1] Lord! are come:" responsive
   thus,
The trinal now, and now the virgin band
Quaternion, their sweet psalmody began,
Weeping; and Beatrice listen'd, sad
And sighing, to the song, in such a mood,
That Mary, as she stood beside the cross,
Was scarce more changed. But when they gave
   her place
To speak, then, risen upright on her feet,
She, with a colour glowing bright as fire,
Did answer: "Yet a little while,[2] and ye
Shall see me not; and, my beloved sisters!
Again a little while, and ye shall see me."
  Before her then she marshall'd all the seven;
And, beckoning only, motion'd me, the dame,
And that remaining sage,[3] to follow her.
  So on she pass'd; and had not set, I ween,
Her tenth step to the ground, when, with mine eyes,
Her eyes encounter'd; and, with visage mild,
"So mend thy pace," she cried, "that if my words

---

1 *The heathen*.] "O God, the heathen are come into thine
inheritance." Psalm lxxix. 1.
2 *Yet a little while*.] "A little while, and ye shall not see me;
and again a little while, and ye shall see me." John xvi. 16.
3 *That remaining sage*.] Statius.

Address thee, thou mayst still be aptly placed
To hear them."   Soon as duly to her side
I now had hasten'd : " Brother ! " she began,
" Why makest thou no attempt at questioning,
As thus we walk together ? "   Like to those
Who, speaking with too reverent an awe
Before their betters, draw not forth the voice
Alive unto their lips, befell me then
That I in sounds imperfect thus began :
" Lady ! what I have need of, that thou know'st ;
And what will suit my need."   She answering thus :
" Of fearfulness and shame, I will that thou
Henceforth do rid thee ; that thou speak no more,
As one who dreams.[1]   Thus far be taught of me :
The vessel which thou saw'st the serpent break,
Was, and is not :[2] let him, who hath the blame,
Hope not to scare God's vengeance with a sop.[3]
Without an heir for ever shall not be
That eagle,[4] he, who left the chariot plumed,

[1] *As one who dreams.*]   Imitated by Petrarch, L. i. s. 41.

—— Se parole fai,
Sono imperfette e quasi d'uom che sogna.

[2] *Was, and is not.*]   " The beast that was, and is not."   Rev.
xvii. 11.

[3] *Hope not to scare God's vengeance with a sop.*]   " Let not him
who hath occasioned the destruction of the church, that vessel
which the serpent brake, hope to appease the anger of the Deity
by any outward acts of religious, or rather superstitious ceremony ;
such as was that, in our Poet's time, performed by a murderer at
Florence, who imagined himself secure from vengeance, if he ate
a sop of bread in wine upon the grave of the person murdered,
within the space of nine days."

[4] *That eagle.*]   He prognosticates that the Emperor of Germany
will not always continue to submit to the usurpations of the Pope,
and foretells the coming of Henry VII., Duke of Luxemburgh,
signified by the numerical figures DVX ; or, as Lombardi supposes,
of Can Grande della Scala, appointed the leader of the Ghibelline
forces.   It is unnecessary to point out the imitation of the Apocalypse
in the manner of this prophecy.   Troya assigns reasons for applying the prediction to Uguccione della Faggiola rather than to
Henry or Can Grande.   Veltro Allegorico di Dante.   Ediz. 1826,
p. 143.   But see my note, H. i. 102.

Which monster made it first and next a prey.
Plainly I view, and therefore speak, the stars
E'en now approaching, whose conjunction, free
From all impediment and bar, brings on
A season, in the which, one sent from God,
(Five hundred, five, and ten, do mark him out,)
That foul one, and the accomplice of her guilt,
The giant, both, shall slay.   And if perchance
My saying, dark as Themis or as Sphinx,
Fail to persuade thee, (since like them it foils
The intellect with blindness,) yet erelong
Events shall be the Naïads,[1] that will solve
This knotty riddle; and no damage light [2]
On flock or field.   Take heed; and as these words
By me are utter'd, teach them even so
To those who live that life, which is a race
To death: and when thou writest them, keep in mind
Not to conceal how thou hast seen the plant,
That twice[3] hath now been spoil'd.   This whoso
    robs,
This whoso plucks, with blasphemy of deed

---

1 *The Naïads.*] Dante, it is observed, has been led into a mistake by a corruption in the text of Ovid's Metam. l. vii. 757, where he found—

> Carmina Naïades non intellecta priorum
> Solvunt.

instead of   Carmina Laïades non intellecta priorum
> Solverat.

as it has been since corrected by Heinsius. Lombardi, after Rosa Morando, questions the propriety of this emendation, and refers to Pausanias, where "the Nymphs" are spoken of as expounders of oracles, for a vindication of the poet's accuracy. Should the reader blame me for not departing from the error of the original, (if error it be,) he may substitute

> Events shall be the Œdipus will solve, etc.

2 *No damage light.*]

> Protinus Aoniis immissa est bellua Thebis,
> Cessit et exitio multis; pecorique sibique
> Ruricolæ pavere feram.   *Ovid, ibid.*

3 *Twice.*] First by the eagle and next by the giant. See the last Canto, v. 110, and v. 154.

Sins against God, who for his use alone
Creating hallow'd it.   For taste of this,
In pain and in desire, five thousand years [1]
And upward, the first soul did yearn for him
Who punish'd in himself the fatal gust.

"Thy reason slumbers, if it deem this height,
And summit thus inverted,[2] of the plant,
Without due cause : and were not vainer thoughts,
As Elsa's numbing waters,[3] to thy soul.
And their fond pleasures had not dyed it dark
As Pyramus the mulberry ; thou hadst seen,[4]
In such momentous circumstance alone,
God's equal justice morally implied
In the forbidden tree.   But since I mark thee,
In understanding, harden'd into stone,
And, to that hardness, spotted too and stain'd,
So that thine eye is dazzled at my word ;
I will, that, if not written, yet at least
Painted thou take it in thee, for the cause,
That one brings home his staff inwreathed with
      palm." [5]

[1] *Five thousand years.*]   That such was the opinion of the church,
Lombardi shows by a reference to Baronius. Martyr. Rom. Dec.
25. Anno a creatione mundi, quando a principio creavit Deus
cœlum et terram, quinquies millesimo centesimo nonagesimo—Jesus
Christus—conceptus.   Edit. Col. Agripp. 4to, 1610, p. 858.

[2] *Inverted.*]   The branches, unlike those of other trees, spreading
more widely the higher they rose.   See the last Canto, v. 39.

[3] *Elsa's numbing waters.*]   The Elsa, a little stream, which flows
into the Arno about twenty miles below Florence, is said to possess a
petrifying quality.   Fazio degli Uberti, at the conclusion of Cap.
viii. l. 3, of the Dittamondo, mentions a successful experiment he
had himself made of the property here attributed to it.

[4] *Thou hadst seen.*]   This is obscure.   But it would seem as if he
meant to inculcate his favourite doctrine of the inviolability of the
empire, and of the care taken by Providence to protect it.

[5] *That one brings home his staff inwreathed with palm.*]   "For
the same cause that the *palmer*, returning from Palestine, brings
home his staff, or bourdon, bound with palm," that is, to show
where he has been.

      Che si reca 'l bordon di palma cinto.

'It is to be understood," says our Poet in the Vita Nuova, § 41,

I thus: " As wax by seal, that changeth not
Its impress, now is stamp'd my brain by thee.
But wherefore soars thy wish'd-for speech so high
Beyond my sight, that loses it the more,
The more it strains to reach it? "—" To the end
That thou mayst know," she answer'd straight,
    "the school,
That thou hast follow'd; and how far behind,
When following my discourse, its learning halts:
And mayst behold your art,[1] from the divine
As distant, as the disagreement is
'Twixt earth and heaven's most high and rapturous
    orb."
    " I not remember," I replied, "that e'er
I was estranged from thee; nor for such fault
Doth conscience chide me."　Smiling she return'd:
" If thou canst not remember, call to mind
How lately thou hast drunk of Lethe's wave;
And, sure as smoke doth indicate a flame,
In that forgetfulness itself conclude

" that people, who go on the service of the Most High, are properly named in three ways. They are named *palmers*, inasmuch as they go beyond sea, from whence they often bring back the palm. Inasmuch as they go to the house of Galicia, they are called pilgrims; because the sepulchre of St. James was further from his country than that of any other Apostle. They are called Romei," (for which I know of no other word we have in English except *Roamers*,) " inasmuch as they go to Rome." " In regard to the word *bourdon*, why it has been applied to a pilgrim's staff, it is not easy to guess. I believe, however, that this name has been given to such sort of staves, because pilgrims usually travel and perform their pilgrimages on foot, their staves serving them instead of horses or mules, then called *bourdons* and *bourdones*, by writers in the middle ages." Mr. Johnes's Translation of Joinville's Memoirs, Dissertation xv., by M. du Cange, p. 152, 4to edit. The word is thrice used by Chaucer in the Romaunt of the Rose.

[1] *Mayst behold your art.*] The second persons, singular and plural, are here used intentionally by our author, the one referring to himself alone, the second to mankind in general. Compare Hell, xi. 107. But I will follow the example of Brunck, who in a note on a passage in the Philoctetes of Sophocles, v. 369, where a similar distinction requires to be made, says that it would be ridiculous to multiply instances in a matter so well known.

Blame from thy alienated will incurr'd.
From henceforth, verily, my words shall be
As naked, as will suit them to appear
In thy unpractised view."   More sparkling now,
And with retarded course, the sun possess'd
The circle of mid-day, that varies still
As the aspect varies of each several clime;
When, as one, sent in vaward of a troop
For escort, pauses, if perchance he spy
Vestige of somewhat strange and rare; so paused [1]
The sevenfold band, arriving at the verge
Of a dun umbrage hoar, such as is seen,
Beneath green leaves and gloomy branches, oft
To overbrow a bleak and alpine cliff.
And, where they stood, before them, as it seem'd,
I, Tigris and Euphrates [2] both, beheld
Forth from one fountain issue; and, like friends,
Linger at parting. "O enlightening beam!
O glory of our kind! beseech thee say
What water this, which, from one source derived,
Itself removes to distance from itself?"
   To such entreaty answer thus was made:
"Entreat Matilda, that she teach thee this."
   And here, as one who clears himself of blame

---

[1] *So paused.*] Lombardi imagines that the seven nymphs, who
represent the four cardinal and the three evangelical virtues, are
made to stop at the verge of the shade, because retirement is the
friend of every virtuous quality and spiritual gift.
  [2] *I, Tigris and Euphrates.*]

> Quaque caput rapido tollit cum Tigride magnus
> Euphrates, quos non diversis fontibus edit
> Persis.   *Lucan, Phars.* lib. iii. 258.

> Tigris et Euphrates uno se fonte resolvunt.
>   *Boetius, de Consol. Philosoph.* lib. v. Metr. 1.

> —— là oltre ond' esce
> D'un medesimo fonte Eufrate e Tigre.
>   *Petrarca, Son. Mie Venturo*, etc.

Imputed, the fair dame return'd: "Of me
He this and more hath learnt; and I am safe
That Lethe's water hath not hid it from him."

And Beatrice: " Some more pressing care,
That oft the memory 'reaves, perchance hath made
His mind's eye dark.   But lo, where Eunoe flows!
Lead thither; and, as thou art wont, revive
His fainting virtue."   As a courteous spirit,
That proffers no excuses, but as soon
As he hath token of another's will,
Makes it his own; when she had ta'en me, thus
The lovely maiden moved her on, and call'd
To Statius, with an air most lady-like:
"Come thou with him."   Were further space
      allow'd,
Then, Reader! might I sing, though but in part,
That beverage, with whose sweetness I had ne'er
Been sated.   But, since all the leaves are full,
Appointed for this second strain, mine art
With warning bridle checks me.   I return'd
From the most holy wave, regenerate,
E'en as new plants renew'd[1] with foliage new,
Pure and made apt for mounting to the stars.[2]

---

[1] *Renew'd.*]   —— come piante novelle
               Rinnovellate da novella fronda.

So new this new-borne knight to battle new did rise
            Spenser, Faery Queene, b. i. c. xi. st. 34.

"Rinnovellate" is another of those words which Chaucer in vain
endeavoured to introduce into our language from the Italian, unless
it be supposed that he rather borrowed it from the French.   "Certes
ones a yere at the lest way it is lawful to ben houseled, for sothely
ones a yere all things in the earth renovelen."
                              The Persone's Tale.

[2 See note to last line of the Hell.]

INDEX OF PROPER NAMES

MENTIONED OR REFERRED TO IN THE
PURGATORIO [1]

Abydos, xxviii. 74.
Achan, xx. 107.
Acheron, ii. 100.
Achilles, ix. 32 ; xxi. 93.
Adam, ix. 9 ; xi. 45 ; xxix. 84 ; xxxii. 37 ; xxxiii. 62.
Adice, xvi. 117.
Adrian v., xix. 97.
Æneas, xviii. 135 ; xxi. 98.
Æthiop, xxvi. 18.
Africanus.   See Scipio.
Agatho, xxii. 105.
Aglauros, xiv. 142.
Agobbio, xi. 80.
Agobbio, Oderigi d', xi. 79.
Ahasuerus, xvii. 28.
Alagia, xix. 141.
Alagna, xx. 86.
Albert i., vi. 98.
Alberto, Abbot of San Zeno, xviii. 118.
Alcmæon, xii. 46.
Aldobrandesco, Guglielmo, xi. 59.
Aldobrandesco, Omberto, xi. 58, 67.
Alexandria, vii. 137.
Alonzo iii., King of Arragon, vii. 116.
Alpine, xiv. 33 ; xxxiii. 110.
Amata, xvii. 34.
Anacreon, xxii. 105.
Ananias, the husband of Sapphira, xx. 109.
Anastagio, xiv. 109.
Andes, xviii. 84.
Antenor, v. 75.
Antigone, xxii. 108.
Apennine, v. 94 ; xxx. 87.
Apollo, xx. 127.
Apulia.   See Pouille.

Aquinum, xxii. 14.
Arachne, xii. 39.
Aragonia, iii. 113.
Archiano, v. 93, 122.
Arezzo, vi. 14 ; xiv. 49.
Argia, xxii. 109.
Argus, xxix. 91 ; xxxii. 63.
Aries, viii. 135 ; xxxii. 52.
Aristotle, iii. 41.
Arnault.   See Daniel.
Arno, v. 123 ; xiv. 26.
Asopus, xviii. 92.
Assyrians, xii. 54.
Athens, vi. 141 ; xv. 96.
August, v. 38.
Aurora, ii. 8 ; ix. 1.
Azzo, Ubaldini of, xiv. 107.

Bacchus, xviii. 93.
Bagnacavallo, xiv. 118.
Baptist.   See John.
Barbarossa.   See Frederick.
Battifolle, Frederigo Novello da, vi. 17.
Beatrice, daughter of Folco Portinari, passim.
Beatrice, Marchioness of Este, viii. 73.
Beatrix, wife of Charles i., King of Naples, vii. 129.
Belacqua, iv. 119.
Benevento, iii. 124.
Benincasa d'Arezzo, vi. 14.
Bernardin.   See Fosco.
Bethlehem, xx. 135.
Bismantua, iv. 25.
Bohemia, vii. 98.
Bologna, xiv. 102.
Bolognian, xi. 83.
Bolsena, xxiv. 25.

1 The references are to Canto and line.

223

PRINTED BY MORRISON AND GIBB LIMITED
EDINBURGH

**THIS BOOK IS DUE ON THE LAST DATE
STAMPED BELOW**

AN INITIAL FINE OF 25 CENTS

WILL BE ASSESSED FOR FAILURE TO RETURN
THIS BOOK ON THE DATE DUE. THE PENALTY
WILL INCREASE TO 50 CENTS ON THE FOURTH
DAY AND TO $1.00 ON THE SEVENTH DAY
OVERDUE.

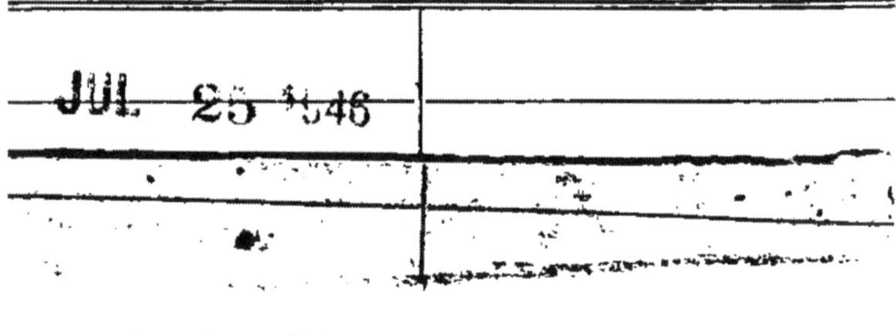

www.ingramcontent.com/pod-product-compliance
Lightning Source LLC
LaVergne TN
LVHW051214190726
843642LV00005B/1648